KU-255-636

Change and Intervention

Change and Intervention: Vocational Education and Training

Edited by

Peter Raggatt and Lorna Unwin

 The Falmer Press

(A member of the Taylor & Francis Group)
London • New York • Philadelphia

UK The Falmer Press, 4 John St, London, WC1N 2ET

USA The Falmer Press, Taylor & Francis Inc., 1900 Frost Road, Suite 101, Bristol, PA 19007

© Peter Raggatt and Lorna Unwin 1991

All rights reserved. No part of this publication may be reproduced, stored in a retrieval system, or transmitted, in any form or by any means, electronic, mechanical, photocopying, recording or otherwise, without permission in writing from the copyright holder and the Publisher.

First published 1991   Reprinted 1994

Library of Congress Cataloging-in-Publication Data available on request

British Library Cataloguing in Publication Data
Change and intervention: vocational education and training.
  1. Great Britain. Vocational education
  I. Raggatt, Peter II. Unwin, Lorna
  375.00860941

  ISBN 1-85000-694-6
      1-85000-695-4 (pbk)

Jacket design by Caroline Archer

Typeset in 10/12 points Bembo
by Graphicraft Typesetters Ltd., Hong Kong

Printed in Great Britain by Burgess Science Press, Basingstoke on paper which has a specified pH value on final paper manufacture of not less than 7.5 and is therefore 'acid free'.

Contents

Contents

List of Abbreviations and Acronyms

AB	Awarding Body
ABE	Adult Basic Education
ALBSU	Adult Literacy and Basic Skills Unit
APL	Accreditation of Prior Learning
ATS	Adult Training Strategy
BGT	Business Growth Training
BTEC	Business and Technician Education Council
CATS	Credit Accumulation Transfer Scheme
CBI	Confederation of British Industry
CEE	Certificate of Extended Education
CELP	College Employers Links Project
CNAA	Council for National Academic Awards
COMETT	Community Action Programme for Education and Training for Technology
CP	Community Programme
CPVE	Certificate of Pre-Vocational Education
C&GLI	City and Guilds of the London Institute
CSE	Certificate of Secondary Education (replaced with GCSE)
DES	Department of Education and Science
DTI	Department of Trade and Industry
ED,TA	Employment Department, Training Agency
EDAP	Employee Development and Assistance Programme
EHE	Enterprise in Higher Education
ERA	Education Reform Act
ERASMUS	European Community Action Scheme for the Mobility of University Students
ESOL	English for Speakers of Other Languages
ET	Employment Training
FESC	Further Education Staff College
FEU	Further Education Unit
FTEs	Full-time Equivalents

GCE	General Certificate of Education (replaced with GCSE)
GCSE	General Certificate of Secondary Education
GLC	Greater London Council (now abolished)
HCTB/C	Hotel and Catering Training Board/C-Company
HESIN	Higher Education Services for Industry in the North
HNC/D	Higher National Certificate/Diploma
HRM	Human Resource Management
ILB	Industry Lead bodies (also called Lead Industry Bodies and, more usually, Lead Bodies
ILEA	Inner London Education Authority (now abolished)
ITB	Industrial Training Board
ITOs	Industry Training Organizations
JTS	Job Training Scheme
LA	Local Authority
LEA	Local Education Authority
LEN	Local Employer Network
LINGUA	Action Programme on Modern Language Teaching
MCI	Management Charter Initiative
MMFITB	Man-made Fibres Industry Training Board
MSC	Manpower Services Commission (now TA)
NATFHE	National Association of Teachers of Further and Higher Education
NCC	National Curriculum Council
NCVQ	National Council for Vocational Qualifications
NEDO	National Economic Development Office
NIESR	National Institute for Economic and Social Research
NJTS	New Job Training Scheme
NROVA	National Record of Vocational Achievement
NTI	New Training Initiative
NVQ	National Vocational Qualification
OECD	Organization for Economic Cooperation and Development
PIC	Private Industry Council
PICKUP	Professional, Industrial and Commercial Updating
PLJ	People, Learning and Jobs
PONSI	Program on Noncollegiate Sponsored Instruction
RDA	Regional Development Agents
RSA	Royal Society of Arts
PSG	Rate Support Grant
RVQ	Review of Vocational Qualifications
SATUP	Scientific and Technical Updating
SCIP	Schools Curriculum Industry Project
SEAC	School Examination and Assessment Council
SCOTVEC	Scottish Vocational Education Council
TA	Training Agency
TDLB	Training and Development Lead Body

TECs	Training and Enterprise Councils
TOPS	Training Opportunities Scheme
TSD	Technical Skills Development
TUC	Trades Union Congress
TVEI	Technical and Vocational Education Initiative
UDACE	Unit for the Development of Adult Continuing Education
UVP	Unified Vocational Preparation
VET	Vocational Education and Training
WEA	Workers' Educational Association
WEEP	Work Experience on Employers' Premises
WRNAFE	Work-Related Non Advanced Further Education
YOP	Youth Opportunities Programme
YT	Youth Training
YTS	Youth Training Scheme

Introduction: A Collection of Pipers

Peter Raggatt and Lorna Unwin

At the 1990 Conservative Party Conference in Bournemouth, Michael Howard, the Secretary of State for Employment, assured delegates that he and John MacGregor, the Secretary of State for Education, did work closely together. His statement came in response to one delegate who, in the employment and training debate, had questioned the effectiveness of having two Whitehall departments seemingly responsible for giving people the relevant skills and opportunities for personal development which together produce a capable workforce. Howard illustrated this ED/DES partnership by announcing that from 1991 all school leavers would carry with them a Record of Achievement whose primary purpose was to give employers a clearer picture of a young person's capabilities. That Howard on the one hand felt the need to give delegates reassurance and on the other that he rather than the Education minister was given the opportunity to announce a school-based measure reflects how far the traditional Whitehall demarcation lines have been blurred. Indeed, Howard's brief reference to a ED/DES partnership obscures a complex structure within which comprehensive and deliverable policies for vocational education and training (VET) are battling for both survival and supremacy.

This book has brought together some key players and key policies which are currently part of that complex structure and presents them for public scrutiny. In the same book, we hear from policy-makers, educationalists, industrialists and training providers. This book does not set out to pursue one ideological argument but presents a series of different perspectives which, taken together, reveal the massive scale of change and intervention currently shaking this country's VET infrastructure.

The constant changes in both VET policy and practice since the early 1970s have been well documented. Some of those changes are the result of direct government intervention in education and training policy, for example, TVEI, YTS and the introduction of a competence-based framework for qualifications. Other changes have occurred as an indirect result of such intervention or have occurred in the ad hoc manner which characterizes much VET practice, for example, the development of learner-centred delivery methods, recognition of transferable skills and modularization of courses. We have reached a position now, however, where those changes are being consolidated through an interventionist strategy which is impacting on VET curriculum and pedagogy both on- and off-the-job, on the way in which individuals and employers pay for training, and on the relationships between business and education at all levels from primary school through to higher education. And, significantly, it is the Department of Employment that is steering the strategy into place.

The rationale for the structural and curriculum developments in VET in recent years has been the increasingly single-minded pursuit of a vocational education and training system that will enable Britain to contend more effectively in the international competition for world markets. The broad goal is the development of a flexible, adaptable workforce which responds positively and enterprisingly to the demands of economic and technological change. Government policies have been directed towards this goal and in addition to the DES two other Government departments, the ED and the DTI, became directly involved with education and training policies: the ED through the creation of the Manpower Services Commission and the DTI first through its 1977 Discussion Paper, 'Industry, Education and Management'. By the end of the 1970s, the principal agent often planning and monitoring the form that intervention would take was the Manpower Services Commission. Created by the Conservative government in 1973 it successfully survived the shift in political philosophy from the corporate state to the neo-liberalism of the Thatcher administrations.

The crucial years were those which followed the election of the Conservative government in 1979. As a major quango it was a likely target for a government committed to a laissez-faire economic policy and the deconstruction of the Welfare State. Rapidly rising unemployment and the MSC's usefulness in cloaking youth unemployment under the respectability of youth training programmes helped it to survive. The early cut in its staff and programmes was quickly reversed and its budget was expanded to provide the Youth Opportunities Programme.

It also seized the opportunity to advance its ideas for a more comprehensive strategy for manpower development. This appeared in *A New Training Initiative: A Consultative Document* (ED/MSC, 1981), which was endorsed by government, and followed by a White Paper based on the Commission's recommendations which outlined the government's programme. The Commission was given 'a central role' in the implementation of the programme.

The key components in the strategy were a system of vocational qualifications based on relevant standards of competence for all skilled occupations and vocational preparation for all young people including those still in school: 'To get a better trained and more flexible workforce we need to start with a better preparation for working life in schools and better opportunities for continuing education and personal development in the early years at work'. Elsewhere in the White Paper the groundwork was laid for another innovation that developed through the 1980s — Records of Achievement and the NROVA or National Record: 'Each young person's progress will be recorded, reviewed and assessed as he or she goes through the programme. A document of progress will be given to the young person on leaving the programme and will record standards achieved in a way which is recogniz- able to both the young person and to potential employers'. The Commission had moved to the heart of vocational education and training policy-making becoming, in effect, the national training agency with a major role in the economic regeneration of Britain through training. The development was formalized in the 1984 White Paper *Training for Jobs* in which the MSC was charged with expanding 'its range of operations so as to be able to discharge the function of a national training authority'.

The decision to give the MSC a leading role in developing and im- plementing a strategy for youth training was also a decision not to give schools (or the DES) a central role. In contrast, France when faced with a similar problem chose to expand technical and vocational provision in second- ary schools and, in 1986, introduced a Vocational Baccalaureat (*Baccalaureat Professionel*), which provides a higher level vocational qualification and gives access to employment and to technical courses in university. The curriculum includes a common core of mathematics, French and a foreign language, and combines a broad vocational education with the mastery of a specialist area.

A school-based model along the lines adopted in France must have held few attractions for the government or the MSC. Seen from an MSC perspec- tive far too many young people left school unqualified, often lacking basic literacy and numeracy skills and effectively immunized against further educa- tion or training. It was these failures of the school system that dominated the MSC's programmes and there would have seemed little point extending the period of compulsory schooling when it was so clearly evident that schools were ill-equipped to provide effective programmes. Moreover, the MSC was functionally related to the Department of Employment and its emerging role as a national training authority stressed skill development and manpower planning. This was very different from the more holistic, developmental and essentially longer-term perspective that continued in the DES despite its acceptance of the contribution that education should make to economic regeneration. There was a further difficulty in seeing the schools as the basis for a reformed vocational education and training system. Responsibility for delivering *educational* policy was largely devolved to Local Education Author- ities and the intentions of government could be too easily thwarted.

In planning a new system for vocational education and training the model provided by the German dual system held more attractions than the school-based model and it is interesting to consider why it was not adopted. Clearly employer support would be essential for the successful introduction of the model and the CBI's role was crucial. Initially the CBI was enthusiastic but this withered as a detailed understanding of the system developed. There were several reasons for this as Keep's (1986) study demonstrates. The absence of an effective existing local or regional mechanism similar to the German Chambers was one difficulty and the CBI did not wish to see the development of a major new role for rival representative organizations such as the Chambers of Commerce.

A larger problem was the very strong opposition to a trade union role in YTS similar to that which the German trade unions had in the dual system. The CBI strongly rejected the notion of co-determination in the field of vocational training. It was in a powerful bargaining position on this because it was clear that the YTS would rely on the participation of small employers, many of whom, it was argued, would not participate if unions were involved, a particularly likely outcome in view of the use by some employers of previous training schemes as an opportunity for job substitution. Nor was the CBI prepared to countenance a statutory framework underpinning youth training as used in Germany, where training contracts are legal documents which set out in great detail the rights and responsibilities of trainees and employers. The CBI was consistently anti-legislation, arguing for a voluntary system in line with its policy of freeing industry from government intervention — a view that fitted well with those of a government that was increasingly committed to a reduction in the role of the state and opposed to the consensual politics that had dominated since World War II. A further difficulty with the German model was that it was very clearly founded on different attitudes on the part of employers. In Germany employers provided the financial support for training; in Britain employers insisted on government funding (and opposed an effective system of monitoring).

In summary the CBI insisted on an employer-led scheme with the work-experience element being completely controlled by employers. Their preferred model was based on the WEEP element of YOPs — which had the added attraction of an early contribution to production by trainees. With the overriding priority of obtaining sufficient training places, the CBI was well placed to resist an effective mechanism for monitoring the new scheme.

Significantly, having made the choice in favour of an employer-led, task-focused model, the story of the 1980s sees the MSC moderating its position as it incorporates elements of a personal development model. In doing this, the MSC sought to blend the two models in order to produce the much heralded flexible and adaptable workforce. The apotheosis of this approach is two-year YTS, introduced in 1986. It is interesting to follow the MSC's shifts in emphasis in youth training. In its early programmes, the task-focused model is dominant right up to and including one-year YTS. The Design Framework of two-year YTS, however, demonstrates a firm commitment to a balanced approach. The Framework gave equal weight to four outcomes: competence in job skills; competence in a range of transferable core skills; ability to transfer skills and knowledge to new situations;

Table 1   *Task-focused model of training*

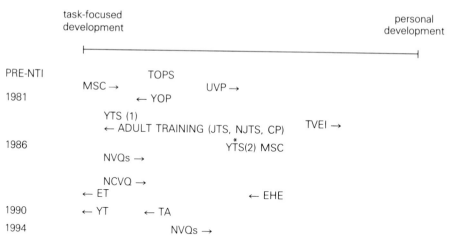

KEY
⇄ General direction during implementation
* The design framework of YTS (2) puts it in the middle of the continuum – its 4 outcomes specified both task and personal development.
   'A' Levels could be seen as completely task-focused but both YTS (1 and 2) and 'A' Levels are transformed/distorted by the nature of their delivery/teaching-training method. Hence YTS could be totally task-focused, 'A' level could develop core skills and be seen as a major vehicle for personal development. The same paradox applies to degrees gained in higher education.
   The same continuum can be used for plotting companies and educational institutions. They too are moving — companies are embracing the concept of a 'learning organization' and educational institutions are 'meeting the needs of the market'.

personal effectiveness. Each of these outcomes can be justified in terms of contributing to the development of a competent workforce but three of the four would also feature in any statement of educational aims.

Ironically, employers ultimately rejected two-year YTS by complaining that its emphasis on the development, assessment and recording of the four outcomes was too time-consuming and bureaucratic. They also objected to the mandatory off-the-job component of the scheme and the MSC's formal monitoring which demanded that all providers achieve Approved Training Organization status. This rejection flew in the face of the demands employers have been making since the dawn of time for employees to possess both occupational competences and transferable skills.

In 1990, the Training Agency capitulated to the employers, replacing YTS with Youth Training (YT). This places only one requirement on employers and providers, that they ensure all trainees follow a training programme which leads towards a Level 2 NVQ. And so we see a return to the task-focused model as shown in Table 1. This table plots the position of a number of education and training programmes in order to illustrate the complexity of VET policies and practices, many of which can be attributed to the MSC and its subsequent progeny. Significantly, at the beginning of the 1990s all the interested parties involved with VET policy and practice are advocating movement into the centre of the continuum. Will this new consensus last? Is the climate now right for the creation of a single ministry for education and training?

The major theme in this book is change and intervention in vocational education and training. Contributors examine individual aspects of policy and practice considering, *inter alia*, three sub-themes. The first is the competence-based approach and its implementation; the second is an exploration of who are the winners and losers as government has placed national economic development at the heart of its policies and programmes for education and training. A third theme is the process of change and intervention itself. While apparent in all the chapters, it is most easily traced in the case studies where policies initiated at national level by government and other bodies are modified by factors in the local context and are implemented in ways which are acceptable to individual organizations.

The NTI, as has already been noted, made competence-based qualifications a key component of its agenda for improving Britain's VET performance. This has now emerged as the pervasive influence on both VET policy and practice and, not suprisingly, features with different degrees of optimism and unease in several chapters. In the next chapter Graham Debling, Head of the Standards Methodology Unit in the Training Agency, describes the methodology for defining standards of occupational competence and argues that such standards are central to securing a competent and adaptable workforce. For Debling, standards must encompass relevant technical skills, transferable skills that underpin the ability to apply knowledge and understanding to new situations, and the qualities of personal effectiveness that are required in the workplace to deal with co-workers, customers and others. By implication this sets out criteria that may be used to evaluate National Vocational Qualifications (NVQs) which are based on standards of occupational competence. Do they, *in practice*, incorporate transferable skills and personal effectiveness or, given the process through which standards are defined by employer-led lead bodies, are they restricted to employers' concerns for the *special* skills needed for the particular job? Do they provide the breadth of training which will help the trainee move to other jobs as changes take place in the industrial structure?

The implications of the competence based approach for higher education are the theme in John Burke's contribution. Burke distinguishes between changes arising from the absorption of new ideas (osmosis) and those which are directed and intentional interventions. A consistent concern in his chapter is the issue of 'core' or 'generic' skills which he examines with reference to the Enterprise in Higher Education initiative. He also considers the indirect effects of the competence based movement on higher education both through the consequences of osmosis as ideas seep into institutions and the pressures from students whose previous experience has encouraged the development of generic skills and autonomous learning.

Richard Guy's analysis focuses on the different interests involved in vocational education and training. Drawing on his experience in the Training Agency and as Chief Executive of one of the first Training and Enterprise Councils he suggests that interdepartmental rivalries produced a plethora of initiatives but made it difficult to identify a clear strategy. Nonetheless it is clear that in the 1980s employers have been seen as the key customer of the educational service and have had a central place in many VET initiatives. This has, in Guy's view, produced a number of benefits, notably the introduction of structured training programmes for young people in companies that had never had them before. The emphasis on serving the employers has, however, tended to divert attention from the needs of individuals. For Guy, the key challenge for the 1990s is shifting the balance of funding and control towards individuals and motivating the very large numbers of young people and adults in dead end, low-skilled jobs to enter training.

Peter Raggatt takes up the issue of competence based standards and argues that the domination of lead bodies by employers has resulted in standards that are too occupationally specific and lack the transferable skills necessary to produce a competent, adaptable workforce. He discusses the relationship between the NCVQ and the Awarding Bodies and questions the adequacy of current procedures for ensuring that assessment to national standards can be delivered correctly and consistently in the many thousands of workplaces throughout the country.

In the next chapter we switch the focus to the United States and discover from Lorna Unwin's account a familiar set of problems and diagnoses. The United States is failing in the competition for world markets; if it is to compete effectively education goals must reflect the needs of business and business must contribute more to education. Her chapter assesses some of the initiatives that have attracted the attention of British policy-makers including Compacts and Private Industry Councils and describes the emerging consensus around the concept of core or transferable skills.

Ian McNay brings us back to Britain and a discussion about the importance of strategic economic planning. He argues that the national government has largely disengaged from economic planning and that the constraints of function and size render local planning ineffective. McNay suggests that this gap can best be filled by collaborative mechanisms between educators and employers at the regional level. Such mechanisms could provide research support for strategic economic planning, an identification of training and development needs and training and updating the workforce in relevant competences. He illustrates what can be done with examples from Britain and Europe.

The next two chapters take up the question of 'who are the winners and losers?' which Richard Guy touched on in his chapter. In Guy's analysis employers have been the winners for much of the 1980s, with adults benefitting least from the range of initiatives that were undertaken. Edwards, however, argues that the central assumption that Britain needs to produce multi-skilled flexible workers, which drives education and training policies for adults, is ideologically loaded. He acknowledges that there are increased opportunities for adults to obtain qualifications but suggests that these gains may be lost if the economic imperative that produced them declines. In contrast, non-work related options taken by the elderly, home managers and so on have become more expensive and less available. Edwards suggests that we need therefore to extend the debate about education and training policy beyond economic need to a discussion about economic and social policy in order to ensure that there are more winners and that the gains are sustained.

John Field continues the theme of 'winners and losers'. He describes the decline of traditional forms of adult education now that direct funding no longer protects the service and explores some of the changes that are taking place in that very heterogeneous area. Most of these are unplanned and unrelated to any government or other intervention agency.

Practitioners working in VET are all too well aware of how policies tend to get recycled and they reel from a sense of déjà-vu as each new initiative is announced. Any ideas which involve a partnership between education and training do require, however, long gestation periods if they are to be really effective. In the next chapter, Lewis Elton describes how the concept of the autonomous learner and its attendant advantages has found a new and nationally-funded voice through the Enterprise in Higher Education programme. The emphasis which Elton places on the individual learner echoes one of Richard Guy's key themes.

Most of the analyses offered in this book have been directed at national policies. Individual programmes and initiatives have been discussed briefly and usually illustratively. The next two chapters are different. They provide a detailed examination of how changes in government policies have affected a college of further education and a manufacturing company. The first chapter is a case study of Newham Community College in the East End of London. In Newham, national policies and new forms of funding were both constraints on what the college could do and how it could do it but also opportunities for extending its services to the community. In practice Newham was able to provide new opportunities and new services for a new adult clientele. This case study relates in a very real sense, at a local level, to the principles discussed in Edwards' chapter.

Companies, too, are affected by national VET policies as the next chapter describes. Lorna Unwin provides a case study of Coventry-based Courtaulds Grafil, a leading manufacturer of carbon fibre. Grafil has introduced competence-based training throughout its plant and, as a result, is completely restructuring shopfloor operations. Like all companies, however,

Grafil's main concern is profits and this study voices the concern of Grafil's Chief Executive that the stockmarket stifles creative training policies by its short-term attitude to investment.

The final contribution brings us back to the national policy level. For much of the 1970s and throughout the 1980s the expressed intention of government has been to increase the effectiveness of vocational education and training, i.e. to increase the stocks of skilled workers. An employer-based model was chosen with training and assessment being largely workplace-based. What are the outcomes so far? Hilary Steedman's chapter is a comparative study of improvements in workforce qualifications in Britain and France from 1979–1988. It is clear from her analysis that France, which developed provision for education and training within the overall objectives of successive national economic plans and adopted a school-based model for vocational education for 16–19 year olds, has been much more effective. It produces larger numbers of more highly qualified young people. Their vocational education has a greater breadth and is fully integrated into the educational system, enabling progression to higher education. In contrast, Britain has developed a segregated system with youth training funded through the Department of Employment and promoted through local Training and Enterprise Councils (TECs) and academic education funded through the DES and delivered through schools.

At the time of writing (Autumn 1990) yet another change has been announced. Vocational education and training (VET) in the United Kingdom is now overseen by a new division of the Department of Employment, the Training, Enterprise and Education Division. At national level, this new ED Division comprises the rump of a once confident and expanding beast which began life as a cross-breed, the MSC. Where once the MSC controlled large budgets for the funding of government-sponsored training programmes, research and development projects and business growth activities, the new Division's primary function is to set the policy criteria within which the TECs will operate. The style, structure and availability of VET will be largely determined by a network of regional, employer-led TECs. In short the 'Skills Revolution' which everyone says is necessary for the country's current and future prosperity, is, for the most part, in the hands of volunteers, that is the unpaid members of the TECs with assistance from local and regional civil servants. Although the Division will keep some money of its own for VET-related research and development, it is the TECs who must carry out the bulk of this work.

Education in general and vocational education and training in particular are very much on the political agenda for the 1990s and have been given a high priority by all three main political parties. It is too early to see how far the rhetoric of recent ministerial and opposition statements will be translated into action, but the shift in current emphasis is in marked contrast to the wilderness years which VET has previously endured. Current wisdom suggests that the majority of British employers have been shown to make little if any investment in training, while educationalists have largely shunned training on the grounds that its purely functional basis is the antithesis of sound educational objectives and processes. This book attempts to explore the reality which has been obscured by such polarized positions and provides positive examples of the ways in which the partners in VET are beginning to work together.

References

AINLEY, P. (1988) *From School to YTS*, Milton Keynes, Open University Press.
ED (1984) *Training for Jobs*, London, HMSO.
ED/MSC (1981) *A New Training Initiative: A Consultative Document*, London, HMSO.
FINN, D. (1987) *Training Without Jobs*, London, Macmillan.
GLEESON, D. (1989) *The Paradox of Training*, Milton Keynes, Open University Press.
KEEP, E. (1986) 'Designing the stable door: A study of how YTS was planned', *Warwick Paper in Industrial Relations*, No. 8.
UNWIN, L. (1990) 'Learning to live under water: The 1988 Education Reform Act and its implications for further and adult education', in FLUDE, M. and HAMMER, M. (Eds) *The Education Reform Act 1988: Its origins and implications*, London, Falmer Press.

Chapter 1

Developing Standards

Graham Debling

This chapter explores some of the characteristics of standards within the education and training context. It describes how Government policy designed to encourage an enhancement of the effectiveness of the nation's workforce has led to a major programme to establish standards of occupational competence, and it concludes by examining some of the implications of this programme to post compulsory education.

Standards in Education

Standards provide an explicit point of reference for making judgements.

Within the context of education and training, standards may relate to different things. For example, one might talk about the standards of teaching or training, or the standards of attainment or learning which result from training and education programmes. Whatever the context, however, standards provide a point of focus, a point of reference. It is by reference to the standard that it is possible to form a view as to the adequacy or excellence of what is offered or delivered, or what is attained.

Standards do not exist in isolation. They have credibility because they relate to a particular purpose or purposes. Teaching or training is about helping an individual, or a group of individuals, learn something this is considered worthwhile. The quality of a teaching or training programme is often evaluated with respect to either a notional or explicit learning expectation. Given that the purpose of the teaching or training is to help others learn, the effectiveness or standard of teaching or training relates directly to the effectiveness of the process in helping the learner to attain or exceed the learning objective.

However, within the context of standards relating to the teaching or training process, measures of the quality of the teaching or training have other important parameters. There is a cost incurred in learning — both for the learner who invests time in learning and for those who facilitate the learning. If the quality of teaching or training were measured solely in terms of attainment of learning objectives, standards could not differentiate between one approach which facilitates learning in an hour, and an alternative approach which does not result in attainment of the desired objectives in under 10 hours. Other important considerations are the starting point of the individual, the context of the learning, and the environment in which the learning is occurring.

Thus, when a view is expressed about the standards of training and teaching, against some notional (often implicit) criteria, it is likely that the observer will be taking into account many different factors. The difficulty with reference to implicit standards is that when two or more people are expressing separate views about the standards or quality of teaching or training, it is not necessarily clear that each contributor is forming a judgement against the same parameters. To effect an enhancement in teaching or training processes, to form comparative views of the effectiveness of different approaches, it is necessary to have more explicit points of reference — more explicit standards.

Standards which Describe Learning

Similar considerations apply to standards which describe learning outcomes. Learning has a purpose or purposes. What is to be learnt, and the level of attainment, are inextricably linked to the purpose(s) of learning.

Much of education is about learning in order to facilitate further learning and it has been suggested this is what distinguishes it from training, in that training is about learning for subsequent application in employment. In reality, however, much of education is also about the acquisition of skills for subsequent application in life as a whole and, increasingly, it is being recognized that training which does not prepare the individual for subsequent experiential learning, at the least, is of limited value. At the extremes it may be possible to differentiate between education and training, but there is much common ground between the extremes.

In describing the desired learning outcome and/or providing points of reference beyond which it is hoped that the learner will progress, standards relate to the purpose of learning. This may be about acquiring the skills of survival and ensuring fulfilment in life, or, more specifically, it may be about acquiring the skills and competences required to generate income in order to sustain body and soul. While such attainment may also provide a foundation for subsequent learning, there is also learning which is specifically about preparing for further learning. When seeking to define standards of learning, it is important to be clear about the purpose of the learning.

Generally, standards in education and training have been implicit rather than explicit. Degrees are considered to be of a higher standard than A Levels but this difference is not described explicitly. An individual who has gained an A Level in French has achieved a higher standard in that language than an individual who has never studied, and has no skills in, the language, despite having a first class honours degree in a science discipline. Clearly the concept of a degree being of a higher standard than other qualifications has to do with notional ideas about academic demand. However, given that it is a notional concept, how consistent is the standard for an award such as a degree in mathematics offered by different institutions? How consistent is the standard between degrees in different disciplines? While it is generally considered that a degree is of a higher standard than a Higher National Diploma, how confident can we be that a degree in one discipline is of a higher standard than a Higher National Diploma in another discipline? Given the variability in the interpretation of standards within a single discipline, it is difficult to see how any claims can be made about the relative standards of different qualifications in different disciplines as long as the standards are notional. To sustain claims of comparability standards need to be explicit.

Standards and Assessment

Sometimes the purpose of learning has been confused with the purpose of assessment.

The sequence of events should be to:

1   Analyse the purpose and identify the desired learning.
2   Design cost effective learning strategies.
3   Design and implement assessment processes which are both valid and reliable.

Assessment can serve different purposes — it can be either formative or summative. It serves a quality assurance role. If valid and reliable it will reveal what has been learnt, and assist in determining what further learning is desirable or necessary. As an outcome of the assessment the individual gains a measure of his or her learning or learning achievement, the teacher or trainer gains insight into the effectiveness of the learning process, and, if the attainment is certificated, there is a public acknowledgement of what has been learned.

Assessment may also be used to differentiate between individuals. Such assessment is important where its primary purpose is to rank individuals. The purpose of the ranking might be to form a view as to suitability for a specific employment or learning opportunity. Ranking is of particular importance where the number of applicants exceeds the number of places. The selection process has at least two parts. First of all there is a need to ensure that individuals meet minimum requirements. Thereafter, in employment, the concern will most likely be to identify the person who will make the best contribution.

In the context of a learning opportunity, the concern may be to identify the individual or individuals who are likely to benefit most from the learning opportunity. There may also be a concern to identify those who will reflect best on the institution through performing exceptionally well during and after the programme of learning. Norm referencing is often used for these purposes. While the cost effectiveness of the assessment process depends very much on the extent to which the assessment meets the purpose, the design of an assessment process for norm referencing often allows considerable compensation between different skills and learning and therefore does not provide a very good vehicle to recognize actual attainment.

It is interesting that in a climate concerned with affirmative action to compensate for other forms of disadvantage or undesirable discrimination, once the minimum expectation has been described, other considerations may come into play, rather than seeking to identify those who will perform best, subsequently.

Both employment and learning require skills, knowledge, understanding specific to the context, and a range of underpinning skills and abilities. There would seem to be no one right profile of underpinning skills or abilities which ensure effective subsequent performance. There is considerable scope for compensation as illustrated by the work of Schroder (1989). Individuals who are good at identifying their own strengths and limitations can often quickly compensate for their weaknesses once they experience the demands of the employment situation or learning opportunity.

National norm referenced examinations would appear to be valid and reliable only at the extremes. It has been suggested that in the middle of the range grades, there may be no more than a 50 per cent probability that an individual will actually be awarded the grade which reflects his or her ability if based solely on performance in a one-off examination. What is particularly clear is that standards established to rank individuals do not effectively represent what has been learned.

It is regrettable that decisions which can impact significantly on the individual's future can depend so heavily on norm referenced assessments. In this context the move towards placing greater emphasis on continuous assessment and the more recent acceleration towards the introduction of criterion referenced assessment practices against more explicit standards can only be welcomed. This of course presents new challenges for those who have depended upon the norm referenced examinations for selection purposes.

Standards for Different Purposes

Reflecting that learning may be for a variety of different purposes, standards which describe desired learning outcomes can also reflect these different purposes. Standards might describe

* desired attainment within an academic discipline
* attainment in a general skill or competence which underpins much of learning and performance (for example, communication, number, problem solving, personal skills)
* attainment which gives insight into preparedness for subsequent employment in one or a number of occupations or employment settings
* occupational or role competence.

Currently there are a number of national initiatives directed towards defining more explicit standards pertinent to a number of the above issues.

The development of Standard Grade in Scotland to replace O Grades in the late 70s and early 80s and the more recent steps in England and Wales to establish grade-related GCSE and the National Curriculum are concerned with defining more explicit standards for attainment in academic disciplines. They also seek to recognize attainment in a range of general skills, competences, or core skills such as communication and number, and in the process skills which are embedded within single or multi-discipline areas.

More recently, at the request of the Secretary of State for Education and Science, the National Curriculum Council and the Secondary Examinations Assessment Council, in association with the National Council for Vocational Qualifications have begun to explore how core skills such as communication, number, problem solving and personal skills might be defined, assessed and certificated, and fostered within the curriculum for the 16–18 age group. The involvement of the NCVQ also suggests that assessment and certification might be facilitated throughout life, given that National Vocational Qualifications are relevant to all ages.

The Employment Department, Training Agency's Higher Education Initiative is, in part, seeking to foster changes in higher education that will give greater prominence to the development of enterprise characteristics which include the core skills described above. This will involve higher education developing explicit descriptions (standards) of attainment in these core skills and competences. It will need to do this to ensure that learning strategies are used which are effective in enhancing these skills and will have to develop more explicit descriptions (standards) of attainment if it is to ensure that learning strategies are more effective in enhancing them.

With respect to occupational standards of competence, the Employment Department, Training Agency, in 1986, established a major programme to foster the development of more explicit standards which describe effective performance in employment. The second part of this paper describes this programme in some detail.

The Occupational Standards Programme

Background

While its specific objectives were restated in slightly different ways from time to time during its life, in essence the Manpower Services Commission (MSC) retained the primary objective of seeking to assist the efficiency and effectiveness of industry and commerce through the development of a skilled and adaptable workforce.

In 1981, through its New Training Initiative, the MSC perceived that vocational education and training needed to be more extensive and enhanced if it was to result in the formation of a workforce fully able to respond to the challenges of the late 20th/early 21st centuries. At the heart of this was a need for standards of a new kind.

The 1986 White Paper *Working Together — Education and Training* (ED/DES, 1986) reinforced the need to have established standards of competence: 'Qualifications and standards are not luxuries — they are necessities, central to securing a competent and adaptable workforce. Economic performance and individual job satisfaction both depend on maintaining and improving standards of competence'.

The National Council for Vocational Qualifications (NCVQ) was established by the same White Paper with the remit to take the lead in the reform of vocational qualifications. A target date of 1991 was set for an operational system of competence-based vocational qualifications which fully reflects the foreseeable needs of modern day employment.

There were a number of developments. The White Paper *Employment for the 1990s* (ED, 1988) was published. It described a new framework for training and vocational education. It was more explicit about the nature of the new standards:

> Our training system must be founded on standards and recognized qualifications based on competence — the performance required of individuals to do their work successfully and satisfactorily.

It was also explicit about who should identify the standards:

> The standards must be identified by employers and they must be nationally recognized. Thus we need a system of employer-led organizations to identify and establish standards and secure recognition of them, sector by sector, or occupational group by occupational group.

The White Paper also expressed the expectation that the standard-setting organizations would provide the lead in establishing arrangements for assessing and accrediting learning achievements, have the ability to influence a significant part of the sector and be seen as the body which can deal with government on training and vocational education matters.

It was not only government who foresaw the need for clear and explicit employment based competences and a framework of qualifications based on such standards. The relevance was also recognized by the Trades Union Congress (1989) in its publication *Skills 2000*, and in the report of the CBI's Vocational Education and Training Task Force, also published in 1989.

Both publications set out what each organization felt was important to achieve modernization of the British vocational education and training system in order to ensure that, as a nation, Britain could compete with the best in the world. The establishment of clear and explicit standards and their incorporation within vocational qualifications was identified as fundamental to quality and quality assurance. The CBI suggested that by 1995, at least half of the employed workforce should be aiming for updated or new qualifications within the NVQ framework.

Also in 1989 the Secretary of State for Education and Science asked the NCVQ to begin discussions with professional bodies as to how their qualifications might be incorporated within the NVQ framework. The Standards Programme had already been taken into this domain in 1988 by the then Council for Management Education and Development which, through its Management Charter Initiative, committed itself to defining standards of competence for all levels of management. In the same year the accounting professional bodies also separately committed themselves to developing standards of competence for their professionals.

The Standards Programme and NCVQ

The Standards Programme, initiated in 1986, is concerned not only with establishing a better definition of effective performance in employment through competence based standards, it is also concerned with the way in which such standards are expressed.

Occupational standards of competence define effective performance. The definition of competence adopted for the standards programme stems from a perception that a competent individual can perform a particular function or satisfy a particular role:

> in a wide range of settings having different characteristics, over an extended period of time, responding effectively to irregular occurrences and contingencies.

Standards of competence must encompass not only the relevant technical skills but also those which underpin the ability to transfer the skills and knowledge to new situations within the occupational area, the skills of organization, planning, innovation and coping with non-routine activities, and the qualities of personal effectiveness that are required in the workplace to deal with co-workers, managers and customers or clients.

Prior to the Standards Programme there were few national standards of occupational competence. Certification, through qualifications, depended upon individuals demonstrating knowledge and understanding, and/or a range of skills. Much of the emphasis in assessment was based on classroom learning and the collection of evidence in the form of written examinations.

The emerging standards of the Standards Programme are designed to serve both the immediate and long-term needs of industry, commerce and the public sector and thereby have currency nationally both within and across occupations and industries. As standards of occupational competence describe effective performance, they should become a primary focus for vocationally related employment and training. Assessment and certification to the standards will attest to competence.

It is envisaged that the primary, national certification process will be through National Vocational Qualifications (NVQs). An NVQ is a qualification, awarded by a national examining or validating body, which has been accredited by the NCVQ. Accreditation depends upon the qualification meeting the NVQ criteria of the NCVQ. Information on the NVQ criteria was first published in January 1988, but of course will be subject to updating and revision from time to time. The criteria specify that an NVQ is:

> A statement of competence, clearly relevant to work and intended to facilitate entry into, or progression in, employment, further education and training, issued by a recognized body to an individual.

An NVQ attests to the individual's competence. Its purpose is to give recognition to an individual who has demonstrated attainment of the standards of competence associated with a qualification.

Thus, the Employment Department, Training Agency's Programme and the role of the NCVQ are closely linked, as was envisaged in the 1986 White Paper.

The objective of the Standards Programme is to ensure that competence based standards are established which relate to the needs of employment, and that employers have a sense of ownership of such standards such that they recognize them and take responsibility for their modernization and utilisation. It is agreed that the standards should be expressed explicitly and transparently so that all — learners, teachers, assessors — can see and understand what is expected and what has been achieved. It was also foreseen that it would be desirable to establish certification which recognizes partial achievement, facilitates credit accumulation, where certification of the individual parts (units) makes sense to, and is valued by, users. In its Criteria and Related Guidance, NCVQ identified that an NVQ Statement of Competence should be expressed in three degrees of aggregational detail:

the NVQ title;

units (of competence);

elements (of competence).

It was foreseen that the NVQ title should denote the area of competence encompassed by the qualification. Units of competence are subdivisions of the qualification comprising of a self-standing area of competence which would be recognized and have value in employment. Each unit should be given a titles which indicates the area of competence encompassed by it. Unit titles are important because they appear in the National Record of Vocational Achievement (NROVA); the mechanism whereby NCVQ would facilitate credit accumulation.

The Programme and Scotland

The NCVQ remit was limited to England, Wales and Northern Ireland. In Scotland, subsequent to the publication of its Action Plan in 1983, the Scottish Education Department sponsored the introduction of a modular, criterion referenced curriculum for Non Advanced Further Education. (This was extended into higher education by a decision of SCOTVEC in 1988).

In 1984 the Scottish Technical Education Council (SCOTEC) and the Scottish Business Education Council (SCOTBEC) merged to form the Scottish Vocational Education Council (SCOTVEC). SCOTVEC took over responsibility for the administration of the new National Certificate.

In Scotland the National Certificate will be extended to include the standards of competence that will emerge from the Standards Programme. Credit accumulation is to be facilitated by the introduction of a Scottish Record of Education and Training.

Lead Bodies

It was envisaged that the standards would be developed by employer representative organizations, subsequently identified as Lead Bodies. In essence, the key characteristics of a Lead Body are that it should

represent the interests of the major users of the standards it defines;

involve the appropriate employer, employee and educational interests;

have the credibility to be able to secure the acceptance by the major users of the standards it develops;

be willing to work with the appropriate Examining and Validating, Certificating and Awarding Bodies to secure qualifications based on the standards;

be adequately resourced to take the work forward.

Lead Bodies are established and recognized by the Employment Department, Training Agency for the specific purposes of identifying and maintaining occupational standards and for developing national vocational qualifications based on them. In general they are not legally constituted entities except where the role is taken on by an organization or body legally constituted for another purpose. Sometimes a Lead Body is a loose federation of separately constituted bodies formed to facilitate cooperation and consultation.

In 1986 the first Lead Bodies were primarily Industrial Training Organizations or employer membership organizations. Subsequently a number of interested groups active in similar or overlapping areas came together to form consortia in order to minimize duplication and identify common needs, for example the Care Sector Consortium and the National Textile Training Group.

In those instances where occupations extend over most employment settings, cross-sectoral Lead Bodies have been established to take forward standards development work. Examples include the Administrative, Business and Commercial Training Group and the Training and Development Lead Body. Standards development work with respect to management was facilitated by the establishment of the National Forum for Management Education and Development, by the CBI, the Foundation for Management Education, and the British Institute of Management.

Some professional bodies have also assumed the mantle of Lead Bodies especially where the Privy Council has recognized the Professional Body as having a licensing role for those pursuing the occupation. However, for some professional bodies, members are employed in diverse situations, perhaps in different sectors of industry, commerce and the public service. Under such conditions, while the prime responsibility for standards development lies with the employer-recognized organizations, they are of course free to consult with, and draw on the expertise of, anybody they consider can make a useful contribution. Indeed, they may well draw on the standards of competence defined by professional bodies for their membership.

Similarly, Lead Bodies may draw on the expertise lodged with individuals and groups in education and training, especially where such groups and individuals are held in high esteem because of the quality of what has gone before. To date, many Lead Bodies have included individuals from the further and higher education scene on committees and working parties.

Government commitment to the Standards Programme is substantial. Ministers have regularly emphasized its importance in public statements; substantial resources running into millions of pounds per year have been provided since 1986 to support the Lead Body work. Research into, and development of the methodology is supported, and Lead Bodies can receive up to 50 per cent of the cost of developing standards and the initial publicising of the standards and resultant qualifications.

By 1990 over 150 Lead Bodies were in action, having developed, or were in the process of developing standards for well in excess of 500 different occupations. Hence in the four years from 1986 when, in response to the needs of the Youth Training Scheme, the standards development work had begun with semi-skilled and craft level occupations, it had progressed steadily to the point where standards development work was underway with respect to higher technician and professional level occupations. By the end of 1992 NVQs will be available for some 80 per cent of the UK workforce. There are, of course, a large number of occupations in which relatively few people are employed.

Looking ahead, it seems that the initial standards development work will continue for much of the 1990s. It is the first time that any nation has attempted to describe effective performance for its entire workforce. The standards themselves will be subject to continual refinement and modification, and the methodology, too, is likely to be subject to further refinement. Moreover, the world of work is constantly changing and there will be an ongoing requirement for the regular revision and modernization of the standards.

Technical Support

Throughout the 1980s MSC sponsored a range of work with different industries and relevant to different occupations. Organizations were encouraged to explore alternative ways in which good quality training and vocational education might be defined. Much was learned from that work. By 1986 the time was ripe to introduce an element of commonality in approach. This was seen as necessary in order to

> facilitate inter-industry recognition and easy interpretation,
>
> to avoid the confusion and costs inherent in asking those who deal with a range of industries and occupations to deal with substantially different approaches,
>
> allow a national approach to credit accumulation.

The objective of the Standards Programme was to foster the development of standards of competence which described effective performance in employment. The early work to establish and describe standards frequently resulted in products which concentrated primarily on separate and isolated skills or knowledge and understanding (perhaps reflecting past practice).

It was recognized that there was a need not only to establish a common approach, but also to instigate a programme of research and development.

This was to provide greater insight as to how standards might be developed which truly reflect a broad concept of competence; explore issues relating to, and develop advice pertaining to, the clear and explicit expression of the standards; and investigate matters relating to valid, reliable and cost effective assessment.

The Employment Department, Training Agency established the Standards Methodology Unit to oversee the work. In its turn it established a Technical Advisory Group including representatives of the major national awarding bodies, NCVQ, and a team of consultants. From the work of this group a series of Technical Guidance Notes were devised on the 'Development of Assessable Standards for National Certification.' A programme of research and development was established and a quarterly bulletin, *Competence and Assessment*, was published to disseminate findings and facilitate networking between Lead Bodies and the consultants assisting them in the standards development work.

In parallel, NCVQ established its own programme of Research and Development which is yielding a series of Research and Development Reports, in order to inform the process of developing and implementing NVQs. In 1989, ED, TA and NCVQ launched a series of joint NVQ information and Guidance Notes. *Competency Based Education and Training* (1989), edited by John Burke provides interesting insight into much of the research, development and debate associated with the Standards Programme and the development of NVQs.

Some Implications for Post-compulsory Education and Training

Occupational standards describe effective performance, over an extended period of time, in different settings. However, competence is more than the performance of isolated tasks or the application of the relevant technical skills. The breadth of occupational competence is described by the Mansfield and Mathews 'Job Competence Model' (1985):

Task Skills — for the performance of relevant tasks.

Task Management Skills — for the management of a group of tasks to achieve the overall job function.

Contingency Management Skills — for responding to breakdowns in routines, procedures and sequences.

Job/Role Environment Skills — for responding to the general aspects of the work role and environment, such as natural constraints and working relationships which might relate to the standards applied and work organization.

Another analysis suggests that occupational competence depends on the individual drawing on

Technical skills, both psycho-motor and cognitive, and knowledge and understanding which might relate directly to the work activity or, being of a more general nature, support a range of work activities.

Environmental awareness — a knowledge and understanding of the work and social context including the expectations and needs of others and the way in which external activities (external to the immediate area of influence) may impinge on the effective performance of the work role.

Intellectual effectiveness encompassing skills such as planning, prioritising, coping with variation, thinking ahead, and making decisions.

Personal effectiveness incorporating the use of initiative, adaptability, self competence, social competence and self awareness.

Socially acceptable behaviours relating to the specific work activity such as attendance, time keeping and personal appearance.

(Derived from the work of Conner and Warr, 1989).

Such analyses of the components of competence serve a number of different purposes. They may be used to interrogate emerging standards (derived from the process of functional analysis — see ED,TA. Technical Guidance Note No. 2 and *Competence and Assessment* Special Issue No. 1 December 1989). Additionally however, such analyses can assist in determining learning needs, structuring learning opportunities, and in the design of valid and reliable assessment strategies.

The analyses also provide insight into the links with other national standards development activities. Academic knowledge and understanding may well underpin and contribute to the development of technical skills and environmental awareness. The enterprise characteristics of the Enterprise in Higher Education Initiative place much emphasis on both intellectual and personal effectiveness. The core skills identified by the National Curriculum Council encompass both problem solving and personal skills, and a range of skill areas which will underpin technical skills (communication, number, foreign languages and information technology).

Providers of learning opportunities are very much concerned with initial assessment, developing learning strategies and carrying out assessment for certification purposes and might be helped in these activities by such analyses.

Initial Assessment

In seeking to ensure precision in their interpretation, or at least adequate consistency, NVQs and the constituent standards are explicit and contain large volumes of information. An NVQ will be made up of a number of units. Each unit reflects an area of competence that, in the eyes of employers, warrants separate certification. A unit is made up of a number of elements of competence. Each element of competence has a number of performance criteria attached to it, and range statements which provide insight into the diversity of conditions, materials, systems, etc. through which the unit and constituent elements seek to define competence. It seems increasingly likely that associated with each unit will be guidance on the assessment evidence that might be collected. Additional insight into the knowledge and under-standing, and possibly technical skills, which underpin, contribute to, or are essential to sustain effective performance might also be provided. Figures 1 and 2 provide examples of the information available for elements of com-petence taken from units pertinent to the provision of financial services and management.

As a general objective, units should be written in a language that is comprehensible to not only those who facilitate learning, but learners and those who use the standards such as employers and gatekeepers to further education. Both the structure of the units and the volume of information can be overwhelming. However, a number of pilot studies into the accreditation of prior learning (APL) against such standards has demonstrated that once individuals have been given guidance on the structure and format of the standards they do not find it difficult to identify where they do and do not already match the standards (MCI APL Project, NCVQ APL Project, SCOTVEC APL Project).

Of course, claims of competence are of limited value if not substan-tiated. The three projects identified above have illustrated that it is possible for individuals to accumulate and present evidence of prior learning sufficient to satisfy assessors of competence in order to warrant certification. However, this entails extensive work on the part of the individual. Where assessment is not for certification purposes, but to assist in making decisions about subse-quent learning programmes and employment choices, self analyses supported by some face to face counselling may be sufficient.

Whether for counselling purposes or to gain credit for prior learning, such processes will be assisted considerably by the NCVQ Database. This database will incorporate the extensive information encompassed within NVQs and their constituent units. Through selection of key words, units can be identified from different starting points. A range of software will be developed to facilitate the full exploitation of the database for a variety of purposes.

Learning Strategies

There is growing interest in exploiting experiential learning. One effective example involving experiential learning in the preparation of medical practi-

Figure 1
BUILDING SOCIETY SECTOR UNIT 3: SET UP, MONITOR AND MAINTAIN CUSTOMER ACCOUNTS

ELEMENT
Amend and update accounts against instructions

PERFORMANCE CRITERIA

(a) revised and existing internal documents/updated files and records are complete, accurate and legible, and are filed in the correct location
(b) all necessary signatures (internal and external) and internal authorizations are obtained to schedule
(c) correspondence to customer (or customer's legal representative) is accurate and complete (all necessary documents enclosed), and despatched promptly
(d) correspondence to other branches of own society or other organizations/professional agencies is accurate and complete (all necessary documents enclosed), and despatched promptly (normally on the same day as completion)
(e) cash transactions and financial documents are processed correctly and treated confidentially
(f) all calculations are correct
(g) computer inputs/outputs are accurate and complete
(h) indicators of problems/contingency situations are referred immediately to an appropriate authority

RANGE OF VARIABLES TO WHICH THE ELEMENT APPLIES

Types of amendment Change of account type; added property insurance; marriage; divorce; death; increased mortgage/loan; closure; overdraft; change of name by deed poll/marriage; change of address; indecision.
Other organizations/professional agencies Valuers; insurance companies; banks; other building societies; solicitors.
Filing systems — computer/manual.
Different classification of changes and authority linked to each e.g. letters, forms, probate letters of administration statutory declaration forms, power of attorney.
Range of customer accounts

EVIDENCE REQUIRED

Performance evidence over time for the range of customer accounts and with different amendments. Simulations may be used to supplement.
Knowledge of the type of amendment that may be necessary and the implications this has for the various accounts will be needed in order to be able to perform.
Knowledge evidence may be used to supplement that available from performance, although as much of the work is proceduralized, valid tests may be difficult to devise.
Plus which knowledge can and should be disclosed to other organizations, societies etc. (pc — c & d): what copies and correspondence should be forwarded to and reasons for this, in terms of building society's relationship to other professionals in the field (pc — d); why files should be in correct location (e.g. for others, for ease of access) (pc — a); why contingency situations (or likely ones) should be referred on (pc — h).

Figure 2

Occupational Standards for Managers
(Management II)

Key Purpose: *to achieve the organization's objectives and continuously improve its performance*

Key Role: *Manage People*

Unit II 6   Develop teams, individuals and self to enhance performance.
Element II 6.4   Evaluate and improve the development processes used.

Performance criteria:

(a)   The applicability and usefulness of development processes are discussed and agreed with all the individuals/teams concerned.

(b)   Where development processes have proved inappropriate and/or the resources used are unsuitable or inadequate, suitable alternatives are proposed, discussed and agreed.

(c)   Where development plans have proved to be unrealistic for whatever reason, appropriate modifications are made following discussion and agreement.

(d)   Information on the strengths and weaknesses of development processes is offered to appropriate people in order to improve overall practice.

(e)   Experience from past development is used to improve current practice.

Range indicators:

Evaluation and improvement relates to all development processes used by the manager whether they are:
- work activities
- formal education/ training
- informal education/ training.

Evaluation of development processes will include analysis which is both:
- quantitative
- qualitative.

Information on which the evaluation is based includes:
- written evidence
- oral evidence
- numerical data.

Discussion and consultation involves:
- higher level managers
- subordinates
- colleagues, specialists, staff in other departments
- external development organization(s).

Information on the strengths and weaknesses of development processes is offered to:
- higher level managers
- colleagues, specialists, staff in other departments
- external development organization(s).

tioners is the Burrows approach at McGill University in North America. It entails confronting students with real patients (or carefully trained actors simulating patients) from day one of their degree programme. Students are helped to identify their own learning needs so that they are able to complete diagnosis and decide on subsequent action.

There is no doubt that individuals can learn much from experience but most effective learning requires a clear insight into what is required and criteria for judging whether or not what should be learned has been learned. The new standards provide the necessary descriptions and the performance criteria needed for this. However, even in the simplest of occupations, competence is not solely about performing a limited range of routine tasks on a day-to-day basis. As suggested by the Job Competence Model, competence also includes planning and organizing responding to contingencies, and recognizing and responding to the job/role environment. The extent to which such constituent skills and associated knowledge and understanding can be acquired through experiential learning in the workplace depends on both the cost of supervision and the added value (or cost of failure) of the work activity.

Where there is significant risk that incompetence could result in a potential safety hazard to the individual or others or significant financial loss, it is likely that the individual would be required to demonstrate an intermediary level of attainment before tackling the full activity. For example, he or she could be assessed on the constituent skills, perhaps through the use of simulations.

Similarly, in the context of pre-employment education and training, learning programmes may be directed at enhancing initial employability without acquiring full competence. Under such conditions it may be desirable to design learning strategies which initially facilitate learning the constituent skills and/or underpinning knowledge and understanding. While the standards themselves have the capacity to provide added relevance, for the learner, there will be much of value in ensuring that the learning occurs in an integrated way which links it as closely as possible to the application. Where young people are in transition from school to work, or where adults are seeking to prepare themselves for a range of promotion possibilities or alternative employment opportunities, they may find it most useful to pursue a learning programme which enhances those broad based or core skills which are relevant to a number of employment opportunities, rather than those which are relevant to a single occupational opportunity.

Higher order occupations, such as higher technician and professional occupations, are often preceded by a programme of full-time vocationally related education. Such programmes can be considerably quicker than those which depend on experiential learning in employment. (This does not, however, deny the value or relevance of such experiential learning). While it would seem desirable for such programmes to provide simulations of the employment situation through both practical and theoretical modelling, it would also seem likely that the major element of such programmes be concerned with developing the constituent skills, knowledge and understanding.

For entrants to such occupations and professions, it is likely that full-time, pre-employment programmes or programmes of pre-promotion education and training, will need to be supplemented by periods of supervised experiential learning in order to develop, and to be able to demonstrate, full competence.

The extent of such post-education experiential learning that would be required, might well reflect the diversity of employment opportunities that is served by the pre-employment programme. The development and application of more explicit standards will make it far clearer to employers what can and should not be expected of candidates, and will provide greater insight into what learning might be required in order to gain full competence.

Finally, within the context of devising learning programmes, the more explicit standards should make analysis of training and education needs far easier. In particular, the more detailed performance criteria provide much greater insight into why competence has not yet been achieved. Remedial learning may be much more clearly focused, and the need for it, and its objectives, better understood by the learner.

Assessment

In essence, certification offers a form of guarantee to other users. Certification of competence recognizes that the individual has presented sufficient, valid evidence to convince a recognized assessor that he or she is able to perform effectively to the standards as defined within the unit. The assessors will be concerned not only with validity and sufficiency but also currency and reliability.

There is no such thing as 100 per cent certainty in assessor's judgements. The collection of diverse, valid and relevant evidence can enhance the reliability of the certification. However, the law of diminishing returns applies and there has to be a balance between the volume and cost of evidence collected and the importance of the certification.

There is likely to be some link between the complexity, diversity, and extensiveness of the assessment processes, and the cost of failure or added value of the role to which a unit applies, or the occupation to which a qualification applies. It is likely that assessment to determine the competence of a potential commercial airline pilot will be far more extensive, possibly more rigorous, and definitely more expensive, than the assessment which might be applied to a shop assistant.

Candidates for assessment may present a diversity of evidence, particularly if they are seeking credit through the assessment of prior learning. On the other hand, structured, formalized education and training programmes will probably have built within them assessment processes designed to yield adequate evidence.

Probably the best evidence of competence comes from effective performance in the workplace. The likelihood that a single workplace can provide an opportunity to demonstrate full competence diminishes as the occupation becomes more diverse and complex. Time constraints may not allow collection of sufficient evidence. In more demanding occupations the challenges which face the individual become more unique, and it becomes more difficult to attribute the outcomes of good or bad decisions to a single person because either they are the outcomes of teamwork, or there is an extended time delay before the rightness of the decision manifests itself. There are also conditions where there is not one right solution, or today's solution may not be the best solution tomorrow. Under all such conditions, evidence of constituent skills, the application of knowledge and understanding, etc., (derived through simulations and case studies perhaps), may have an important part to play in forming views as to competence. Similarly, under some conditions, it may also be valuable to seek evidence of explicit knowledge and understanding of fundamental concepts and principles.

For any unit, there may well be a preferred balance of evidence. Such a balance may include essential evidence acquired from the workplace or a near simulation, and other evidence that might be acquired from performance, or alternatively through simulations and case studies, possibly supplemented by assessment of knowledge etc. For the new entrant to an occupation, particularly in more demanding occupations, it is likely that there will be considerable emphasis on collecting evidence of the constituent skills, knowledge and understanding supplemented by evidence of effective performance in the workplace. However, the more mature applicant, with extensive employment experience, able to present evidence of effective performance over an extended period of time, perhaps in a diversity of contexts, might need only to present limited evidence of the underpinning skills, knowledge and understanding in order to satisfy an assessor of his or her competence. Such matters are discussed in more detail in the reports of the APL project referred to previously.

Amongst those who facilitate learning in education and training contexts, there are very different levels of expertise in assessing core certification purposes. Few, if any, have extensive experience in assessing against competence based standards. Where assessment is to national standards, for certification purposes it has either occurred as an integral part of a learning process or has been characterized by a one-off, short duration test. Neither condition has sought to collect evidence of competence, neither has required the assessor to form a judgement on the sufficiency of evidence, balancing evidence derived from performance in employment, in simulations of case studies, or derived through oral questioning or written responses. Where assessment has been an integral part of a learning programme, if developed and delivered locally, the assessor has been able to control the evidence that it presented through the structure of the assessment process. Where assessments are set (and often judged) centrally, they have been characterized by those things which are easily designed and administered under such conditions. Of course, preconceptions as to assessment processes and expectations have dominated what have been learnt.

All of this implies that not only will there be a need for those who deliver assessment to be adequately briefed on the new standards, there may well also be a need for training so that they can better design and deliver relevant assessment processes and evaluate, with adequate consistency, diverse evidence. It is significant that, where NVQs are being established, it is not unusual for Lead Bodies and Awarding Bodies to require that those who deliver assessment should have demonstrated competence as assessors. Looking ahead, it seems unlikely that all teachers will simply be assumed to be competent to assess for certification purposes.

There are also new challenges for Awarding Bodies. Current developments imply a greater emphasis on locally delivered assessment, by recognized assessors, subject to external verification procedures. Given the costs of external verification, it would seem likely that nationwide external verification may depend upon on effective local verification. Traditionally such verification has been an integral part of the activities of the teaching institution. It is dependent on peer scrutiny and support. It is likely that, where there are candidates or assessors (for example in a specific workplace), there will be a need to establish low-cost verification, perhaps through facilitating the local networking of a number of workplaces. Clearly, there will be a range of marketing opportunities for educational and training establishments to provide assessment and verification services. However, from what has been said already, it is probable that, to deliver such services, institutions will have to invest in further staff development. Indeed, in some ways, it is unfortunate that the current initiatives in education to develop more explicit standards to describe expected learning and the move towards criterion referenced assessment did not occur 10 years earlier. If it had done so, many in education would already have much of the expertise necessary to support, contribute to, and indeed, carve out a clear role within, the move towards establishing qualifications which attest to occupational competence. The current developments within the context of NVQs and occupational standards of competence draw heavily on research that has been carried out in the context of education over the past three decades or more. Perhaps, for too long, there has been a tendency in higher education to ignore the expertise lodged within its fraternity — within the schools of psychology and education. Current developments reflecting concern with quality, and giving a higher focus to staff development, provide the opportunity to redress the balance.

References

BLACK, H. and WOLF, A. (1990) *Knowledge and Competence, Current Issues in Training and Education*, Sheffield, ED,TA and COIC.

BUILDING SOCIETY LEAD BODY (1989) *Financial Services — Building Society Sector Standards*, London, BSCB.

BURKE, J. (1989) *Competency Based Education and Training*, London, Falmer Press.

CONFEDERATION OF BRITISH INDUSTRY (1989) *Towards a Skills Revolution*, London, CBI.

CONNER and WARR (1989) Private Communication, Sheffield University, Social & Applied Psychology Unit, Dept of Psychology.

EMPLOYMENT DEPARTMENT (1988) *Employment for the 1990s*, Cm. 540, London, HMSO.

EMPLOYMENT DEPARTMENT/DEPARTMENT OF EDUCATION AND SCIENCE (1986) *Working Together: Education and Training*, Cm. 9823, London, HMSO.

EMPLOYMENT DEPARTMENT, TRAINING AGENCY (1987) *Competence and Assessment, A Quarterly Bulletin*, Sheffield, ED,TA.

EMPLOYMENT DEPARTMENT, TRAINING AGENCY (1988–91) *Development of Assessable Standards for National Certification*, Sheffield, ED,TA.

MANAGEMENT CHARTER INITIATIVE (1990) Experienced Managers Project 1990, private communication, (report expected in the Autumn 1990) London, MCI.

MANAGEMENT CHARTER INITIATIVE (1990) *Occupational Standards for Managers*, London, MCI.

MANSFIELD, B. and MATHEWS, J. (1985) *The Job Competence Model*, Bristol, FESC.

MANPOWER SERVICES COMMISSION (1981) *A New Training Initiative*, London, HMSO.

NATIONAL COUNCIL FOR VOCATIONAL QUALIFICATIONS (1988) *The NVQ Criteria and Related Guidance*, London, NCVQ.

NATIONAL COUNCIL FOR VOCATIONAL QUALIFICATIONS (1990) *Database of Qualifications*, London, NCVQ.

NATIONAL COUNCIL FOR VOCATIONAL QUALIFICATIONS/SUSAN SIMOSKO (1990) *Report of the NCVQ APL Project*, Sheffield, ED,TA.

SCHRODER, H. (1989) *Managerial Competence — The Key to Excellence*, Dubuque, Kendall/Hunt.

SCOTTISH EDUCATION DEPARTMENT (1983) *16–18s in Scotland* — An Action Plan, Edinburgh, SED.

SCOTTISH VOCATIONAL EDUCATION COUNCIL (1989) *Report of the SCOTVEC APL Project*, Glasgow, SCOTVEC.

TRADES UNION CONGRESS (1989) *Skills 2000*, London, TUC.

Chapter 2

Competence and Higher Education: Implications for Institutions and Professional Bodies

John Burke

Introduction and Background

The consequences of nearly twelve years of Thatcherism have been felt in virtually every aspect of life in the UK, and after experiencing the savage rounds of 'cuts' during the 1980s, the universities no longer feel immune from the demands of the market economy. With the loss of the premium in overseas student fees, lower levels of funding, new forms of acceptability and the necessity to explore new sources of income merely to survive, Higher Education has been forced — and continues to be forced — to review its policy and practice.

Some of the reforms and some of the new trends have been viewed with considerable apprehension and suspicion, for very good reason. The short-term needs of economy cannot be permitted to so dominate the concerns of HE that it loses sight of its essential mission, but some significant change or realignment appears necessary if it is to play its part in contributing to the well-being of society, a society which reflects the concerns of a trading nation which must compete in international markets if it is to survive in recognizable form.

Change Conceptualized as Intervention and Osmosis

McNair (1989) characterizes changes in terms of External and Internal Pressures; I adopt a similar but significantly different conceptualization: change in terms of Intervention and Osmosis.

Interventions may be divided into (a) Interventions already taking place and (b) Interventions planned but not yet put into effect.

The most obvious examples of 'Interventions' in the first category are various HE research projects, focusing on competence, sponsored or directed by the Training Agency (TA). The impetus for this work arises outside HE — external pressure in McNair's term — but is taken up by HE and, as we shall see, transformed or transmuted in the process.

The most significant intervention in the second category is the extension of the National Vocational Qualification (NVQ) Framework above Level 4, encompassing graduate and professional qualifications.

Osmosis refers to changes which 'seep' into HE and may be seen as arising as a response to internally recognized needs. I see 'osmotic' changes occurring in HE as a result of features of competency based approaches being 'absorbed' into HE, largely as a result of what is happening in terms of NVQs and parallel developments in the National Curriculum. It will be noticed that developments in HE have close correspondences with developments outside HE; the diffusion of competence based approaches through what had been conceived as the impermeable membrane of HE suggests an apparent reversal of the causal relationship which has previously obtained.

Intervention may bring about rapid and directed change as a result of **policy** initiatives. Osmosis is a more gradual process of absorption as new ideas permeate an environment; this may bring about a climate of change, a supportive ethos and an embedding in **practice**; this may precede policy. When the change process is handled with sensitivity, duly acknowledging Adam's principle of enlightened 'self interest', symbiosis or mutual reciprocity and reinforcement may occur.

National Vocational Qualifications will impact on HE in the very near future. Although conceptualized as an intervention (above), NVQs should benefit not only from the pioneering work in HE projects sponsored by the TA but also, clearly, from osmosis. At the time of writing (July, 1990) there are some 170 NVQs which have been accredited, estimated to encompass 30 per cent of the workforce. As the standards development programme (see Chapter 1) bears fruit, there should be a rapid growth in the NVQ framework.

By January 1992, Jessup (1990a) estimates there will be nearly 900 NVQs covering the employment functions of up to 80 per cent of the working population. By that time, the gaps in provision will largely relate to Level 5 and specialized occupations. With this rapid growth in the NVQ programme, there will be two notable effects: (1) many of the ideas underpinning the notion of NVQs, at present seemingly arcane or esoteric, will have filtered into public consciousness; (2) development work will be well under way in extending the NVQ framework to graduate and professional qualifications (this remit was enjoined in February, 1989).

Any new technical development involving new ideas and unfamiliar language may well appear opaque and complicated at the outset. This is certainly true of NVQs with their detailed specificity. There is a lead time before these concepts become familiar and what once appeared complicated becomes much less so as the same pattern of units, elements, performance criteria and range statements consistently reoccur. At a deeper level, ideas about demystified and 'open' assessment, increased trainee or student autonomy, and clear target setting will be common coinage, if only because so large a part of the working population will have been and continue to be affected by them at work, at FE colleges and even in pursuit of some recreational activities. Even if NVQs were never introduced above Level 4, these ideas would affect HE as they featured in public debate about education and training, especially as this is an issue of increasing importance on political agendas; there has never before been such a convergence of views from different political parties and both sides of industry, the CBI and TUC. Further, new entrants to HE (and especially entrants from vocational routes) will have developed certain expectations about the outcomes of learning, born of their earlier experience, and they will be equipped with their new skills.

For the purposes of this chapter, I will illustrate some of the recent **interventions** in HE by reference to two projects. I will then go on to examine two issues which feature prominently in these projects: the notion of outcomes and skills, tracing their parallel development in lower-level NVQs and the National Curriculum. This will set the scene for a discussion of higher level NVQs, and their implications for HE institutions and professional bodies.

Interventions in HE: Two Research Projects

(a) Learning Outcomes and Credits in Higher Education

This two-year project was set up in 1989 by UDACE on TA funding to investigate and evaluate learning outcomes in HE. It began its work by developing descriptions of learning outcomes in five subject areas:

— Design
— Engineering
— English
— Environmental Science
— Social Science

with staff drawn from ten universities and polytechnics.

Three perspectives are being investigated, the views of:

(a) the teacher or course provider
(b) the student, and
(c) the employer.

The first task was to develop draft statements of what different departments expect students to learn and know — the outcomes. The project was designed to embrace a number of different disciplines and different degree structures so that different learning styles and forms of assessment could be investigated.

The work is well under way, and a number of interim reports have already appeared in different subject areas, including a 'statement' outlining the general characteristics of each area, the 'key purposes', major activities and the learning outcomes in relation to these activities.

The Design Group makes the point:

> ... it is important that the definition of learning outcomes should not inhibit, or constrain, or merely provide criteria for failure, but should positively facilitate the identification of a student's particular strengths, given that there may be a variety of equally valid routes to a design solution, and open out design education opportunities.

This is very much in line with the recommendation from the HE White Paper (DES, 1987) which argues that in HE standards and quality of teaching need to be judged by reference mainly to student achievement. Numbers and class of degrees and non-completion rates do provide a measure of success but 'standards of attainment in the specialist knowledge and competence associated with the particular subject of study are the key criteria' (3.15).

UDACE (1989, p. 6) comments:

> Measuring the increase in knowledge would appear to be a fairly straight forward process, and one in which there is already consider-able experience and expertise ...

> Competence is more problematic. (...) Definitions of competence in vocational education are often based on performance to a standard which excludes elements of achievements like the development of learning skills, persistence or teamwork.

Since this was written, the NCVQ and NCC both produced their reports on core skills; the NCVQ report addresses this issue directly in proposing the development and assessment of core skills in NVQs as common learning outcomes in both A/S and A levels and NVQ 3s as well as lower-level core skills, which goes some way to meeting this criticism; the NCVQ also proposes to develop core skills in levels above 1–3, which will reflect a range of more demanding skills. This area of enquiry has also become the main focus of the second project, Enterprise in Higher Education, which is considered in the next section.

(b) Enterprise in Higher Education

When the Enterprise in Higher Education (EHE) Initiative was first launched by the TA, the concept of 'enterprise' was not defined with any precision.

This allowed a range of possible interpretations. With the benefit of nearly two years of experience, the TA distinguished three strands of meaning:

1 Entrepreneurship: the qualities and skills which enable people to succeed in business enterprises.
2 Personal effectiveness: the qualities and skills possessed by the resourceful individual.
3 Transferable skills: the generic capabilities which allow people to succeed in a wide range of different tasks and jobs.

Each strand of meaning is clearly focused on skills, which were recognized as 'generic skills':

Enterprise skills are the generic skills which are needed in all jobs. They include effective communication and problem solving, the ability to create and seize opportunities, to think creatively and take calculated risks where necessary. Enterprising people take the initiative and are pro-active, can work co-operatively with and through other people, can manage resources and assume responsibility. (TA, 1988, p. 52)

The rationale behind the project is outlined by the TA:

Employers often find graduates strong on subject knowledge and analysis but lacking in the personal skills and the understanding of working life which would make them fully effective people, ready to take responsibility forward effectively with others. Enterprise in Higher Education is an initiative intended to change that, across UK higher education. (TA, 1990)

Support for this view is strongly expressed in a report issued by a joint working party set up in November 1989 by the Institute of Physics, the Standing Conference of Professors of Physics and the Committee of Head of Physics in Polytechnics to consider the future pattern of degree courses in the light of curriculum changes taking place in schools and the advent of the single European market in 1992.

The report notes that both students and employers have already indicated that the present courses are far from satisfactory: physics students said in a recent survey carried out by the Council for National Academic Awards that they did not feel they had gained much from their courses by way of self-confidence, communication skills and the ability to absorb information as did students in other disciplines; industrialists claim that new graduates lack communication skills and aptitude for solving the kinds of problems industry tackles. (Unsigned article, *Physics World*, June 1990)

But there are broader implications arising from present practice. Not only are students not developing the skills they will require when they seek employment, but their experience of working in an academic environment divorced from 'real-life' constraints is a further hindrance:

> The scientist who enters industry must therefore be prepared to work with partially defined systems (...) Thus the solution to key problems which may be encountered in industry frequently comes from the amalgamation of different specialist knowledge. This again contrasts markedly with the requirements of academia in which progress is more often marked by the collaboration of like-minded and similarly trained specialists. (Grayson, 1990)

Vella (1989) identifies a number of skills which are necessary not only as a practising scientist, but also as a biochemistry student. The honing and enhancement of these skills is particularly important from the perspective of a professional, who has a life-long practical (and ethical) obligation to up-date knowledge and keep abreast of developments within his or her profession. Six skills are singled out:

(i) Skills required for continuing self-education (i.e. the ability to learn from printed and oral sources).
(ii) Skills of critical thinking.
(iii) Skills which relate to productive scientific work (planning, co-operation, creative imagination, problem solving, discerning opportunities, explanation of alternatives, and choosing, generation and evaluation of hypotheses and models).
(iv) Skills of communication (oral, written and electronic). Computer skills.
(vi) Technical and manual instrumentation skills.

As the project became embedded in different institutions, different facets of 'enterprise' began to emerge.

> (EHE) is about developing all forms of enterprising skills, not just entrepreneurial skills, in addition to **academic skills**. Indeed the emphasis that has emerged is on personal transferable skills, **learning skills** and the ability to operate effectively with colleagues. (Faulkner, 1990, emphasis added)

Leeds Polytechnic was even more explicit:

> *The Enterprise Project is about curriculum change.* It is a central feature of the commitment by Leeds Polytechnic to the successful accomplishment of learning by all its students.
>
> (The Enterprise Unit, Leeds Polytechnic, 1990, original emphasis)

This emphasis on 'learning skills' is also clearly expressed in the Open University's proposal (1990):

> The University intends to strengthen the support it provides to students in the identification and development of skills relevant to their personal and career goals. This will be achieved through a programme which develops the concept of the 'enterprising learner'.
>
> In initiating this programme, the University's central concern is with the relationship between the concept of enterprise and the processes involved in learning. In our view these processes are shared by students, staff and employers ...
>
> The Enterprise Programme will have three aims:
>
> — to support students through a process of self-assessment and target-setting leading to the identification of clear personal and vocational objectives.
> — to support staff as they create opportunities for students to become enterprising learners.
> — to maximize the potential and current opportunities within the existing curriculum which encourages students to be enterprising.

Judging from the way the EHE project appears to be unfolding in different institutions, learning skills and a raft of personal skills are being identified and enhanced across each discipline within the participating institutions. Each institution is required to:

1 target learning outcomes for students;
2 devise new curricula for all students in all disciplines within the institution;
3 encourage students to take a more active part in 'ownership' of their learning;
4 arrange project work in partnership with employers, providing students with an opportunity to experience 'real life' problems.

To bring this about, institutions are required to initiate staff development programmes and adjust management structures which encourage and ensure delivery of the project objectives so that they are integrated in the institutional curriculum.

Osmosis: The Competence Based Movement

The competence based movement is most visibly represented in the National Council for Vocational Qualifications (NCVQ), which has brought about a 'quiet revolution' (Burke, 1989a, pp. 1–2) in vocational education and training (VET). It is important to appreciate that the NVQ framework is not simply one development in a series of short-lived reforms (cf. Burke, 1989b, pp. 121–2). It is a fundamental reorganization and reorientation in vocational education and training with major, far-reaching consequences. In comparison, previous attempts at reform in terms of new initiatives, curricula and examinations appear as 'tinkering' with details in the superstructure. Originally inspired by the seminal White Paper *A New Training Initiative* (ED, 1981), and reinforced by White Papers in 1984, 1985 and 1986, NVQs involved a radical reconceptualization of the purposes of education and training, the needs of the individual, the technical requirements of assessment, set in the context of national needs now and well into the next century.

Among the many developments within NVQs, we may focus on two which have already translated themselves into HE and which are likely to become increasingly important: a concern with 'outcomes' and 'generic competences' or 'core skills'. While neither is exclusively linked to competency-based approaches, both feature as important developments.

(a) Outcomes

The clearest and most comprehensive account of the thinking behind NVQs is by Gilbert Jessup, Director of Research, Development and Information at the NCVQ, but writing here in a personal capacity. *Outcomes: NVQs and the Emerging Model of Education and Training* is a personal statement and does not necessarily reflect NCVQ policy. Its publication (1990a) marks a subtle but significant shift in emphasis from the early work, as is signalled by the title. The emphasis is on **outcomes**, the focus on education and training, not, significantly, **vocational** education and training. This allows him scope to broach all outcomes (not exclusively 'competency based') and all education and training. A focus on the outcomes of learning is listed as the second fundamental criterion underlying NVQs but Jessup sees it as the **key** concept in the emerging competency based model because it confers a vital principle of coherence on all the activities which characterize the NVQ approach, most notably:

A genuinely comprehensive Framework, where individual qualifications (and even 'part qualifications') relate to each other;

Open access, and progression;

The Accreditation of Prior Learning;

> Independence of mode of learning, or attendance;
> A 'demystified' assessment process which is open, and equitable and 'fit for purpose'.

These are not just desirable characteristics, they can be shown to follow logically and coherently from the adoption of 'outcomes' as the organizing principle. For the first time in the history of education and training in this country, it is becoming possible to plot the contribution and the relationship between different kinds of qualification. With the creation of the NCVQ Database, anyone with access to a terminal is empowered to interrogate any of the qualifications within the framework and to make the best use of provision in terms of his or her needs, his or her career goals. This will give an increasingly large number of HE entrants experience of the control over their own learning, previously inexperienced by any student group; it is surmised they will not wish to yield this control as they progress.

Jessup (1990a) recognizes that in promoting competence, there may be legitimate and worthwhile objectives other than competency:

> In many areas, particularly at the higher levels of competence, there is a related body of knowledge and theory which underpins a wide range of competent performance. This body of knowledge would normally have its own internal coherence and should be acquired and understood by students. It would not be appropriate to perceive it, and assess it, simply in relation to elements of competence. (Chapter 18)

The important point for Jessup is that education and training should be **goal-directed** towards explicit outcomes, although, again, he is quick to assert that pre-determined outcomes are not necessarily the only worthwhile outcomes:

> Whether pursuing general or specific objectives individuals will learn more effectively if they are clear about the targets or learning outcomes they are trying to achieve. Learning is a purposive activity and should be targeted on explicit outcomes. This should not discourage incidental and additional learning taking place en route which is not part of the plan. Nor should it stop people following tangential lines of enquiry out of curiosity. In fact, such additional learning is more likely to be stimulated within the context of a learning plan. (Chapter 1)

This argument is set in a context where the actual outcomes of learning may be negligible or even counterproductive. He emphasizes this by distinguishing aims and objectives from outcomes:

... the way Shakespeare or poetry are taught in schools may actually put more people off these pursuits as adults than the number it stimulates to continue. This is not to question the aim of such education, only the outcome. (Chapter 1)

It is also set in a context where the outcomes of HE may be counterproductive:

Too often new graduates leave universities with a patchy or *even wholly misleading view* of what life is like as a physicist in one of the largest sectors of potential employment: manufacturing industry ... (Editorial, *Physics World*, June, 1990) (emphasis added).

This 'subtle shift' has considerable implications for HE. It refutes the common assumption that NVQs are necessarily limited in their applicability to education by their provenance in training. The direct and broad focus is firmly placed on the development and assessment of competence as an outcome. In NVQ levels 1–4, the focus is targeted on 'occupational competence' as the desired outcome to be assessed, while acknowledging that other valuable intended and 'unintended' (in the sense of unprespecified) outcomes may accrue. Above level 4, the nature of the competence to be assessed may still be 'occupational competence' as this is the established domain of the different professions with a responsibility for licensing and overseeing the professional competence of their members. In fact some professions have independently developed a sophisticated competency based approach, for example The Chartered Society of Physiotherapists, and other professional training groups, such as commercial airline pilot training, clearly have a paramount competency focus. It may still be the focus of graduate and postgraduate disciplines in HE where the discipline is clearly vocational, for example Veterinary Surgery, Dentistry, Law. Again, in the USA, it is already possible to qualify as a physician through competency based training. But there are some disciplines in HE for which a focus on occupational competence would not be appropriate, for example Philosophy or Classics.

We may acknowledge that on a continuum between, say, Dentistry and Philosophy, the majority of disciplines will have a clearly vocational stratum but will have other desirable outcomes which go far beyond any particular occupational requirement. The identification, description and analysis of these competences is just beginning.

While Jessup's focus on outcomes clearly acknowledges that all outcomes in NVQs will not be occupational competence outcomes, he draws out attention to a further point: among prespecified outcomes there should be some outcomes which have (broadly defined) occupational relevance, no matter what the subject or discipline studied. The point is that even the study of philosophy is instrumental and vocational in so far as it is perceived by its students as a means to an end, a satisfying career. In philosophy, analysis and communication are honed very carefully within the contextual ambit of the discipline. With little effort, the context could be enlarged so that students were reflexively aware of the value of these skills in the world of employment. Employment, presumably, is a desired (eventual) outcome of their course. It is reasonable, therefore, to suggest that all courses should effectively contribute to that outcome. Such skills are known variously as 'core' skills or 'generic' competences and are highly valued in employment (cf. CBI, 1989; ICI, 1989; Institute of Physics, 1990); again, these concerns are taken up when we consider HE Projects.

(b) Core Skills or Generic Competences

In March, 1990, the National Curriculum Council (NCC) issued a report *Core Skills 16–19*, a response to the Secretary of State recommending that six core skills: communication, problem-solving, personal skills, numeracy, information technology, modern language competence, 'should be incorporated into the study programmes of all 16–19 year olds' (NCC, 1990, 3.11)
   The report continues:

> The six core skills identified by NCC should be embedded in A and AS syllabuses wherever possible and be a requirement of syllabus design. They overlap and reinforce one another, but their separate identification is essential in curriculum planning and for assessment and reporting. (Para 3.12)

The NCC divided these skills into two groups, the first of which

> **communication, problem solving and personal skills** should be developed and embedded in every A and AS syllabus. These skills are continuously developed through life. They are fundamental to learning and used in all occupations. (Para 4.12)

The NCC acknowledges that numeracy, information technology and modern language competence, although equally important, could not be fully developed in every subject but where possible they should be included.
   Almost simultaneously, the National Council for Vocational Qualifications (NCVQ) published a report *Common Learning Outcomes: Core Skills in A/AS Levels and NVQs* (Jessup, 1900b). This report endorsed the NCC recommendations and went some way forward in describing the technical requirements for a framework of core skills which would be common and transferable between NVQs and A and AS levels and the mechanisms which might be employed in assessing these skills in NVQs.
   In a paper to Council (July, 1990) Jessup proposed to initiate a joint development programme with SEAC and others to create a progressive

structure of core skill outcomes, giving priority to the areas of problem solving, communication and personal skills within the first three levels of NVQs.

These initiatives stemmed from a growing recognition of the importance of bridging the divide between academic and vocational education, and school and employment. The (then) Secretary of State for Education, Mr Kenneth Baker stressed the importance of identifying core skills in a speech in February, 1989. The Confederation of British Industry (CBI) issued a report in October, 1989, calling for a 'skills revolution', 'offering more relevant transferable skills and broadbased qualifications'. In November 1989, the new Secretary of State, John MacGregor asked the NCC and SEAC, in consultation with others (including the NCVQ), to prepare proposals for incorporating core skills and assessing them in the National Curriculum. SEAC is about to publish its own recommendations and these are understood to be in line with both the NCC and NCVQ reports. The implications for HE institutions are obvious. Future cohorts of students will enter HE conscious of the importance of core skills in learning programmes, and, it is surmised, increased skills in these areas. In particular, with better communication skills and an ingrained problem-solving approach, these more autonomous learners will demand (and deserve) a specifically pedagogic response. This may affect styles of teaching and learning, but it may also make demands for innovative curriculum content, and more equitable and meaningful processes of assessment. Students will be more conscious of the world of employment, and the perceived relevance of the kind of learning they are about to experience. (See Elton, Chapter 9, this volume, for a further discussion of this and related points).

It should, perhaps, be noted that the rationale underlying the provision of Access Courses is that they develop the core skills considered essential for performance as an undergraduate, or at least provide the foundation skills necessary in making a 'bridge' to undergraduate level study. Over the past decade, access to HE has considerably widened in terms of entry qualification. This trend was affirmed by the 1987 White Paper *Higher Education: Meeting the Challenge* (DES, 1987), which commented on the three generally recognized routes:

— traditional sixth form qualifications, i.e., A levels, with the recent addition of AS Levels, and Scottish Highers
— vocational qualifications
— access courses.

This should be read in conjunction with the White Paper's projections of entrants to HE:

Of potentially greater impact, however, is the assumption underlying Projection Q (the optimistic projection) that there will be a significant increase in the proportion of qualifying young people who enter higher education. This will depend very largely on continuing growth in demand for higher education from young women, *alongside increases in the proportion of higher education entrants with vocational and technical qualifications (...) The development of the Technical and Vocational Initiative (TVEI) and the two year Youth Training Scheme (YTS), and the streamlining associated with the National Council for Vocational Qualifications (NCVQ) and the Scottish Action Plan, should increase the proportion of young people gaining qualifications and is likely to motivate more of them to seek entry to higher education.* (DES, 1987, 2.8, pp. 6–7, emphasis added).

Summary of Osmotic Influences

The 'osmotic' Influences may be summarized:

— Wider access will mean more students entering HE from vocational routes. HE will need to build on their experience and go some way to meet their well-rounded and legitimate expectations about learning.
— Students who enter HE by the traditional academic routes will share some of these expectations.
— Students will have experience of working to targeted outcomes, in the form of statements of attainment in the National Curriculum or units of competence in NVQs.
— Students will have an awareness of core skills, and, it is surmised, increased proficiency as autonomous learners, problem solvers and communicators, among other skills.
— Students will have an increased awareness, and a broader experience, of the process of assessment, demystified assessment. They will have experience of continuous assessment, and expect some kind of record of achievement.
— Students will have greater choice. Some institutions may feel immune from this pressure over the short term, with many more applicants than places but they will know (cf. White Paper, 1987) that accountability is very much linked to founding. With an increased awareness of 'industry needs' (translated as career expectations), students will want to make connections between what is on offer and what they see as relevant.

Higher Level NVQs

In February, 1989, the Secretary of State for Education extended the NCVQ remit to include professional and graduate qualifications. Because of the daunting task of getting the lower-level NVQ framework up and running by 1992, higher level qualifications have been temporarily relegated to the back-burner, though some preliminary negotiation, especially with professional bodies, has taken place. Although problems associated with assessing knowledge and understanding in both professional and graduate awards may be of similar complexity, in one respect professional qualifications are very much more straightforward, for two reasons: (1) as professional bodies tend to control and license their members in terms of occupational groupings, they present themselves as obvious 'Industry Lead Bodies' (See Debling, Chapter 1, this volume, for a description of Lead Bodies) in determining standards; (2) the concept of 'occupational competence' (the first fundamental criterion underlying NVQs) is especially relevant for virtually all professions.

In contrast, 'occupational competence' may be very inadequate when applied to many academic disciplines, which lack an occupational focus. The nature of the competence to be assessed in HE needs to be determined. The UDACE research into outcomes in HE and the EHE project should provide valuable pointers and experience on which to build.

At the time of writing, the UDACE project has not yet reached its half-way point but two concerns need to be noted. (1) The description of current outcomes is obviously very useful as a starting point in specifying outcomes; it is very much less useful if it does not move on to set targets rather than merely state what is being done. (2) The process of assessment in NVQs has become an intregal part of the learning process and has enjoined a rigorous reappraisal of examinations; the eventual success of this project must be judged, at least in part, by its success in overcoming the formidable problems involved in breaking out of the self-imposed straitjacket of undergraduate final examinations, limited, in most disciplines, to essay writing.

The EHE project, focusing on skills, is clearly preparing the ground for the eventual introduction of higher level NVQs. It is stimulating a fundamental reappraisal of purpose and process and it is doing it by seeking to gain consent across institutions, an extraordinarily difficult task to accomplish within the cultural traditions of HE, and especially difficult in universities with their jealously guarded and highly prized autonomy.

In the meantime, a raft of technical issues to do with the assessment of knowledge and understanding (cf. Black and Wolf, 1990), the nature of the competence to be assessed and the derivation of standards in HE await resolution, although it is assumed that HE will make an increasing contribution to these debates as they acquire a more immediate relevance for all HE institutions.

Implications for Institutions and Professions

I noted earlier an important difference between the implications for professions and the implications for HE institutions: the immediate relevance of occupational competency to all professions but its more problematic relationship with many (but not all) HE disciplines. Among other obvious differences, the kind of knowledge required and valued by professionals is very striking. Eraut (1985) makes the point very succinctly:

> New knowledge is created both in the research community and in each professional community. But each places different valuations on different kinds of knowledge in a way that minimizes their inter-pretation. The particularistic nature of knowledge gained by practis-ing professionals presents yet another barrier to knowledge creation: both its exchange with other professionals and its incorporation into theory are limited by its specificity, and often by its implicitness.

Eraut argues that we should recognize that much of the relevant expertise lies outside HE, but that its development is limited by the lack of appropriate structures for knowledge exchange.

The problem is exacerbated because the way knowledge is *used* by professionals often bears little relationship to the way it is organized and taught within HE, as is amply demonstrated by Boreham (1989 and 1990). He cites the example of clinicians in prescribing drugs for epilepsy; not only did they not use the theory they had learned at university but found it could not be used in practice. Other examples abound. Nearer home, the mismatch between theory and practice in education used to be a bye-word in staff rooms, although that dysfunction has been recognized and at least partly rectified with the emergence of 'classroom studies' employing an ethno-graphic perspective to what is actually going on. Grayson (1990), quoted earlier, furnishes a further recent example.

In my view, the solution to these problems lies in closer collaboration between HE and the professions, with professional bodies taking a more active role in specifying needs and assisting in more meaningful assessment procedures. The need for active cooperation is recognized in a recent report in the *UK Press Gazette* (1990):

> Once the NCTJ proficiency test is replaced by the NVQ (. . .) editors would have to stop criticising the NCTJ and get involved far more. The new tests would be university-based and unless editors were prepared to let college staff take over they would be needed at local universities to act as invigilators.

Not only invigilators, I suggest, but assessors and designers, and even occasional teachers. In the meantime, the fate of professional education is very much tied into HE provision, so the remaining implications may be appropriately considered as applying to both, *mutatis mutandis*.

A number of issues may be highlighted and briefly considered under six headings:

(a) Fundamental reappraisal of purpose,
(b) Suspicion,
(c) Inertia,
(d) Consent,
(e) Staff training,
(f) Funding.

(a) Fundamental Reappraisal of Purpose

In 1987, a government White Paper reaffirmed its commitment to HE, but also made some significant demands:

> The Government takes a wide view of the aims and purposes of higher education. It adheres to the Robbins Committee's definition (...) but above all there is an urgent need, in the interests of the nation as a whole, and therefore of universities, polytechnics, and colleges themselves, for higher education to take increasing account of the economic requirements of the country. Meeting the needs of the economy is not the sole purpose of higher education; nor can higher education alone achieve what is needed. But this aim, with its implications for the scale and quality of higher education, must be vigorously pursued. (...) The Government and its central funding agencies will do all they can to encourage and reward approaches by higher education institutions which bring them closer to the world of business. (DES, 1987, 1.2–1.7)

These 'significant demands' presage a shift in emphasis which has already taken place below HE. A number of initiatives aimed at taking an 'increasing account of the economic requirements of the country' have embedded themselves in the schools sector over the past ten years. TVEI, for example, may be seen as an attempt to make the school curriculum more relevant to the needs of employment. FE, too, culturally and traditionally more responsive to 'industrial needs', has been transformed. The prospects of a huge number of 'early school leavers' and people in employment have been the focus of attention from the MSC and, later, the TA. The creation of the NCVQ in 1986 marks a watershed. It was set up to bring about a fundamental reform of vocational education and training, with an emphasis on competency, to meet the real needs of industry by opening out opportunities for individuals to increase their skills and knowledge, and thereby enhance their employability. Shortly afterwards, the National Curriculum Council (NCC) and the School Examination and Assessment Council (SEAC) were set up, to bring about the changes of the 1988 Education Reform Act (ERA). Many of these initiatives started independently — that is, they were not the result of an overall 'masterplan', but reflected a growing consensus on trends and needs largely shared by all political parties, the CBI and the TUC. Thus Faulkner (1990), discussing the Enterprise in Higher Education (EHE) initiative, comments:

> It should be noted that the EHE initiative is not an isolated initiative but one of a number including TVEI, NVQs, GCSEs and the National Curriculum, which aim to improve the nation's skills to meet the challenges of a fast changing world. It is also part of an increasingly international move towards the development of personal skills.

Pressures for change

Pressure for change in HE has been mounting slowly. Slee (1990a) characterises the 1980s as a time of retrenchment and instrumentalism:

> In the 80s, there was no radical shift in culture . . . no major shift in perceived function . . . the reverse was true. Confused policy initiatives engendered powerful reaffirmation of cultural mores and a strengthening of belief in traditional functions.

These years may be likened to a developing wave, a drawing in and building of pressure. In the 1990s, the wave is likely to break. McNair (1989) sees a combination of demographic and economic external pressures leading to change throughout the adult education sector:

> These pressures will call for the development of a system of education and training which will:
> * be clearer about the objectives and outcomes of what is offered to learners;
> * offer modular structures of delivery linked credit accumulation and transfer;
> * place a heavier emphasis on the accreditation of competence, rather than on course completion;
> * stress the development of 'enterprise skills' (in the broad sense — qualities like initiative creativity, research and organizational skills) and transferability of skill and knowledge.

At the same time, internal forces will bring about change:

> Development will be encouraged and/or constrained by the tensions between three forces within the education and training system. These are:

* learners, who are concerned with their personal development and relevance to the opportunities open to them, in life and employment;
* those who pay for education and training (the 'customers' — including government, employers and individuals) who are concerned with 'value for money' and the assessment of outcomes;
* those who are concerned with the growth and survival of their organizations.

He goes on to suggest that the most rapid and positive development is likely to occur when the needs of all three are recognized; where one attempts to dominate the system, there will be powerful resistance from the others. (cf. Edwards, Chapter 7 and Field, Chapter 8, this volume).

Although McNair's analysis is directed to the whole of adult education and training, and not specifically to HE, it holds good for both HE and the education and training needs of the professions. This is evidenced in the growth and development of a number of initiatives in HE, and the initiatives in FE and the schools' sector (already mentioned) which will eventually feed into HE with predictable effects.

Changes already underway in HE

There is already considerable movement specifically in HE towards the kind of changes envisaged by McNair; his predictions may be usefully compared with what is already happening in HE:

'... a system clearer about objectives and outcomes ...'

An HE project co-ordinated by UDACE is examining learning outcomes across a broad spectrum of degree programmes in universities and polytechnics.

'... modular structure of delivery linked credit accumulation and transfer'

An increasing number of HE institutions have adopted modular programmes and have made reciprocal arrangements for transfer of credit among themselves, CATS (Credit Accumulation Transfer Scheme), while the Council for National Academic Awards (CNAA) is exploring the broad issue of competence in undergraduate programmes and the accreditation of prior learning.

'... emphasis on the accreditation of competence, rather than on course completion.'

> Virtually all HE courses have traditionally placed a heavy emphasis on assessing attainment rather than counting course completion (in contrast to much adult education). But, quite apart from possible requirements for inclusion in the higher level NVQ Framework, there has been an increased interest in specifying outcomes; cf. UDACE, above for example.

'Stress the development of 'enterprise skills' . . . and transferability of skill and knowledge.'

> In 1987, the Training Agency launched its massive project aimed at promoting 'enterprise' in HE and there is also considerable interest (and investment) in management competences conceived as core skills (cf. ICI, 1990). The University of Sheffield has set up a Personal Skills Unit to pioneer work nationally throughout HE in the development of transferable personal skills among undergraduates. Other projects, with a more focused orientation towards professions, include the Management Charter Initiative and Competences in School Management, mounted by School Management South, which represents a consortium of LEAs in the south east. (McNair, 1989)

The changes which are taking place, and are about to take place, need to be considered in a context where there is a good deal of suspicion in some quarters, and a feeling of complacency resulting in inertia in others.

(b) Suspicion

There is undoubtedly a huge fog of suspicion and misunderstanding enveloping the response of many well-intentioned teachers in HE. This extends from knee-jerk reactions to anything to do with training, through deep rooted suspicion of anything perceived as 'government' or politically inspired intervention, the erosion of academic independence and freedom, to well-grounded apprehensions about the purpose and mission of HE. Berger (1966) suggests that the first wisdom of sociology is that 'things ain't what they seem' and a healthy scepticism is endemic to academic life. But Berger's dictum cuts both ways. While motive may be endlessly discussed and debated, some attention should be directed to what is actually going on, and the reasoned arguments which support such change. The huge programme of change in NVQs is open to inspection, supported by a developing and critical literature; the EHE initiative has encouraged a wide interpretation in possible responses. The need for change is extensively and reliably documented, and supported by all political parties and both sides of industry. There is growing academic support from completely independent sources (of Physics Professors *et al.*, already quoted). But suspicion persists, as may be obliquely inferred from an article in *Enterprise at Nottingham Polytechnic* and a paper presented at an Enterprise conference at Durham University.

First, the polytechnic article:

What Isn't The Enterprise Initiative?

At this stage it may be helpful to review what Enterprise at the Polytechnic is not:

it is NOT part of the Department of Trade and Industry's Enterprise Initiative.

it is NOT related only to industry but to all forms of employment.

it is NOT about one political view point but about developing students able to contribute to a rapidly changing world.

above all it is NOT directly about income generation, as many assume, though it will, hopefully enhance our own income generating capacities. (Nottingham Polytechnic, 1990)

Second, the Durham paper; Dr Peter Slee is Director of the Durham University project which appears to have been notably successful (Barber, Hayward and Slee, 1990). He distinguished three notions of 'enterprise':

(a)   entrepreneurship;
(b)   industrial liaison;
(c)   developing skills in students.

Slee enlarges on these categories:

('Entrepreneurship') has some adherents. Not least at Whitehall. But not enough to make this a banner to march a programme under. Certainly in the 11 universities and most of the 12 polys this definition of enterprise is to rallying cries what lead balloons are to aviation, or chocolate fireguards to safety. Indeed, in Nottingham Poly's roguish 'course guide' on how to cock-up an EHE project, there is a section ranking in order of magnitude the ten strategies guaranteed most effective in raising apoplexy, wilful negligence, and pet-lips in academic colleagues. Constant use of the word 'entrepreneurial' came top of the list! This, of course is not surprising. Notwithstanding its ideological overtones in this context, entrepreurship simply does not square with traditional academic objectives. In short, this definition is highly exclusive. It does not square with most disciplinary hierarchies. It is therefore marginalised to a handful of business schools.

The second interpretation is more complex in Slee's account. He divines two main categories of liaison, differentiated by objective:

(a) first, 'relevance assurance'. Liaison that encourages HE to become more relevant to employer needs (project work, vacation placements, site visits, lectures).

(b) second, resource generation. There are two strands to this (1) control; employers have a say in what they pay (2) replacement of public expenditure.

He comments:

> The key strand of 'relevance assurance' stems from Callaghan's Ruskin speech. It has since been applied to range of schemes designed to rid industry and commerce of its tainted image among the young. It has been applied particularly powerfully to school programmes like Mini-Enterprise and TVEI (Mark 1) where there were expectations that 'real world' experience makes school more meaningful to the less well motivated pupil. (Barber *et al.*, 1990)

Slee likens this conception of 'EHE' as 'TVEI for HE'.

The third interpretation is the 'Enterprising Student (...) who develops the core skills, qualities and attitudes necessary for personal success in the world of employment'. This is, now, widely accepted as the 'preferred view' among participating institutions.

(c) Inertia

This is a particular problem in HE institutions which are prestigious or particularly successful in attracting students, or both. If the institution is successful, why bother? The Enterprise Director from one such institution advanced four arguments, centering on more open and fairer assessment, enhanced learning skills producing better results, an increased share in the student market at a time of demographic decline and the link between accountability and funding. The first three arguments fell on deaf ears, but most academics were particularly sensitive about the fourth. As each HE institution is now subject to external 'visitations' for an audit, it was pointed out that unless the institution could demonstrate its perceived success by acceptable criteria, some 'external criteria' might be imposed. It was therefore in everybody's interest to clarify the learning outcomes it was promoting and to provide some record of its students' success (record of achievement or 'profile') in developing the kind of learning skills which most academics claimed were already implicit in all their activities. This, then, is a useful strategy. It provides an 'efficient cause' (in Aristotle's term) to move from inertia to activity. The identification, recognition and enhancement of such skills follows in consequence, and further entails the examination of possible deficiencies. Teaching, learning and assessment strategies are reviewed.

In discussing undergraduate biochemistry, Green (1990) reflects on the 'mutually reinforcing dynamic' which begins to unfold once the process is started:

> If we now analyse *what* is taught/learned (*content*) with *how* it is taught/learned (*process*) we begin to see the twin activities of know-ledge accumulation and skill acquisition potentially provide a mutually reinforcing dynamic. Whatever the preferred end of the programme of study, whether it be the pursuit of scientific excel-lence *per se*, the attainment of a desired professional position, or a good all-round intellectual training, then the means by which this end may be most effectively attained is via the optimal infusion of knowledge with skill. Without 'know how' (the positive enhance-ment of information accumulation through skill development) knowledge remains at the level of a commodity. In this case the teaching/learning focus is a simply to *transfer* information from sender to receiver thus *shaping* or *moulding* the knowledge base. The teacher thus defines and determines the narrow intellectual range available to the learner.

Most teachers in HE would claim they are aware of these relationships. Most, however, would concede that many students do not share their vision. M. Jourdain in *Le Bourgeois Gentilhomme* makes an arresting discovery when he realizes he has been speaking prose all his life. The *recognition* that skills are being learnt, and the formative assessment of such skills, enhances skill acquisition, and, as HMI (1988) note, such skills need to be assessed if they are to be accorded importance by students who tend to prioritize work loads for very instrumental reasons. Indeed, Smithies (1990), writing on the need to bridge the academic/vocational divide in schools, reminds us: 'It is a great mistake or plain wishful thinking to assume that learning is natural and enjoyable. We carry on because we can see the good it will do us'.

As part of the academically successful and privileged 15 per cent, HE students may have a better appreciation of such skills, but they need to be aware of them and their perceived utility. Relevance does not inhere in content like some magical property — it is the connection one makes be-tween content or process and possible usefulness; making these vital connec-tions confers relevance and boosts motivation.

(d) Consent

All HE institutions are complex organizations and all would claim a demo-cratic form of management; this is reflected in the work of the myriad committees which are essential to the running of such communities. In this kind of milieu, the implementation of a change policy is contingent on consent, unless it is externally imposed. At one HE institution, the Enterprise Director explained that the EHE initiative had involved the creation of over 35 new committees and working groups and itself reported to a further 40. Any HE institution embarking on a similar initiative — or responding to an invitation to embark on higher level NVQs — will need to think carefully about communications and resourcing; in the current round of EHE initiatives, resourcing needs are reflected in up to £1m funding over five years. The EHE initiative demonstrates that it is possible to gain an over-all institutional consent to proceed, although in many HE institutions there well may be as many opinions and degrees of consent as there are academics. This points up the importance of the next concern, staff training.

(e) Staff Training

Writing in another context, Nash (1990) makes the point that the grandest design is of little use unless the action is underpinned by a philosophy that has been thrashed out by the main participants. A common ethos is essential both as a backcloth indicating common intent and as a unifying factor. There will be disagreements but they should not be over fundamental issues.

The extent to which anyone might reasonably expect a unified, shared vision across departments or faculties in HE is very problematic. But some sharing is plainly essential. The best example of an HE institution embracing a through-going competence based approach is Alverno College, Milwaukee, USA. The Carnegie Foundation recently deemed Alverno to offer one of the three most effective undergraduate programmes in the USA, ranked with Harvard and Chicago. But Alverno went through an extraordinary period of internal dissension lasting many years (including legal confrontations) before it was effectively transformed. Alverno provides an attractive possible model, but there are so many differences between Alverno and any British HE institution of which I am aware that extreme caution needs to be exercised in trying to graft on many of its singularly successful distinguishing characteristics. However, much may be learned from the Alverno experience; to this end, the Training Agency arranged a number of conferences for September 1990 to disseminate these ideas and promote discussion and debate, so Alerno should be well known by the time this book appears.

(f) Funding

Funding has already been alluded to, above. I mention it here merely to underscore the importance of this dimension, and to emphasize the scale of change necessary to bring about the kind of transformation envisaged.

References

BARBER, J.P., HAYWARD, J.C.F. and SLEE, P. (1990) *Enterprise in Higher Education Annual Report*, Durham, University of Durham.

BERGER, P.L. (1966) *Invitation to Sociology*, Harmondsworth, Penguin.

BLACK, H. and WOLF, A. (1990) (Eds) *Knowledge and Competence: Current Issues in Training and Education*, Sheffield, Careers & Occupational Information Centre.

BOREHAM, N.C. (1989) 'Modelling medical decision making under uncertainty', *British Journal of Educational Psychology*, 59, pp. 187–99.

BOREHAM, N.C. (1990) An Investigation of the Methodological Issues Relating to Specifying Professional Competence, unpublished report to NCVQ.

BURKE, J. (1989a) 'Introduction', *Competency Based Education and Training*, London, Falmer Press.

BURKE, J. (1989b) 'Attitudinal change in FE in response to the introduction of NVQs', in BURKE, J. (Ed.) (1989a).

CONFEDERATION OF BRITISH INDUSTRY (1990) *Towards a Skills Revolution*, London, CBI.

DEPARTMENT OF EDUCATION AND SCIENCE (1985) *Education and Training for Young People*, Cmnd 9482, London, HMSO.

DEPARTMENT OF EDUCATION AND SCIENCE (1986) *Working Together: Education and Training*, Cmnd 9823, London, HMSO.

DEPARTMENT OF EDUCATION AND SCIENCE (1987) *Higher Education: Meeting the Challenge*, Cmnd 114, London, HMSO.

EMPLOYMENT DEPARTMENT (1981) *A New Training Initiative: A Programme for Action*, Cmnd 8455, London, HMSO.

EMPLOYMENT DEPARTMENT (1984) *Training for Jobs*, Cmnd 9135, London, HMSO.

ENTERPRISE UNIT, LEEDS POLYTECHNIC (1990).

ERAUT, M. (1985) 'Knowledge creation and knowledge use in professional contexts', *Studies in Higher Education*, 10, 2.

GRAYSON, S. (1990) 'Working in industry', *The Biochemist*, 12, 1, pp. 12–13.

GREEN, S. (1990) 'Know-what, know-how and transferable personal skills in biochemistry', *The Biochemist*, 12, 1, pp. 9–11.

ICI (1989) *Core Development Programme*, London, ICI.

JESSUP, G. (1990a) *Outcomes: NVQs and the Emerging Model of Education and Training*, London, Falmer Press.

JESSUP, G. (1990b) *Common Learning Outcomes: Core Skills in A/AS Levels and NVQs*, R&D Report No. 6, London, NCVQ.

NASH, C. (1990) 'Flexible learning and the management of change', publication forthcoming.

McNAIR, S. (1989) *Trends and Issues in Education and Training for Adults*, Leicester, UDACE.

NATIONAL CURRICULUM COUNCIL (1990) *Core Skills 16–19*, London, HMSO.

NOTTINGHAM POLYTECHNIC (1990) What isn't the Enterprise Initiative?', *Enterprise Newsletter*, 1, 2, Feb.

OPEN UNIVERSITY (1990) *EHE Proposal to TA*, Milton Keynes, Open University.

PHYSICS WORLD (1990) 'Undergraduate curriculum: departments support reduced degree', pp. 6–7, and Editorial: 'Industrial betrayal', June 1990.

SHEFFIELD CITY POLYTECHNIC AND LIVERPOOL POLYTECHNIC (1990) *Learning Outcomes for Design*, UDACE Project Interim Report, Leicester, UDACE.

SLEE, P. (1990a) 'Enterprise in Higher Education at the University of Durham', unpublished conference paper, CUA 23/03/90.

SLEE, P. (1990b) 'Apocalypse now: The future of HE', forthcoming conference paper.

TRAINING AGENCY (1988) *Enterprise in Higher Education*, Sheffield, TA.

TRAINING AGENCY (1990) 'Enterprise in Higher Education: Background note for visit to USA, Spring 1990,' unpublished paper.

UDACE (1989) *Understanding Learning Outcomes*, Leicester, UDACE.

UK PRESS GAZETTE (1990) 'NVQ will be the final arbiter', April 16, Vol. 15.

VELLA, F. (1989) 'Teaching biochemistry for the 21st century', *Biochemical Education*, 17, 1, pp. 6–8.

Chapter 3

Serving the Needs of Industry?

Richard Guy

The 1980s may well be remembered as the decade of initiatives and initials in education and training. NTI, YTS, ATS, RVQ, NCVQ, WRNAFE, TVEI, PICKUP, REPLAN, EEI, LEN, and COMPACTs were all launched, usually preceded by a relevant White Paper. Each of these initiatives in turn spawned a number of developments concerning analysis of the curriculum, assessment and learning. Basic Skills, Core Skills, Functional Analysis, Generic Competences, Workplace Assessment, Individual Action Plans, Records of Achievement, Open Learning, Distance Learning, Resource Based and Project Based Learning.

This was also the decade which witnessed both the dramatic rise in influence and the ultimate demise of one of the key institutions involved — the Manpower Services Commission (MSC). At times, this array of initiatives, changes and developments may have seemed uncoordinated and unnecessarily 'bitty' to the observer. It is as if the whole area was searching for an overall strategy and direction for long term development with nobody in a position to either define it or fund it. Yet on closer analysis, it is possible to identify a degree of coherence with perhaps three key themes for the 1980s, within a strategy largely led by the MSC:

— the New Training Initiative itself which has provided the framework for nearly all MSC activity,
— the reform of education, and more particularly vocational education, to bring about greater responsiveness and more relevance to the world of work. Associated developments have included defining 'breadth' in courses and qualifications and, more particularly, the place of knowledge and generic skills,
— change in institutions and the 'system' including a redefinition of who does what at national, sector and local level.

If there have been common themes and aims adding up to a strategy of sorts, why the plethora of apparently disparate initiatives? There are perhaps four main reasons.

First, a trio of Government Departments have been involved, namely the Department of Employment (and the MSC), the Department of Education and Science (DES) and the Department of Trade and Industry (DTI) with a corresponding succession of Ministers. Interdepartmental rivalry has been a significant factor particularly in the latter part of the decade where the demise of the MSC together with renewed activity at the DES have led to a situation with no clear leadership — each Department has its own strategy with similar or at least, overlapping aims.

Second, funding for action on this front has been steadily increasing throughout the decade. The MSC proved itself particularly adept at procuring funds, for the overt purpose of alleviating unemployment in the short term, but using them in pursuit of its strategic goal of developing better vocational education and training arrangements. It is inevitably easier to procure public funds for very specific initiatives than for a strategy, particularly in a situation where each Department has its own priorities.

Third, the period in question has seen much emphasis placed on the development of new and hopefully improved approaches and methods. It is one thing to state in NTI that training will be 'to standards', quite another to develop institutions, systems and methods for setting standards and assessing their achievement. It is one thing to say that Further Education colleges do not respond well to the needs of employers, quite another to develop in practice a fully effective response. The approach has been one of trying something which seems sensible and modifying, adding to or replacing it (sometimes only part way into its implementation) — a process of iteration.

Last, whilst an initiative can be implemented and its results seen, in a relatively short period of time, a full blown strategy must necessarily take longer to emerge.

We are now into the 1990s and one thing is very clear; that the performance of, and investment in vocational education and training, are woefully inadequate when compared to that of other similar nations. This view appears now to be shared by all branches of Government, the Opposition, the CBI, the TUC and the Education Service. The activity which took place during the 1980s is largely responsible for this consensus. There is also agreement as to what the aims and objectives should be, but the consensus starts to break down in determining what precisely should be done.

Over recent years education and training have developed a high profile. This has many benefits, but it also means that the political debate will focus on the differences in policy rather than the (greater) areas of agreement. The polarization at least serves to clarify the policy jungle. However, a high political profile may also mean a focus on the short term, a problem which the UK suffers in other areas. Any dramatic improvement in our vocational education and training must be a long term process with attitudinal and cultural issues being as important as systems, methods and funding.

It is not difficult to demonstrate that industry has been increasingly 'brought into' many of the new and developing arrangements for education and training. It seems that we have arrived at a position whereby Government clearly believes that industry knows best: but is industry able to express its needs and, more importantly, is it in the best position to make crucial decisions in education and training?

Industry Involvement in Education and Training

Education and training providers are in a remarkably complex market situation when compared to other suppliers of services. Their customers are the individual learners (and their parents where young people are concerned), business and Government. Each of these groups in itself represents a complex array of different needs and wants. Nor do the sources of income correspond to the importance of each of the customer groups.

It is not surprising that this situation has all too often led to a supplier centred approach. When this is combined with a lack of clarity of objectives about learning (for life or for economic life?) the providers of learning can easily see themselves as custodians of all that is good and forget that this often corresponds to that which is good for them.

In the 1980s the employer was seen as the key customer of the education service as young people approach working life. It has been felt that it is employers who benefit most and should therefore express the need and for that matter stump up much of the funding. This employer role as key customer and part funder has been the main reason for the increased employer involvement in the 1980s initiatives, together with an apparent desire on the part of Government to bring about a more commercial, business-like approach to the situation.

It was perhaps thought too difficult to offer the same central place to the other customers, learners themselves: how could the demand be clearly articulated and how could they be involved in decision making?

Three themes for the 1980s were identified earlier. Industry was brought in as the leading customer within the initiatives relevant to each theme.

These three themes are taken here separately with NTI dealt with first not only as the most important but also as the foundation for much that followed.

The New Training Initiative

Published in 1981, the NTI set out three objectives for the decade:

— to reform and increase skill training in order to end the reliance on time-serving and introduce training to standards,
— to equip all young people for work,
— to widen opportunities for adults to train and re-train throughout their working lives.

The first of these was to involve the creation of occupational standards to define acceptable skill targets for training so that for both apprenticeship and adult training acceptable outcomes could be defined without reference to time-serving, mode or place of learning.

During the early 1980s little happened on this front except for some exemplar and pilot work and the continued work of the relevant ITBs. However, in mid-decade the 'Review of Vocational Qualifications' (RVQ) was begun. This was instigated in order to rationalize the jungle of vocational qualifications and because the development of YTS had shown clearly that although some occupations were served by a very wide range of qualifications, many, especially those below 'craft' level, were not linked to a qualification at all. The standard setting requirement was high on the agenda of the officials concerned but assumed lesser importance for many of the various interests involved, ITBs, Trade Unions, parts of the Education Service and some Awarding Bodies. Many organizations were keen to see standards set but as an addition to access, time-serving and course requirements rather than an alternative.

Nevertheless, the RVQ recommended the establishment of a National Council for Vocational Qualifications and a standards setting programme was established, based initially on the needs of YTS and later a wider range of occupations and NVQs.

The setting of standards for each occupation is carried out by a Lead Industry Body which is defined as 'employer led'. These standards are then incorporated into assessment and certification structures usually involving an Awarding Body like RSA, City and Guilds or BTEC, so producing an approved NVQ for that occupational area. The idea was (and still is) that this process would lead to a rational set of portable transparent qualifications, based on the needs of industry and free of prescribed duration, mode or method of learning or restrictions on access. Rationalization would also demand a reduction in the number of awards.

Whilst such an outcome represents excellent news for businesses and individuals, it is rather less helpful to the various interests within the system. It represents a major reform, again benefiting the two customer groups but set against powerful interests on the other hand. As such, Government has not understood the inevitable resistance and the need for significant backing. In particular, the extent of the need to change attitudes and actions of the three key interests has been dramatically underestimated:

— the existing industry bodies have not necessarily been representatives of the whole of an industry, and sometimes have an interest in maintaining current training patterns;
— the training providers (principally, but not only, the FE colleges) demonstrate a tendency to be resistant to change especially here, where the effects are radical;
— the awarding bodies who respond opportunistically to a market for

'easier' qualifications have been very reluctant to rationalize their awards or to adopt assessment methods free of course definition.

A great deal needs to be done in relation to the first two groups but positive attitudes are now evident and change will come over time. In the case of the Awarding Bodies, RSA, City and Guilds and Pitmans have generally responded well, and of course the new voluntary Industry Training Organizations are very often involved as the awarding body for part or all of their standards. However, even these bodies are unlikely to be willing to give up their non-NVQs, and BTEC has been largely allowed to ignore the reform process.

From the view point of the individual, NVQs provide great benefit:

— credit accumulation
— open access
— inclusion of prior learning from any source
— a structure of levels and standards providing 'portability'
— reward for practical achievement
— qualifications for occupations not previously covered.

For industry the standards are perhaps the key benefit. They can be used for:

— recruitment
— analysing training needs
— planning training
— providing and buying training
— assessing and recording progress and achievement
— ensuring the relevance of training and maximizing the role of on-the-job training.

The lessons in this reform process could be summarized as:

— industry can play a crucial role if widely consulted and represented;
— Government needs to do more to effect the changes against powerful special interests;
— the individual as key beneficiary has exercised almost no power in the development process.

Massive progress has now been made in the development of NVQs and, more than ten years after NTI, standards based arrangements are a reality in many sectors. Even that great bastion of time serving, the Construction Industry, has just about been reformed.

The MSC's basic response to NTI Objective 2 was of course, the Youth Training Scheme, first one year, and then up to two years of support. This was, in some ways unfortunately, introduced at a time of high unemployment, although this, of course, was the main reason why funding was available. The ambitious design framework for the scheme was never fully realized except in the very best of provision. The principal intention to involve many employers in direct contracts with the MSC gave way to the massive use of 'umbrella' managing agents as the main deliverer with smaller employers, and voluntary sector organizations were left to deal with the most disadvantaged.

It was often the case that FE colleges decided to segregate YTS trainees, as in the early days they were relatively few in number and the design framework included a great emphasis on 'life and social skills'. This resulted in colleges often keeping trainees apart from their normal vocational day-release courses and putting them into special programmes for very low achievers involving broad-based basic skills training. Not surprisingly, this frequently led to demotivation in young people, often putting them off college attendance while also failing to directly meet employers' needs. Nevertheless, the scheme has introduced structured training arrangements into companies and sectors where they never previously existed and has turned hundreds of thousands of young people from demotivated school leavers into eager learners and achievers. In the latter part of the decade, as the focus moved towards vocational qualifications (through the NVQ process) the scheme gradually converged with the traditional vocational apprenticeship; the principle difference being that now such an apprenticeship is available in all sectors and occupations and is not based on time serving but on the acquisition of standards of competence.

The key issue now is not unemployment, rather it is how to get training to the very large numbers of young people who enter dead end, low skill jobs. The emphasis now is to be placed on motivating the individual just as much as the employer via the 'Training Credits' initiative. Here at last, we may see a balance between the two key customers, both having part funding and control and both involved in the purchase of the training itself. This had not previously been true of YTS where the employer has been seen as the main relevant customer, leading to an emphasis on assessing young people for recruitment rather than on their training to a significant level of achievement.

Points worthy of consideration here would appear to be:

— The MSC, had the best of intentions but these can sometimes be lost with the need to create programmes in a very short period of time — very high volume delivery structures develop which are best at delivering objectives which were not meant to be the fundamental purpose of the programme.
— Employers who are convinced of the value of training represent a strong and helpful customer group; those who are being introduced to training for the first time may well become good trainers but some will use such schemes for other purposes.

— Again, involvement of young people themselves as a key customer has been lacking until the new Training Credits arrangements.

NTI Objective 3 concerned itself with widening opportunities for adults. This was always a fairly limited objective which acknowledged the fact that the MSC had a small influence on employer based training. In the early part of the decade the MSC was reliant on its TOPS programme, together with the activities of the ITBs and ITOs. TOPS placing rates in employment were fairly low during the recessionary period but the scheme was being more and more focused on skill shortages, and placing rates and unit costs had been improving for a number of years when it was decided to use the MSC's adult training funds for a new set of initiatives under the umbrella of the Adult Training Strategy.

One of the perceived problems with TOPS was that although the public queued up to join it to the tune of three people to every place, once in training the immediate effect on the unemployment register was not great since programmes were short and of high quality and largely off-the-job. Its effect on the register itself was felt to be doubtful because of unknown factors such as whether the people concerned would have obtained jobs anyway, and it certainly did not focus large amounts of money on the long term unemployed. Nevertheless, the programme remained in place and was called the Job Training Scheme within the new Adult Training Strategy. The three other key initiatives within the Adult Training Strategy were a much keener focus on Enterprise Training, the development of more courses in work skills and job finding for the longer term employed (Work Related Skills and Assessment courses) and Grants to Employers for consultancy, recruiting and training unemployed people and training employees.

Nationally, action with the Industry Training Organizations continued. The Open Tech was making a major contribution to widening opportunities, and activities from the DES such as PICKUP and REPLAN were also beginning to support the process.

Many people felt that this range of approaches, although complex, had a significant effect. However, from a Treasury point of view there was not enough focus on unemployment. At the same time, an acute tension developed between the need for flexibility for local MSC offices (which was very great within this system) and the desire at national level to produce branded products which tended to tie down local deliverers.

Following a re-examination of the unemployment situation it was decided to try a new scheme, the New Job Training Scheme with a focus on lower cost (per week), longer duration work-based training (and therefore, hopefully, a higher effect on the unemployment register), a higher performance in terms of getting jobs, together with a concentration on long term rather than general unemployment. By this time long term unemployment was causing considerable concern both socially and in terms of its effect on labour supply and hence inflation when an upturn occurred.

Delivery of the New Job Training Scheme did not go well, with resulting low volumes. Surprisingly, contracts were issued not to existing YTS managing agents with experience but rather to new bodies, each individually set up to deal with almost every occupation which exists; the notion of the Training Manager as opposed to the Managing Agent was born. This idea had not been tried or tested anywhere and led to a lack of structure and focus in the training arrangements. It was also impossible for individuals to know what they were applying for since training was usually set up after recruitment. Hence the queues which had developed to join the old Job Training Scheme were not keen to translate their interest to the new arrangements and those who did sign up were often 'stacked', awaiting real training places.

This scheme was running alongside the Community Programme and, in time, it was decided that large amounts of money being spent on the Community Programme might be better combined with that available for training to produce a new scheme rather like the New Job Training Scheme but to be called Employment Training. The delivery and contracting process was in fact made worse by this decision since the various Community Programme Managing Agents came into the scheme with their lack of experience in training and with very high fixed costs within their arrangements for the delivery of projects. Projects were as much a focus of many of these agents as was training and job finding for participants.

As this was happening, Enterprise Training was proving to be something of a success. Perhaps a key lesson can be drawn here for the whole process. Within the Enterprise Training field, the customers are obvious, they are the Owners/Managers of the businesses being started or developed — they are both the learner and the employer. It has therefore been absolutely necessary that the providers and the MSC gear Enterprise Training to not only the perceived needs but the actual desires of this group of people, many of whom are very articulate and would simply not attend if what was provided was not to their liking. Enterprise Training since its conception in the early 1980s has therefore been a significant success and the lesson is perhaps that the individual as the customer has been heavily involved.

As a tool to initiate increased employer training the grant schemes within the adult training strategy were thought to involve a great deal of waste (in paying for training which would have occurred anyway) and hence the development of Business Growth Training (BGT). This demands half funding by the employer and an emphasis not on training itself but on a change process within firms towards training as an integrated part of business management.

Key lessons in NTI Objective 3 for our theme therefore appear to be:

— a tension between the aims of the MSC, the many officials and many people involved, of improving the training system and dealing with skill shortages, and the Government's point of view that spending in this area should not be concerned only with unemployment and more

particularly with long term unemployment. The initiatives within NTI Objective 3 were particularly Government-led in their
development

— employers find it very difficult to take unemployed trainees unless
they already have substantial skills, hence employer acceptance of the
TOPS and old JTS idea and their general difficulty with the new JTS
and ET designs

— when the individual is involved and given the power of a key customer then it is possible to produce a programme which, whilst at
least part funded by the Exchequer, meets the needs of the customers
involved.

*Reform of Education to Produce Greater Responsiveness and Relevance
to the World of Work*

The key initiatives during the 80s in this area were:

— the Technical and Vocational Education Initiative (TVEI),
— the planning of Work Related Non Advanced Further Education
(WRNAFE),
— Professional, Industrial and Commercial Updating (PICKUP).

Both TVEI and WRNAFE planning were mechanisms devised during the
period when David Young was at the MSC and subsequently Secretary of
State for Employment and Sir Keith Joseph was Secretary of State for
Education and Science. This was, of course, prior to any notion of the Core
Curriculum which developed during the latter part of the decade.

TVEI seemed to begin as an attempt to introduce technical and vocational elements into the curriculum which were to be just that. It was,
however, gradually transmuted to a 'process' which was to have an effect on
the way learning took place. TVEI has had a major effect on the introduction
of such things as work experience and Records of Achievement for the
under-16s. It has had far less effect on introducing vocational elements into
the curriculum and, so far, on those young people in the A level route.

It appears then that TVEI's basic aim is to help to develop 'generic skills'
in young people. Here, the researched demands of employers are interesting
and consistent across a range of investigation.

A number of surveys during the 1980s of employers' perceptions of their
requirements from the education system, identify clearly that they are less
interested in academic and occupational achievement and far more interested
in the achievement of such things as:

— Basic skills e.g. numeracy, literacy and hand skills;
— Personal effectiveness including problem solving and the ability to
manage a range of tasks

— The ability to work alone and in teams
— The ability to take responsibility for one's own learning.

The lists of skills and abilities identified have been slightly different with each survey but the common themes have been clear.

TVEI has lacked clarity in its aims which has meant that in some areas it seems to have lost its way. At its best however in those Authorities and schools where the process is taken seriously it has produced great change. This change has hopefully helped to produce young people whose generic skills are of a higher level than they might otherwise have been.

The planning of Work Related Non Advanced Further Education (WRNAFE) on the otherhand, appeared at first to have a very different purpose. When first mooted, the idea was that colleges did not offer those courses and programmes which were in tune with the needs of the local labour market. In this sense the original idea was that MSC local offices would purchase individual courses/programmes and groups of courses at Colleges to produce the maximum change within the system based on the MSC's developing labour market intelligence systems.

The politics involved in the introduction of the arrangement were, however, very difficult and culminated in a situation where WRNAFE funding would be routed through the LEA and not direct to the college concerned in order to produce, develop and maintain a process of planning provision by the LEA with its colleges, in line with labour market needs. Thus from the employers' perspective it had a very different purpose, indeed, employers' involvement has always been indirect. Their involvement has been with the surveys and the labour market intelligence arrangements that exist to feed in to the planning system. One unfortunate side effect of the arrangements has been that Local Education Authorities have actually had to introduce more onerous planning and management information systems for colleges than was previously the case. This means that although the year's programmes and courses may be well planned, the ability of colleges to be flexible, to change in year and to innovate may actually be diminished. Many college departments already had excellent links with industry but these can now take second place to the planning system. TVEI is now being extended to the whole cohort of young people and WRNAFE planning is now likely to be devolved to Training and Enterprise Councils.

So here the idea that 'industry knows best' both in terms of the need for generic skills and particular FE courses has been paramount. Once again, what of individuals and Government? For individuals, this takes us into the age-old education vs training debate. If it is agreed that generic skills are of prime importance then the purpose of an academic or vocational focus is concerned as much as anything with motivation of the individual. Many young people are motivated strongly by the pursuit of academic subject knowledge, understanding and development. They get little chance of learning with a vocational focus. Many other young people are strongly motivated by pursuit of knowledge, understanding and skills in a vocational area. They get little chance of this pre-16 and later little chance of learning with an academic focus. What is more, it is the academic or the vocational which we generally accredit and reward, not the generic skills which span the two.

It is these skills which make for an effective career and in no small way for satisfaction in life. In this situation employers, whether they know best or not, have little choice but to either:

— use academic achievement as a proxy for intelligence and ability to learn and so recruit people who at least are likely to develop generic skills and are easy to train and/or,
— to train directly for an individual occupation in the most cost-effective way with all that this implies for lack of breadth, knowledge and progression.

Both cases lead to fear of 'poaching' as a major disincentive to train one's own employees too well. Again, the individual is not really taken into account.

From a Government perspective neither TVEI nor WRNAFE required additional financial resources as both were essentially fund transfers. As to whether Government has been satisfied in this context it is impossible to say because there was a lack of clarity of objectives at the outset.

Both business and individuals stand to gain from a greater emphasis on generic skills. However, the providers of learning, and particularly their staff, find it far easier to concentrate on the occupational or the academic or, where an attempt is made, to try to turn generic skills development into a separate learning programme. Fortunately, a great deal of work is now going on to integrate such skills into the accreditation process. (See Debling, Chapter 1, Burke, Chapter 2 and Elton, Chapter 9, this volume).

The Training System

At the beginning of the 1980s a number of ITBs were still in existence but, with a few notable exceptions these were not supported by their industries. However, it could be said that most of the firms with a voice were good trainers and the remainder may have felt that they could feed off the good training of others. National policy was described in the Industrial Training Act 1974. The MSC was a board of businesses, trade unions, education and other interests and at local level the Area Manpower Boards 'advised' the MSC (but not the ITBs). Educational initiatives were funded by the Local Education Authorities with some funds (for FE) coming from the ITB and MSC direction.

At the end of the decade we have a very different system. Here is a quote from the 1989 White Paper 'Employment for the 1990s':

A modern training system must be able to provide industry and individuals with the skills they need to meet the demands of the 1990s. Britain needs a framework which can help to deliver relevant and effective training where it is needed, is responsive enough to adjust to changing labour market conditions both nationally and locally, and helps employers and individuals to make the right decisions about their training needs. That system must be planned and led by employers, because it is they who are best placed to judge skill needs; it must actively engage individuals, of every age, background, and occupation, because they have much to gain from appropriate investment in their own training and skills; and it must co-operate with the education service.

The Government will now be working through the Training Agency and the new National Training Task Force to establish a framework to meet the training needs of the economy in the 1990s. The crucial components of this framework will be effective local bodies led by employers and charged with ensuring the effective delivery of training programmes within the local labour market, and industry level organizations which command the support of employers and which are charged with establishing recognized standards and promoting training within their sectors. The Government believe that this framework will make it possible to achieve a more highly trained workforce able to meet the demands of an expanding economy (ED, 1989).

Industry is thus involved directly at the second and third levels, and is involved in the first via organizations such as the CBI, as well as through TECs and ITOs.

All of this involvement is formal and again it relates partly to the idea of the key customer role of employers in standards setting, local training arrangements and informing Government of overall needs. However, there are other key issues:

— who within any given firm is most suitable to take part?
— the choice of employers to lead TEC boards also concerns their abilities as managers and strategic thinkers.

Employer membership of ITOs varies but often represents a personnel or training specialist from bigger firms. Sometimes such people can have an interest to defend, perhaps a training centre or method of training, and hence are not always ideal representatives of the employer or customer. Nevertheless, standards are usually established by a process of research and consultation concerning the job content in the real world, so ITO membership does not usually have a big effect. It does, though, when the standards are ready to be incorporated into an assessment and accreditation structure to become a vocational qualification.

At this point the long term income requirements of the ITO become an issue and on becoming either a part or whole Awarding Body, the ITO secures a long term income for itself. This often turns out to be a good thing, considering the ITO's interest in the real use of the standards produced. It does serve to emphasize, however, that the ITO at this stage could be dominated by a supplier rather than customer interest.

This problem has been partly dealt with in the TEC movement by making sure that only people from the top level of their organizations join TEC boards. This has often meant the introduction of people who:

— are 'heavyweight' and can open doors for the TEC itself;
— think strategically and decisively;
— can effectively manage as non-executive directors at a strategic level.

Their approach to the subject has so far been clearly shown to be conscientious, committed, innovative and decisive.

Lessons here for our theme might be:

— Government might need to take a stronger lead;
— one way of involving employers (and, potentially, other customers) is to properly research their needs;
— there are differences between the roles and levels of people from industry — it is no simple solution to 'involve industry';
— although individuals as customers are represented by trade unions and other organizations on lead industry bodies and TECs, the individual is not directly represented — again a case for more market research as well as direct involvement in the process.

The Future

The 1980s have taught us a great deal about how to improve education and training. Particularly strong lessons from a whole range of initiatives would appear to be:

— Government needs to take a long term strategic overview. This need not necessarily involve huge extra amounts of money but leadership and well articulated and defined leadership is clearly necessary;
— Industry can play a very effective part, both as customer and in the machinery of the education and training system. It is necessary however, to be clear to whom within industry we are looking to take part and to make a greater use of research and particularly market

research, rather than asking the opinions of people who may seemingly represent industry but may sometimes have a particular interest in mind;

— we must find ways of involving individuals far more heavily in decisions about their own development. Recent research, including the 'Training in Britain' survey has shown an increase in the amount of learning taken up by individuals on their own account in recent years. We must build on this and put power into the hands of individuals in order to give them a feeling that their development is something about which to make choices and to be motivated.

What is proposed, therefore, for the future is what has already been partly developed, that is, a partnership between Government, businesses and individuals. Our new machinery involving Government at the top level, voluntary Industry Training Organizations in defining their industry's needs, and the TECs in local delivery structures should give us the machinery for the future. The involvement of employers within this machinery is already substantial, the involvement and the power of the other customer, the individual, is not yet established. New arrangements for Training Credits for young people may well provide a model which can be taken further into the world of adult learning both for the employed and the unemployed.

If this balance can be found within the machinery and between the customers and funding organizations involved, then we might well, in the medium term, turn the UK's base into something much more approaching that of our industrial competitor nations.

Reference

EMPLOYMENT DEPARTMENT (1989) *Employment for the 1990s*, Cmnd 540, London, HMSO.

Chapter 4

Quality Assurance and NVQs

Peter Raggatt

The introduction of competence based qualifications may well be the last chance the UK has of developing a credible high quality vocational education and training system capable of producing the highly skilled, versatile and flexible workers needed if the UK is to compete effectively for world markets. The changes, initiated and orchestrated by the Training Agency in its various forms, have gone a long way towards giving employers what they have long demanded: a system of vocational qualifications based on 'standards of competence' required by industry and commerce. Moreover, the key recommendation that assessment of competence should, wherever possible, be based on performance in the workplace has given employers a major role in delivering national vocational qualifications. The success or failure of the reform is, to a very large extent, in the hands of employers in a multiplicity of companies and workplaces around the country.

This chapter examines the reforms in terms of quality assurance. Two perspectives are offered. First, I consider the idea of employment-led national standards, identifying some of the apparent tensions and contradictions between policy-makers at the national level and employers' needs, and question whether the policy will deliver the national goal of producing a competent and adaptable workforce. Second, the analysis focuses on the practicalities of delivering national standards through many thousands of local centres with varying degrees of experience in assessment. Here the concern is with the credibility of the new system which will rest very largely on the consistency with which national standards of competence are assessed, i.e. on the guaranteed quality of the assessment. From time to time the approach adopted in the UK will be contrasted with that in other countries.

Employment-led National Standards

National Vocational Qualifications (NVQs) are based on employment-led standards. These are defined by Lead Bodies (see Chapter 1) assisted by the

Training Agency and NCVQ. The shift to this standards-based approach was first mooted by the then Manpower Services Commission in *A Programme for Action — Training for Skills* (1977). This proposed a reform of training based on:

- the introduction of definable and testable standards of occupational competence (in place of time-serving apprenticeships)
- improved training opportunities for young people, access of adults to training and access to qualified status.

The programme favoured an industry-by-industry approach rather than a uniform solution and introduced the concept of industry lead bodies ('lead boards'). Both of these features have been carried through to the present day with minor clarifications and accommodations.

This agenda was more fully set out in the 1981 White Paper from the Department of Employment: *A New Training Initiative: A Programme for Action* (ED, 1981). The key policy issues were identified as:

- the development of skill training to be based on standards of competence by 1985. (This included the reform of the apprenticeship system, reducing the barriers to vocational qualifications and facilitating progression to higher level qualifications)
- the opening of widespread opportunities for adults, whether employed or returning to work, to acquire, increase or update their skills and knowledge during their working lives.

In due course, and with the experiences of the 'competence based' approach gained from the Youth Training Scheme, YTS (1), this led to a review of vocational qualifications under the Chairmanship of Oscar de Ville. In the Report (MSC/DES, 1986), the Working Group argued that there were many weaknesses in the existing system of vocational qualifications. It was held to be a jungle of qualifications, lacking any clear pattern, subject to considerable overlap and duplication and incapable of recognizing learning achievements gained outside formal education and training. Moreover, it offered very limited access to qualifications particularly for those outside the 16–19 window of opportunity; there were inadequate arrangements for progression and transfer of credit, and, crucially, it used asessment methods that were biased towards the testing of knowledge rather than skill and competence. In aggregate this resulted in a low take-up of vocational qualifications and an inadequately qualified workforce, which was a key concern for national policy makers. This concern was echoed at the local level where individual employers complained that newly qualified recruits were unable to perform competently in their job.

The Review Group proposed a major reform of the structure of vocational qualifications. The key points were that:

- vocational qualifications in England and Wales should be brought within a new national framework to be called the National Vocational Qualification (NVQ)
- a new National Council for Vocational Qualifications (NCVQ) should be set up to secure the necessary changes, to develop the NVQ framework and to ensure that standards of competence are set.

The recommendations of the Working Group were endorsed by Government in a White Paper, *Working Together*, and the National Council, working with the MSC, industry and education interests, was given the task of 'establishing a clear focus for national action to secure the specification of standards of competence by effective and appropriate industry bodies' by 1991 (ED/DES, 1986). This, and the guidance provided in the Working Group's review, led to a definition of a national vocational qualification by the NCVQ as 'a statement of competence which is clearly relevant to work and incorporates specified standards in the ability to perform in a range of work-related activities and in the skills, knowledge and understanding which underpin such performance in employment'.

The work of the Training Agency and NCVQ is complementary. Staff in the Training Agency help to establish the necessary industry lead bodies, work with them to specify the standards at NVQ Levels 1–4 and advise on implementation. NCVQ staff assist with the process of constructing the NVQ qualification and ensuring accreditation. An NVQ is a statement of a person's competence to carry out a specified range of work activities. Each NVQ is an aggregate of units of competence, normally 4–25, with the average NVQ comprising 10–15 units. Each unit is itself an aggregate of associated elements of competence. Competence in an element is assessed against specified performance criteria and, if it is to match the demands of actual jobs, should involve assessment of performance in a range of working contexts, conditions and situations. To obtain the NVQ the candidate must be assessed as competent for all required units.

The actual process through which standards are developed is has been described by Graham Debling (Chapter 1, this volume). The work is supported by the Technical Advisory Group which has drawn up criteria for the setting of standards and has issued a series of Guidance Notes. The 'Code of Practice' set out in the first of these embodies the key provision that 'Competences should enable the assessment of performance and should define achievement in terms of outputs' and that 'Wherever feasible, performance in the workplace should be the basis of assessment' (MSC, 1988). The emphasis on workplace assessment was further encouraged by NCVQ which commented favourably on the practice in YTS of assessing the trainees' competence at scheme level, 'ideally in real work situations'. Workplace assessment or assessment under realistic working conditions became an important feature in the system developed by NCVQ.

If we examine these specifications against the goal of producing highly skilled, adaptable and flexible workers, three problems are evident. The first problem is the narrowness of the approach. The process of formulating an NVQ is occupationally specific; standards for individual industrial and commercial sectors, often single industries such as catering, are defined in terms of contemporary occupational activities. The Working Group and the 1986 White Paper refer to competence in relation to 'tasks'. This narrow perception of competence was influenced by the experience gained through YTS, which was dominated by semi-skilled and craft level trainees, and a consequence of vocational education and training policy being single-mindedly directed to serving the perceived needs of employers. The domination of lead bodies by employers, the hasty definition of standards and the commitment to assessment in the workplace were further guarantees that it was the short-term training needs that would be pre-eminent.

A more balanced and thoughtful approach would have incorporated the effects of technological change on work organization and work roles. Standards would have been set which would have used the experience of successful companies which increasingly emphasize working as a member of an interdisciplinary multi-skilled team, processing information in new ways, process control, and encouraging individual initiative and creativity. The implications of such an analysis would have been inescapable: policy must be directed as much towards developing individual potential as to training workers to complete their tasks competently. This would not have denied the competence approach but would have extended it beyond occupational skills to life skills. It would have established that education and training are related processes and that sharp distinctions between occupational and life roles are unrealistic (FEU, 1984). Debling (Chapter 1, this volume) takes a similar view and his account of the Standards Programme makes it clear that it has the potential and the capacity to provide descriptions of competence that reflect this broader definition. This is now an important feature of the Programme, as is shown, for example, by the Enterprise in Higher Education Inititative and the interest in core skills.

The lack of breadth in training might be understandable if the British workforce had benefited from a long period of general education prior to entering work as is the case with Japan and the USA. However, as is well known, the participation rate of 16- and 17-year-olds in education is lower in Britain than in any of its competitors. Until 1989–90 England was the only major industrial nation in which the majority of 16-year-olds left full-time education and training.[1] In many instances participation of 16–18-year-olds in full-time education (for example, Japan and the United States) or in a combination of apprenticeships and part-time education (for example, in what was West Germany) is above 90 per cent. Moreover, as studies by the NIESR have shown, the educational attainment of those who enter apprenticeships is below that of their peers in competitor nations (Prais and Wagner, 1983).

In the absence of an extended and effective period of general education before entering work it is necessary to emphasize breadth in post-school education and training. This strategy is pursued in West Germany where the off-the-job curriculum for young trainees has been increased from 1 to 1½ or 2 days per week (or its equivalent in periods of block release). The extra time is given both to general education, e.g., foreign languages, and to extended theoretical studies relating to the trainee's occupation. The trend towards increasing breadth is also evident in the emergence of polyvalent training in which the first part is general to a number of occupations. This has been facilitated by the policy of the Federal government to consolidate the number of skilled occupations, thus providing the opportunity for broad-based foundation training serving a number of occupations (Raggatt, 1988). In France, too, where some 71 per cent of 16–18-year-olds were in full-time education in 1987 (compared with 31 per cent in Britain), there is an emphasis on breadth in vocational education combined with the mastery of a specific skill. Moreover, all 16–19-year-olds take a common core of mathematics, French and a foreign language. This, as Prais (1989) points out, enables candidates to proceed to higher levels of vocational qualification where these general educational subjects are valuable facilitators and reduces the division between vocational and general qualifications.

There are now clear indications of dissatisfaction among policy makers at the national level about the narrowness of the standards specified by lead bodies which provide the basis for NVQs. The CBI (1989) has ruefully noted: 'the emphasis on standards setting by separate industry bodies has not naturally led to the development of cross sectoral "generic" competences' and has argued that all education and training should be designed to develop self-reliance, flexibility and broad competence as well as skills. The report continues:

> As employers increasingly require the skills for adaptability and innovation in employment education and training needs to be broadly based, concerned not just with technical understanding of the job but competence in the broader work context. Broader occupational competence should be concerned with adaptability, management of roles, responsibility for standards, creativity and flexibility to changing demands. Task competence is not enough to meet this need although some employers concentrating on their short-term needs may believe it is.

A similar refrain was heard from Kenneth Baker (1989), then Secretary of State for Education and Science, speaking at the annual conference of the Association of Colleges of Further and Higher Education, who called for *broadly-based* qualifications and flexibility to meet changes in the employment world, 'Otherwise, the next wave of technology will leave [young workers] stranded'.

The preferred solution to this problem is the notion of a common core of skills. This is by no means a new idea. It was a feature of the TSD's Grouping of Skills project in the 1970s which sought to define 'transferable skills' — skills which are common to behaviour in a variety of contexts and offer the potential for transfer to other contexts and situations, i.e. to an array of situations in working life and life outside work. This led to the core skills and personal effectiveness component in the YTS (1) programme which died with the advent of YTS (2), largely it seems because there was no concept of standards for core skills and they therefore did not fit into the design framework for the competence based YTS (2), nor did they reappear with NVQs. The importance of such skills, if they can be defined and are transferable, is that they would be a key feature in any attempt to develop a flexible and adaptable workforce. Individuals, when changing occupations or progressing to higher levels in the same occupation, would already own some of the competences required for the new position and training could build on existing strengths.

A new consensus is now emerging among groups within education and training, employers and government for the inclusion of a set of core skills, 'generic competences' or 'common learning outcomes' in all general and vocational education programmes and is being viewed as a mechanism through which general and vocational education and training can be more closely integrated. In November 1989, following the publication in October of the CBI Vocational Education and Training Task Force interim report, *Towards a Skills Revolution — A Youth Charter* (CBI, 1989), which proposed a set of 'common learning outcomes' for use with all 14–19-year-olds, the Secretary of State for Education and Science wrote to the National Curriculum Council (NCC) and the School Examination and Assessment Council (SEAC) in November 1989 inviting the NCC and SEAC to consider how core skills could be incorporated into A and A/S levels (Jessup, 1990).

NCC and SEAC worked with NCVQ in developing the report. Subsequently the Secretary of State invited NCVQ to report on the scope for building core skills into NVQs. NCVQ had already undertaken some work on this issue but was conscious that 'The extent to which a minimum achievement in specified core skill areas becomes a requirement in NVQs at certain levels is a policy decision which has wide implications' (Jessup, April 1990). Working closely with SEAC, NCC, FEU and the Training Agency, the National Council reported in two months with a proposal for a joint programme to develop common core skills which would be led by SEAC and NCVQ. The joint programme would 'create a progressive structure of core skill outcomes (in the form of attainment/elements of competence' through GCSE/National Curriculum Levels 1 and 2 and A/AS and NVQ Level 3. Jessup goes on to assert that core skills at NVQ Levels 4 and 5 would have relevance to the Higher Education Enterprise programme (see Burke, Chapter 2, this volume). A coordinated schedule for the introduction of further developments was suggested: 'The operational date of September 1994 is proposed to synchronize the wider introduction of core skills to NVQs with that proposed for A/AS examinations, which NCVQ understands will not be made a requirement in programmes before those starting before September 1994'. The very close association of the major agencies delivering vocational and school-level academic qualifications and the common purpose of a closer integration of the two systems through common skills is underlined in the covering letter: 'If the core skills are common to both A/AS qualifications and NVQs we feel it will provide a major step forward in bridging the gap between general and vocational education' (De Ville, 1990) and 'will facilitate progression from NVQs to higher education' (NCVQ, 1990).

The clearest formulation of core skills has been provided by NCVQ. Six skills have been identified and agreed with NCC. Communication skills, problem solving and personal skills, are 'primary' core skills. They are regarded as the most fundamental, ubiquitously relevant to work and education and capable of being defined in the form of competences whose performance can be assessed in occupational and educational settings. Primary core skills would be embedded in all NVQs and be part of the assessment of occupational competence. A secondary set of core skills — information technology, the application of mathematics and foreign language competence — are of a different order 'in that they do not underpin performance almost universally, as do the first three core skill areas' (NCVQ, 1990). Opportunities might be created for people to gain unit credits in these areas though they would not necessarily form part of NVQs, except where the occupational competence incorporated such a requirement. The crunch question, however, is what use lead bodies will make of core skills. As NCVQ notes: 'The inclusion of core skills in all NVQs may only be effected by redrafting the NVQ criteria. The implications this would have for industry lead bodies setting standards and the take up of NVQs by employers and others, will need to be carefully examined' (NCVQ, 1990).

This would, however, be of little consequence if employers had a firm commitment to human resource development and, as a matter of course, encouraged trainees to include such credits in their qualifications. But this is where the second problem lies: historical and contemporary investment in education and training has been very poor. This is confirmed in a number of studies. The important MSC/NEDO (1984) report, *Competence and Competition*, revealed that employers in West Germany spent nearly three times as much on initial and continuing vocational education and training as did employers in the UK. Elsewhere it has been estimated that British companies spend 0.15 per cent of turnover on training whereas France, Japan and West Germany spend 1–2 per cent (Anderson, 1987). NIESR studies, too, show that training in France, where it takes place mainly in schools, and Germany, where it is predominantly through apprenticeships, is both broader and of a higher quality and leads to higher productivity and to more flexible responses to customers in a variety of industries (Steedman, 1986; Steedman and Wagner, 1987; Prais, Jarvis and Wagner, 1989).

It is not that British employers are unaware that other industrial countries have a higher commitment to training, but they believe that the level of training in their own company is about right — even though there is 'widespread ignorance among top management of how their company's performance in training compared with that of their competitors — even those in the UK ... and a suprisingly high proportion of senior executives ... had only a limited knowledge of the scale of resources devoted to training within their own company' (Coopers and Lybrand Associates, 1985). The reasons for under-commitment to training are complex, involving cultural and structural factors but are beyond the scope of this chapter.[2]

As the CBI points out, many employers remain narrowly concerned with task competences and concentrate on short-term needs (CBI, 1989). The short-term perspective of most British managers, reinforced, as Finegold and Soskice (1988) point out, by the pressure to maximize profits, is one of several factors acting to reduce commitment to training — the benefits of which, by definition, tend to be medium- and long-term. Moreover, some employers regard broad based training providing the adaptability and flexibility sought by policy makers as a threat because it will make their (well trained) workers more marketable and liable to poaching by other employers. The tendency in Britain, more than it is in France and Germany, is for specific company needs to direct training policy (Steedman, 1986; and personal research).

The modular structure of NVQs may well exacerbate this problem. Some employers already provide support for employees to work towards NVQs. These numbers will grow as more employers see real and potential benefits through higher productivity, lower labour turnover, attracting higher quality recruits, a better corporate image and so on (HCTC, 1990; Unwin, Chapter 11, this volume). As yet, however, very few employers have the commitment of Boots the Chemists which is introducing NVQs for all its new full-time sales assistants — some 6000 per year (Financial Times, 4/7/90). Other employers are likely to use the public specification of units and elements of competence as a guide for identifying the competences relevant to the tasks employees perform in the company and could choose to provide or sponsor training only for those competences that are of direct and immediate benefit to them, as implied in the CBI observation that many employers remain narrowly concerned with task competences, and as seems likely from Steedman's study (1986). Whether or not this will lead to a part-NVQ will depend on the arrangements the employer chooses to make for assessment. Small employers may be particularly attracted to the selective use of NVQ units, being unable to provide assessment for the complete NVQ and unwilling to sponsor supplementary provision, for example through off-the-job training, group training workshops as in Germany (Munch, 1984) or by arrangement with a managing agent.

It is probable that with the encouragment of TECs, the support of public funds and continuing political concern for the young, NVQs will become widely accessible to young people over the next few years. But in the absence of a culture of training in British companies it seems unlikely that NVQs will be as readily available to adults. The point was clearly expressed by the Training Manager of a leading retail company who pointed out that companies were commercial, not training, enterprises. Adults were appointed to do a job. They were given sufficient training to carry out that job competently according to company procedures and were then placed on a till point or work station. They were given additional training according to company needs, for example, if they were moved to a different department or company procedures changed, but they were not, and would not be, placed on an NVQ (Retail Certificate) programme for the foreseeable future. It would be costly for the company because of the additional administrative and assessment demands — including record keeping and assessor training — and there would be major difficulties in proposing an expansion of training to the Board unless it could be shown to pay for itself by higher productivity or that it was very important for the corporate image. Moreover, there was an explicit concern that a national qualification would increase the employee's chances of getting a job elsewhere.

Looking ahead, in the absence of legislation there seem only three ways in which companies will facilitate access to NVQs for adults. The first is that it provides a means of recruiting and retaining staff by giving individuals the opportunity to achieve higher qualifications and to progress to higher levels of pay, status and responsibility — i.e., it is part of a employee package of good working conditions. This is likely to become more important as the number of young recruits falls in the years ahead. The second may come from employee demands if young people with NVQs start to gain preferment over older workers who do not have qualifications. The third is through extending the training voucher scheme to adults in employment.

The third problem concerns the ability of management either by qualification or experience to make judgements about training. This is closely related to the previous point but, where that was a consequence of cultural and structural factors mitigating against a commitment to training, here it is the competence of managers to make decisions about training when they are so poorly qualified themselves that is being questioned. Mangham and Silver's study, for example, shows that over one half of all UK companies, irrespective of the type of industry, make no formal provision for the training of their managers; one fifth of companies employing more than 1000 people made no provision for training their managers in 1985; and fewer than one in ten of these large companies provide training for their senior managers. Thompson's survey, conducted for the British Institute of Managers and the CBI report (Constable and McCormick, 1987) revealed that, for those companies engaged in management training, the mean expenditure on management training was £482 per year. The body of evidence available suggests that the UK has not yet developed any widely used, clearly understood method for educating and training its managers (Constable and McCormick, 1987). Given that the majority of UK managers have little or no personal experience of training and that there is the very low level of commitment to management training by companies, it must be doubted whether managers are equipped to understand and promote a human resource development strategy or, even if they did, whether their companies would support it.

NCVQ and the Awarding Bodies

Setting aside the question of whether NVQs as presently conceived will produce versatile, flexible workers imbued with a positive attitude towards change and ready to learn new skills, we turn now to an equally important though narrower issue of whether national standards can be accurately and consistently applied in a multitude of local assessment locations across the country. It is an issue central to the credibility of NVQs. If the standards set by lead bodies are not implemented consistently the reform of the vocational education and training system will collapse. If it is to work, occupational competence must mean the same in Llandudno as it does in Ramsgate. Two principal agencies are involved: the NCVQ and the Awarding Bodies.

The National Council for Vocational Qualifications

NCVQ's role is that of an accrediting organization; it is not another Awarding Body (AB) like City & Guilds (C&G) and the Business and Technician Education Council (BTEC). The ABs submit proposals to NCVQ of the qualifications based on national standards that they wish to offer as NVQs. The proposals will include details of the units and elements of competence, the performance criteria that will be used to assess competence and the methods of assessment that will be used, including the procedures for verification. Increasingly, as lead bodies provide such specifications, the ABs also include range statements, i.e. an indication of the range of variables to which the elements apply — products and services, types of customers, situations, etc. 'Range statements' have added a degree of sophistication to the primitive use of performance criteria as the test of competence. They provide guidance to ABs and to assessors about what evidence, including what evidence of knowledge and understanding, is needed to certificate competence. Range statements are also a useful aid for staff concerned with designing learning (or training) programmes and materials. They are not, however, always available.

A submission to NCVQ passes through a number of stages. It is discussed first with an Officers' Advisory Group, following which, in amended form, it goes to the Accreditation Advisory Group which is a formally constituted sub-group of the Council. This makes recommendations to Council on whether or not the qualification be approved or referred back. In the latter case the AB could, if it wished, still offer it as a qualification but it would not be an NVQ. Comments on proposals are not confined to standards and assessment but also deal with the issue of access. Officers and the Council may seek assurances from the AB that it is moving to remove barriers to access. This is a key pressure point in the serious attempt to increase opportunities for the working population and for other groups such as women returners to become qualified.

Most current NVQs are conditionally accredited; indeed out of about 240 NVQs accredited by October 1990 only a handful were fully accredited.[3] Conditional accreditation, which may be given to proposals that do not fully incorporate employment-led standards, is still a major strand but will reduce in significance as more standards are defined by lead bodies. At one level the use of conditional accreditation is entirely understandable. When NCVQ was established in 1986 there were no agreed standards for industry, indeed the Standards programme was only just beginning. It followed that no qualification could be endorsed as a full NVQ. At another level, the policy of conditional accreditation offers an insight into the relationship between NCVQ and the ABs.

When NCVQ was first established it was under pressure to show rapid progress in the development of the new system of competence based qualifications. A rainbow file of Green Papers, White Papers, other official documents, speeches and research was asserting the need for a much greater commitment to training and for a reformed system of vocational education and training. 'Our competitors in other countries ... invest heavily in training. They are pulling away from us and we must overtake them.... Our vocational education and training system is not — and never was — the envy of the world. But we must make it so.' (ED/DES, 1986) There was no time to be lost. Conditional accreditation was a function of the need to show progress, progress which was as necessary politically, with training high on the agenda of Government and Opposition parties, as it was in economic terms.

There was a further pressure on NCVQ. It was charged with becoming self-financing by 1991 (subsequently this was deferred to 1992 and is likely to be deferred until NVQs 1–4 are complete). In order to do this it had to establish its credibility and it had to do so quickly if it were to have any chance of becoming self-financing in the time scale it was given. It needed to be visible and seen to be making progress. Above all it needed to sign up Awarding Bodies. In doing so it it could generate momentum and encourage others — politicians, employers, other Awarding Bodies, colleges, etc. — to take NCVQ seriously. In the context of a decade in which a multitude of acronyms had been generated to cover the annual change in vocational education and training policies as weaknesses were revealed — WEEP, TOPS, YOP, YTS (1), YTS (2) — NCVQ had to demonstrate to a now suspicious public that it was here to stay and represented a serious and permanent change.

A further factor influencing development in the same direction was a commitment to giving ABs a sense of ownership of the new system. It certainly could not work without their support and it was, to many within NCVQ, important to involve ABs in the formative process of policy development. There is then a sense in which NCVQ is in a dependent relationship with the ABs. Is it symbiotic; are the ABs also dependent on NCVQ?

The current system is voluntary. The previous system of vocational qualifications remains alongside NVQs. They continue to have high credibility, particularly in some industries. To take one example, City & Guilds offer 706/2 Food Preparation which is widely understood and recognized by the hotel and catering industry as a useful qualification. It also offers a Joint Certificate which combines the City & Guilds knowledge test with a modular competence-based programme which was developed by the Hotel and Catering Training Board — Caterbase. The Joint Certificate is awarded by City & Guilds and is accredited by NCVQ. A fee is paid for each candidate for the award and for the accreditation. The costs of the Joint Certificate are therefore higher than for the C&G 706/2. There are also a number of other costs, e.g., the charge for Passbooks for recording candidate's progress towards competence. While an AB may encourage employers and candidates to use NVQs it is also a commercial organization, in business to provide the service which the customer wants. NVQs compete with two natural preferences — to work with a known and, in many instances, a trusted system and to keep expenditure to a minimum. NVQs may be promoted as providing a value-added product but, crudely, to join the NVQ system you have to pay for the privilege. There is, then, a built-in disincentive to move to NVQs if a parallel acceptable system exists.

To summarize, regardless of any advantages the NVQ system has, the voluntary nature of the system, combined with the requirement that NCVQ become self-financing weakened NCVQ in its dealings with the ABs, particularly in its responsibility for quality assurance.

The Awarding Bodies

In the *Review of Vocational Qualifications in England and Wales* (MSC/DES, 1986) the established system was described as 'disparate, complex and large'. It comprised examining and validating bodies which awarded about 1.5 million certificates each year and had a combined income of about £25m; around 250 professional bodies and about 120 industry training organizations. The initial efforts of NCVQ (and the Training Agency through its Standards Methodology Unit) were directed towards developing NVQs at Levels I–IV which was the domain of the examining and validating bodies and Industry Training Organizations.

Each of these Awarding Bodies had its own methods of working and corresponding strengths and weaknesses. Most were examination bodies. Candidates worked to externally set syllabuses and their performance was assessed through externally set examinations. Practical assessments were made *in situ* by, for example, college lecturers. External moderation for the examining bodies was largely carried out by lecturers from other colleges. Experiences differed between courses and awarding bodies but there was no shortage of criticism about the lack of visits by moderators and the poor quality of moderation — with some moderators apparently knowing less about the course than the lecturers they were there to advise. Quality control was based on measures of output. Awarding bodies also had very varied policies and practices in the training of moderators. In some instances it was required, in others it was voluntary. In aggregate this posed questions about the reliability of assessment procedures and hence the credibility of qualifications but the unease expressed was at a low level and to a large extent contained because the relatively small numbers of assessment centres — mainly the colleges — had considerable experience and expertise in assessment.

BTEC, however, operated as a validating body by establishing a contract with a centre to deliver an approved programme. Centres, wishing to offer a BTEC qualification, design their own course and apply for BTEC approval. Quality controls are built into the approval stage through requirements that applications set out how the centre intends to involve local employers, the aims of the course, its structure, the intended learning strategies, course management, methods of assessment and an outline of the evaluation proposed. BTEC publishes its criteria for standards in these areas, including guidelines for evaluation. 'Moderators' visit centres to discuss the presentation of the course, focusing on course management, teaching and learning strategies, assessment and, in the latter stages of the course, on course evaluation. In effect, a process model of control is used.

The reputation of ABs varied. Most made a serious attempt to consult with industry through advisory committees and adapted their syllabuses to meet changing demands. The ABs were, however, vulnerable to criticisms that their qualifications were essentially knowledge based and that employers could not be confident that successful candidates would perform competently in the job for which they were apparently qualified. The ABs encouraged colleges to establish consultative committees for the occupational sectors that they served. The colleges, however, often encountered serious difficulties in sustaining the interests of employers in these committees. This was very largely a consequence of the marginal role that colleges prescribed for employers. They were regarded as the receivers of trained people, not as partners professionally involved in the content and delivery of vocational education and training. The relationship that the colleges fostered was, in consequence, social rather than professional and employers never developed a stake or sense of ownership in the vocational education and training system.

The introduction of NVQs has necessitated major changes. NVQs are assessment driven. Quality assurance is directed towards ensuring that organizations deliver assessment consistently and accurately to specified occupational standards. If consistency is not guaranteed the system will lose credibility and it will be difficult and probably impossible to recover.

What is now required is more complicated than it was. First, the emphasis on standards of occupational competence implies that for assessment to be valid it should take place under realistic working conditions. Indeed, NCVQ and the Training Agency both stress the virtues of assessment in the workplace: 'the ability of an individual to perform in the work role is the primary requirement of an NVQ and this should be reflected in the assessment' and 'As a general rule assessment of performance in the course of normal work offers the most natural form of evidence of competence and has several advantages, both technical and economic' (NCVQ, 1989). This is further encouraged by the admirable emphasis on access to qualifications. For many workers the only access will be through assessment at work.

Awarding Bodies have responded quickly to this and a substantial number of companies have registered with ABs as assessment centres (though none has so far submitted a proposal to NCVQ to deliver NVQs itself). But while workplace assessment satisfies concerns about the validity of assessment of units and elements of competence, it raises serious questions about the reliability of assessment. A short list of the potential difficulties, each of which has implications for quality assurance, includes:

many more people will be involved in assessment most of whom will have had no previous experience in assessing on a formal basis;

there will be a tension between in-company standards and national (occupational) standards;

assessors will be inexperienced in the use of documentation;

assessors will be inexperienced in interpreting training language;

assessors will need to find additional time for assessment;

if assesors are trained it will add to operating costs; if they are not, they may not have the level of competence required to deliver assessment.

The two principal mechanisms used by ABs to provide quality assurance of assessment is through validation and verification (or moderation). Validation, as may be seen from the reference to BTEC above, involves checking that a potential assessment centre *can* deliver assessment in the form and to the standards required. It is essentially a gate-keeping process, admitting those that seem likely to be able to do the job required and keeping out those which probably cannot. Verification provides a check that assessment *is* being conducted as required.

Validation procedures vary. Some ABs spell out in considerable detail the criteria that are applied to centres wishing to deliver assessment. For example, Caterbase, which is controlled by the HCTB/C, must include details about where Caterbase will be offered, i.e. in which units, sites, etc.; the names, qualifications, positions and locations of workplace assessors and Countersigning Officers (who monitor and support the work of the assessors); the modules which the Centre wishes to offer; any training requirements for nominated participants, together with a schedule for implementing them; and an outline of the arrangements for monitoring the quality of assessment and for assessor support. All assessors must be trained.

Some ABs, however, are only now beginning to move towards defining the criteria that should be applied when evaluating an application to become an assessment centre. Recent discussions with an experienced official from a major AB indicated that no criteria had been established and that the AB relied solely on the judgement of the individual representative who visited the site. The AB concerned is now taking urgent steps to rectify this by defining validation criteria.

As yet, however, there is very little evidence as to what should be the key criteria for validation. The Accreditation of Work-based Learning project undertaken by SCOTVEC and covering a number of different occupational fields is the most substantial and solid research we have so far. That suggests that the competence of the assessor in applying the procedures of workplace assessment in different occupational sectors is a key variable (Miller, 1989). Additional evidence to this effect comes from the HCTB *Take-up of Caterbase* study which confirmed the importance of assessor training to help assessors understand and apply the processes of workplace assessment and, not least, to help assessors come to terms with the concept of *national* standards of competence which are usually somewhat different from company standards (HCTB, 1989).

Awarding body policies on assessor training vary. Some require it, others do not. As we have seen, Caterbase, controlled by the HCTC, insists that assessors are trained. By contrast the RSA, which is the largest single provider of certification for office based occupations in the United Kingdom, has no such requirement though training is available on a voluntary basis. Most ABs are somewhere between requiring smaller amounts of assessor training than Caterbase and often provided in-house through a cascade model. Such variation in policies and practices is suprising and worrying given the central position that workplace assessment has in the new system of competence based vocational qualifications.

Verification procedures are adopted by all Awarding Bodies. A three-tier system is often used. This comprises a workplace assessor (usually a supervisor or manager), a countersigning officer or internal verifier (usually a senior manager or a member of the training department) and an external verifier (representing the AB). The verifier appointed by the AB normally visits the Centre two or three times each year. During the visits she/he will check that the assessment procedures are being implemented as agreed and that standards of competence are being correctly and consistently applied in the appropriate environment.

Comments from assessment centres suggest that verifiers interpret their role and apply procedures in different ways and also hold different expectations — even when working for the same Awarding Body. Some look at trainees' work, their 'Record of Achievement' or Pass Book and talk to the staff involved in assessment, others restrict themselves to the documentation and a discussion with the Centre Contact, and others appear to view their main role as moderating the assessments made by company staff. These variations in practice may diminish as verifiers pool their experience, exchange ideas on good practice and discuss issues that arise during verification visits in the sessions which most ABs organize. At the core of such sessions one would expect to find training on what is expected of assessors.

Verification is necessarily based on small scale sampling; it would be prohibitively expensive to do otherwise. The effect is to place the front line and major responsibility for ensuring that NVQ standards are being attained on the company. This practice was identified in an HCTB study where a number of Central Contacts expressed concern that quality in assessment rested very largely on the conscientiousness of assessors and countersigning officers. This, however, seems likely to emerge as the predominant model. In the case of large companies which are assessment centres, the candidates are often widely distributed in smaller units or individual stores around the country. It is simply not feasible for an AB to sample more than a tiny fraction — as few as two or three locations — and the emphasis will be put on a quality assurance audit of the procedures, documentation and practices used by the company. Small companies will have to work through umbrella organizations — colleges, managing agents and TECs — because it would not be possible to deliver validation and verification procedures economically.

Verification practices could be extended beyond the technical aspects of ensuring that assessment is being conducted correctly and consistently to national standards to include, particularly, the issue of equal opportunities. Training Agency policy stresses equal opportunity and it is included as an element of competence in the Training and Development Lead Body (TDLB) draft standards: 'assessment methods do not discriminate on the basis of race, religion, sex, marital status, culture, unrelated physical or intellectual ability'. NCVQ, too, specifies that access must be open. It has not, however, translated this into a requirement. What should be the limits of the verification process? Should verification and sampling go beyond the technical concerns outlined above and include data on access to NVQs for different groups?

More specifically, should verification encompass policies and provision for delivering equal opportunities?

Costs

Underlying the quality control measures being developed is the issue of cost. British companies have no tradition of investing in training. Employers and managers hold a short-term perspective, sustained, as Finegold and Soskice (1988) point out, 'by the pressure to maximize immediate profits and share-holder value'. It is a perspective which is inimicable to investment in training, which is necessarily long term in the returns that it offers. But this is also the context in which NVQs are being introduced and in which Awarding Bodies must develop systems for verifying the quality of the qualifications they are delivering. On the one hand they must develop and operate a system which ensures the credibility of NVQs, on the other hand the system must be cheap otherwise they will have no customers. As commercial organizations competing in the marketplace for customers, they have difficult judgements to make. But so, too, does NCVQ which is the custodian of the reform — an easier role if it did not have to be self-financing.

Workplace assessment will be expensive, particularly for employers that have made little previous investment in training. Competent assessors will be the cornerstone of the system. They will need to be trained and this will add to the initial costs of the system. That said, one of the most curious features of the change to competence based training and workplace assessment is that assessor competences were not defined at an early point in the reform. The Training Agency did not initiate any work on this nor did the TDLB draft competences have much to offer. This is a most extraordinary omission. Why then has the Training Agency been so silent on this issue? Was it overlooked? Or did the TA choose to do nothing because the costs of training assessors to deliver an effective and reliable workplace assessment to national standards might frighten employers and undermine the NVQ approach?

The issue is an interesting one because it illustrates the power of the TA to set the agenda for development work in the Standards programme. In this case the apparent lack of interest meant that no funds were available to sponsor the development of assessor standards. Eventually, NCVQ stepped into the void and brought the major ABs together to draft competences for assessors, including face-to-face assessors, coordinators and verifiers. This group has now been constituted as a sub-group of the TDLB and there seems every likelihood that competences will be agreed and that the validating criteria used by ABs will increasingly require assessment centres to have qualified assessors. NCVQ will, no doubt, encourage this development and is in a position to deny accreditation for qualifications offered by the ABs unless they are backed by qualified assessors. If this does become a requirement it will add to employer costs. Historically, employers in Britain have been notoriously reluctant to invest in human resource development; whether they will be prepared to meet the costs of assessor training will be an interesting test of their commitment to the goal of developing a well trained workforce.

Summary

The reform of the old system of vocational qualifications to one based on standards of occupational competence is still in its infancy. Measured against the national goal of creating a competent, adaptable and flexible workforce it has an inherent weakness: the standards of competence, as currently defined, are too occupationally specific. They provide no basis on which workers could transfer the competences that they develop to different occupational sectors as industries decline and new ones develop. The inclusion of core skills in NVQs is now under discussion. If, as seems likely, the proposal is accepted for 1994, core skills may provide the necessary continuity and congruence across the education and training system and will facilitate both horizontal movement between occupational sectors and vertical progression within an occupation. This would bring us closer to the national goal. We must, however, ask why it took so long. How far did the ideological commitment to employer control over the definition of standards impede the realization of an effective vocational education and training system?

Notes

1 This excludes those who were in publicly funded youth training programmes.
2 See Weiner (1981) for an exploration of the cultural issues and Finegold and Soskice (1988) for a useful review of structural factors including the financial pressure on British managers to maximize short term profits, the lack of national agreements between the state, employers and trade unions on a coordinated training strategy which could be contrasted with the widespread notion of a social partnership between the state, employers and unions in the EC — and the absence of training as an issue in collective bargaining.
3 This system is changing.

References

ANDERSON, A. (1987) 'Adult training: private industry and the Nicholson letter', in HARRISON, A. and GRETTON, J. (Eds), *Policy Journals, Education & Training UK*, pp. 67–73.
BAKER, K. (1989) *Further Education: Towards a New Strategy*, London, HMSO.

CONFEDERATION OF BRITISH INDUSTRY (1989) *Towards a Skills Revolution — A Youth Charter*, London, CBI.

CONSTABLE, J. and McCORMICK, R. (1987) *The Making of British Managers, A Report for the BIM and CBI into Management Training, Education and Development*, Corby, BIM/CBI.

COOPERS AND LYBRAND ASSOCIATES (1985) *A Challenge to Complacency: Changing Attitudes to Training*, Sheffield, National Economic Development Office/ Manpower Services Commission.

DE VILLE, O. (1990) Letter to the Secretary of State for Education and Science, 23rd July.

EMPLOYMENT DEPARTMENT (1981) *A New Training Initiative: A Programme for Action*, London, HMSO.

EMPLOYMENT DEPARTMENT/DEPARTMENT OF EDUCATION AND SCIENCE (1986) *Working Together — Education and Training*, London, HMSO.

FINANCIAL TIMES, 4th July 1990.

FINEGOLD, D and SOSKICE, D. (1988) 'The failure of British training: Analysis and prescription', *Oxford Review of Economic Policy*, 4, 3, pp. 21–53.

FURTHER EDUCATION UNIT (1984) *Towards a Competence-Based System*, London, FEU.

HOTEL AND CATERING TRAINING BOARD (1989) *Influencing the Take-up of Caterbase*, Stage One Report, London, HCTB Research Department.

JESSUP, G. (1990) *Common Learning Outcomes: Core Skills in A/AS Levels and NVQs*, NCVQ R&D Report No. 6, London, NCVQ.

MANPOWER SERVICES COMMISSION (1977) *A Programme for Action — Training for Skills*, Sheffield, MSC.

MANPOWER SERVICES COMMISSION: TECHNICAL ADVISORY GROUP (1988) *A Code of Practice and a Development Model*, Guidance Notes 1, Sheffield, MSC.

MANPOWER SERVICES COMMISSION/DEPARTMENT OF EDUCATION AND SCIENCE (1986) *Review of Vocational Qualifications in England and Wales, Report by the Working Group* (The De Ville Report), London, HMSO.

MANPOWER SERVICES COMMISSION/NATIONAL ECONOMIC DEVELOPMENT OFFICE (1984) *Competence and Competition: Training and Education in the Federal Republic of Germany, the United States and Japan*, London, MSC/NEDO.

MILLER, C. (1989) 'Assessment in the Workplace — Quality Issues', *Competence and Assessment*, Issue 9.

MUNCH, J. (1984) *Vocational Training in the Federal Republic of Germany*, Berlin, CEDEFOP.

NCVQ (1989) *Assessment in National Vocational Qualifications*, NCVQ Information Note 4, London, NCVQ.

NCVQ (1990) 'Core Skills in NVQs: Response to The Secretary of State for Education', July, London, NCVQ.

PRAIS, S.J. (1981) 'Vocational qualifications in the labour force in Britain and Germany', *National Institute Economic Review*, 98, pp. 47–59.

PRAIS, S.J. (1989) 'How Europe would see the new British initiative for standardizing vocational qualifications', *National Institute Economic Review*, August, pp. 52–4.

PRAIS, S.J. and WAGNER, K. (1985) 'Schooling standards in England and Germany: Some summary comparisons bearing on economic performance', *National Institute Economic Review*, May, pp. 53–76.

PRAIS, S.J. and WAGNER, K. (1985) 'Some practical aspects of human capital investment: training standards in five occupations in Britain and Germany', *National Institute Economic Review*, 95, pp. 46–65.

PRAIS, S.J., JARVIS, V. and WAGNER, K. (1989) 'Productivity and vocational skills in services in Britain and Germany: Hotels', *National Institute Economic Review*, November, pp. 52–74.

RAGGATT, P. (1988) 'Quality control in the dual system of West Germany', *Oxford Review of Education*, 14, 2, pp. 163–86.

STEEDMAN, H. (1986) 'Vocational training in France and Britain: The building trades', *National Institute Economic Review*, May, pp. 45–55.

STEEDMAN, H. and WAGNER, K. (1987) 'A second look at productivity, machinery and skills in Britain and Germany', *National Institute Economic Review*, November, pp. 84–95.

UNWIN, L. (1990) 'We're all qualified now: the competence race' in CORBETT, J. (Ed.) *Uneasy Transitions*, London, Falmer Press.

WEINER, MARTIN (1981) *English Culture and the Decline of Industrial Spirit*, Cambridge, Cambridge University Press.

Chapter 5

Meeting the Needs of a 'Global Society': Vocational Education and Training in the United States of America

Lorna Unwin

Nothing is more important than education. And today more than ever, education is not just an issue for children. We must be concerned about people of all ages and backgrounds, citizens and newcomers, those who are literate and those who are not. The future of America depends on it. (Barbara Bush, *BusinessWeek*, 1989)

Our nation is at an educational crossroads. Education must prove that it is equal to the challenges of technology and the information age. The success of our economy and indeed, the survival of our democracy have become more dependent than ever before on each individual's ability to master increasingly complex knowledge and skills. (Educational Testing Service, 1989)

We are students of words: we are shut up in schools, and colleges, and recitation-rooms, for ten or fifteen years, and come out at last with a bag of wind, a memory of words, and do not know a thing. We cannot use our hands, or our legs, or our eyes, or our arms. We do not know an edible root in the woods, we cannot tell our course by the stars, nor the hour of the day by the sun. It is well if we can swim and skate. (Emerson, 1844)

In March and April 1990, the main television channels in the United States of America broadcast nightly a series of advertisements exhorting the business community to become much more closely involved with its local schools and colleges. Much of the rhetoric used in this campaign is similar to that used in ministerial statements and Training Agency, TUC and CBI reports published in Britain. The message, for both Britain and America, is seemingly clear — for both nations to compete effectively in world markets, educational goals must be based on the needs of business, and, in turn, business must contribute to and be actively involved in education. This chapter examines that message in its American context and considers some of the initiatives it has spawned. In addition, this chapter will also compare those initiatives to their current counterparts in Britain.

Facing the Facts

Part of the television campaign urged Americans to face some educational facts:

* School dropout rates hover above 25 per cent nationally and exceed 50 per cent in many urban centres.
* An estimated 25 million Americans are illiterate.
* At age 10, American students rank seventh in a field of 15 countries in terms of scientific knowledge. By age 15, Americans rank 15th of 16 nations.
* Each year 74 per cent of American high school seniors graduate compared with 94 per cent of their Japanese counterparts.
* About half the nation's 17-year-old students lack the mathematics skills commonly taught in junior high school.

This apparent decline in standards and achievement had been highlighted seven years earlier in 1983 with the publication of *A Nation at Risk* which attacked what it saw as a dangerous American complacency which ignored the increasing economic success of other industrialised nations:

> Our once unchallenged preeminence in commerce, industry, science, and technological innovation is being overtaken by competitors throughout the world. If an unfriendly foreign power had attempted to impose on America the mediocre educational performance that exists today, we might have viewed it as an act of war. (NCEE, 1983, p. 5)

The foreign competitor most referred to in reports and articles which warn of America's decline as an economic power is Japan. Taxi drivers in Washington DC talk about the Japanese buying large chunks of real estate in New York, Chicago and other key business and industrial locations as if ready to march in once their economic dominance is complete. *Newsweek* (1990) compounded this seeming obsession with Japanese success by publishing a lengthy account of how the Japanese view Americans. Subtitled *A Nation of Crybabies*, the article reveals that the Japanese see major problems endemic in the American workplace. Those problems include lazy workers, drugs and alcohol addiction, not enough long-term investment, too much greed on the part of bosses and workers, a crumbling education system, crime-ridden cities and a complacency born of decades of affluence. Toshio Yamaguchi, a former Minister of Labour, sums up the general tenor of the article:

> If America's system is an industrial castoff, Japan's is at the leading edge. (*Newsweek*, 1990, p. 24)

The language of politicians, industrialists and education policy makers is that of the sickroom. America is described in terms usually reserved for the underprivileged, as being 'at risk', ailing and in need of urgent treatment:

> The problems of schooling are of such crippling proportions that many schools may not survive. It is possible that our entire public education system is nearing collapse. (*BusinessWeek*, 1989)
>
> Recent improvements are evident and represent significant national accomplishment. But progress falls short of what the times require. Much more progress is needed for the economic development of our nation and the intellectual well-being of the next generation. (ETS, 1989)
>
> America's dismal productivity performance during the 1970s and 1980s is the nation's chief economic disorder and should be the chief concern of economic policymakers. (Binder, 1990)

Alongside the lists of educational statistics and adding to the overall picture of an ailing society are the same factors which currently occupy the thoughts of politicians and employers in Britain. Those factors include the demographic downturn, the effects of scientific and technological changes in the workplace, and the competitiveness of goods in terms of availability, quality and price. The demographic pattern, like each of those factors, has been slow to seep into national consciousness; not surprising in a country which coined the term 'baby-boomer'.

> Americans are predisposed to the view that there are too many qualified people and not enough jobs to go around. Our recent history encourages us to believe that people are superfluous while machinery, financial capital and natural resources are hard to come by. However, things are rarely as they first appear. Closely examined, the apparent excess of American workers proves illusory. In the future, there will likely be too few well-educated and trained Americans looking for their first job. (Carnevale *et al.*, 1988, p. 11)

The number of Americans between the ages of 20 and 29 will fall from 41 million in 1980 to 34 million in the year 2000. The proportion of workers aged 16 to 24 will drop to 16 per cent of the workforce by 1995, down from

24 per cent in 1975. Replacing the traditional supply of young workers will mean recruiting more women, more people from ethnic minorities and making more effective use of an existing ageing workforce, changes which demand a corporate response:

> What those numbers mean is a workforce characterized by fewer skilled workers at entry levels, a glut of mid-level managers ready for promotion, and an overall diversity of cultures, by ethnicity and age. That spectrum will require corporate cultures that make new employees feel valued and give them access to both formal and informal channels of information and career growth. Changes also must come in training and development interventions. Programs will need to fit different learning styles, economic backgrounds, and levels of familiarity with electronic media. How well a company's programs match workers' desires for career development will determine its recruiting and retention success. (Kimmerling, 1989, p. 50)

The discovery by the American business community and many politicians that the United States is not just comprised of white, male, white-collar workers seems startling given the nation's history of immigration, yet published responses to the changing demographic situation indicate just how much some employers and policy-makers need to learn about their country's working population. Interestingly, this discovery of America's diversity is being harnessed in the public relations drive to heighten awareness of the country's need to compete, for example:

> Rising from the ashes of defeat following World War II, the Japanese turned their attention to rebuilding, and as they invested in the infrastructure — creating physical capital — so, too, did they invest in 'human capital'. They did both in precisely the same way — borrowing the best practices from abroad, and adapting them to Japan's special circumstances. Are the Japanese a fair comparison? Can a continental democracy made up of all races and ethnic groups, pluralistic and heterogeneous, fairly be compared to a homogeneous people with widely shared values and a high degree of social consensus? There are two answers: No one said the world was fair. And we can do the Japanese one better. Our pluralism, our diversity, our heterogenity are pearls beyond price. We are the global society. Our differences do not diminish us, they strengthen us. (*BusinessWeek*, 1989, p. E18)

The record of investment in American human capital shows, however, that the different sections of that 'global society' have had very different opportunities in terms of benefiting from that investment:

Employers tend to train their best-educated employees: 79 per cent of college graduates receive training, compared to only 71 per cent of high school graduates and only 45 per cent of high school dropouts

... Economically disadvantaged Americans ... are the least likely to receive training; only about 10 per cent receive postsecondary training of any kind and less than 3 per cent receive training from their employers. Non-white employees are less likely to be trained than whites, and women are less likely to receive training than men. (CBCAEL, 1989, p. 2)

Such figures mask the huge amounts of money spent on training. By the late 1980s, American employers were spending an estimated 30 billion dollars per year in direct costs for formal training courses and up to 180 billion dollars for informal training that they either provided themselves or bought from outside providers. Most of that training — 68 per cent — is for employees aged between 25 and 44. The least trained groups include machine operators, service workers and labourers (Carnevale, 1989, pp. 17–18). Despite the large financial outlay, however, much training is ad hoc and not necessarily designed to meet the long-term needs of the companies which fund it:

... employers retain a certain mindset toward training: training tends to be utilized only when skill needs cannot be fulfilled by hiring from the outside or be redeploying personnel internally. Many employers still rely heavily on informal on-the-job learning rather than structured training and remain unconvinced of the need for in-depth, structured, comprehensive training for many employees. When in-depth training (such as apprenticeship) is utilized, it frequently is to train a small cadre of elite technical personnel — perhaps first-line supervisors, or highly skilled mechanics than can troubleshoot difficult problems. (USDLETA, 1989, p. 7)

Solutions and a Sense of *déjà vu*

The most well-known American solution to its educational problems is the concept of business/education compacts, the first of which, in Boston, Massachusetts, became the model for similar partnership activity in Britain. The Boston Compact was first established in 1982 to improve performance in local schools. The goals of the Compact were expressed in three bilateral agreements between business and schools (1982), colleges and universities (1983) and building and trade unions (1984). Those goals were:

* Improve daily attendance by 5 per cent each year.
* Reduce the high school dropout rate by 5 per cent each year.

* Improve academic performance by producing graduates who are at least minimally competent in mathematics and reading.
* Improve college placement rates by 5 per cent each year.
* Improve job placement rates by 5 per cent each year.

In 1985, the Boston Private Industry Council (PIC), itself an example of yet another solution to America's 'ailing society', reviewed the Compact's targets. Despite the fact that the PIC committee found evidence of 'a strong alliance among the signers of the agreement, and that significant accomplishments had been achieved, especially around the Compact's employment objectives', it concluded that:

> The dropout rate remains alarmingly high. The Class of 1985 posted a dropout rate of 43.6 per cent. For the Class of 1987, the dropout rate rose to 45.1 per cent. Despite minimum competency standards in reading and mathematics, 45 per cent of all seniors score below the 40th percentile on the Metropolitan Reading Achievement Test. At 10 of the 14 non-examination schools, one-half of the seniors are below the 40th percentile ... real school improvement remained an unfulfilled promise. (Boston PIC, 1989)

In March 1989, the Compact's steering committee set new targets summarized as follows:

* To improve the quality of education by enabling each individual school to be responsible for the quality of education it provides. Each school will, therefore, manage its own budget, staff appointments and curriculum development.
* To increase local parental involvement by giving parents increased opportunities to enrol in education and job training programmes.
* To create a comprehensive follow-up programme that assists students for up to four years after graduation, especially for those who experience problems finding work.
* To cut in half the number of students who drop out of the Boston Public Schools over the next five years and to double the number of alternative education opportunities available to youth who have dropped out.
* To ensure that Boston students have the academic skills needed to achieve their potential in a competitive society.

From a set of numerically-based targets, the Compact has considerably broadened its demands. Significantly, for British observers, those new demands are similar to targets now being set by the newly emerging Training and Enterprise Councils (TECs) whose creation was inspired by the American PICs. We seem to have come full circle in this transatlantic game of copycat. The Boston Compact encouraged the Thatcher Government in 1986 to fund, via the then Manpower Services Commission, a series of similar partnerships in urban centres in Britain, despite the warning signs from Boston that all was not well. Norman Fowler, the then Secretary of State for Employment, was obviously developing a taste for the American way. Not only had he been impressed with the concept of Compact, he carried home admiring reports of the PICs he had visited.

Private Industry Councils were established in the USA 1983 following the 1982 Job Training Partnership Act which made changes to earlier federal training and employment legislation for the unemployed. The main changes can be summarized as follows:

* the states became responsible for functions previously carried out by the US Department of Labor, such as approval of local training programmes and monitoring their performance.
* Federal funds had to be spent on training programmes rather than creating extra jobs.
* The private sector was given an increased role in local policy-making with a majority of PIC members representing local business.

The PICs are largely concerned with providing training programmes for the unemployed though they can also support customized training events which respond to the specific needs of local employers. There are now some 600 PICs but their effectiveness is restricted by their federal funding, as the Director of Atlanta's PIC explains:

The JPTA funding received by most PICs allows them to serve no more than two or three per cent of the eligible populace, which is estimated at 100,000 in Atlanta, or 20 per cent of the population. Those limited funds combined with the emphasis on performance, may conflict with the Act's emphasis on service to those who are most in need. (Montgomery, 1988)

Though the Compacts and the PICs are often quoted in Britain and have led to the creation of British versions, they reflect the more publicized tip of a dynamic iceberg. The rationale of the TECs is dealt with in detail in Richard Guy's chapter in this book and they will clearly differ in many ways to their American counterparts. Significantly, however, many Americans to whom I spoke in national government, in education and in business, were surprised that both the Compacts and the PICs alone should have been chosen as suitable models for the British to emulate. They pointed instead to the myriad schemes which exist across the United States, some of which are effective, some failures but each of which might have something to offer. It should be noted that the TECs are contracted to respond to local labour market needs, but their structure and funding have been devised by central

Government and it remains to be seen how far this will prevent them from being truly responsive.

There are, of course, problems in having too much diversity as the *Business-Higher Education Forum* highlighted:

> The remarkable education reform movement of the 1980s has been fragmented and often at odds with itself. If our leaders and our people believe broad consensus exists on how to proceed, they are, unfortunately, mistaken. The point is made dramatically in a background paper prepared for the Forum. Some 20 major reports on education and the economy were examined; together they offer 285 discrete recommendations. Among these 285, only nine enjoy the support of five or more of the 20 reports. More to the point, over 70 per cent of the specific recommendations have only a single champion standing behind them. It is little wonder that progress in raising student achievement has been much too slow. As different pilots seize the helm of educational reform, the ship goes round in circles. (CBCAEL, 1989, p. 5)

The different pilots keen to make their mark on the future of education and training in the United States include industrialists, local and national government, community leaders and the many business organizations such as the Committee for Economic Development, the National Alliance of Business and the US Chamber of Commerce. That such a wide range of people and organizations can affect change is largely due to a long standing commitment in the United States to the concept of 'local control'. As a spokesperson for the American Council on Education in Washington DC emphasized:

> You have to remember that the smallest school or college in the smallest town in most of the States is able to pursue its own vision in terms of the curriculum, its links with business and its use of resources. Whatever ideas the national government has, ultimately local preferences prevail.

This makes the federal government's role somewhat equivocal. It can produce well-received and authoritative reports such as *A Nation at Risk* (NCEE, 1983) and can provide funding for the necessary research and development arising out of such reports. The US Constitution, however, makes no reference to education, responsibility for which lies with each individual state. George Bush has stated on more than one occasion that he wants to be known as the 'Education President' but he and his officials have no way of introducing a federal curriculum or federal standards. When I discussed the introduction of a National Curriculum and National Vocational Qualifications with Americans at local and national level, they repeatedly referred to the major cultural differences between the New and Old Worlds. Yet they also emphasized the desire for coordination and for the federal government to play a much more decisive role in reshaping both school education and post-compulsory education and training. In the midst of this state versus Federal impasse, the business community has been taking on an increasingly influential role.

Call to Action — The Business-led Crusade

Business and education have been bedfellows since the end of the eighteenth century when increasing industrialization forced American employers to address the question of skills training. Originally a nation of farmers and craftsmen, America entered its industrial revolution with a labour shortage and without a system of state education. This meant employers were forced to find solutions:

> Training had to be within a company or a trade group and such programs were hardly just lofty exercises in benevolence and self-improvement. They were an absolute necessity. Industries, such as the Lowell mills, wanted a certain type of worker and they created circumstances that would ensure that they got that type of employee. Specialized workers' groups wanted a particular quality of employment and they took similar steps on their own behalf. (Eurich, 1985, pp. 29–30)

This recognition by both employers and workers of the need for mass education and training led to the creation of Mechanics Institutes, schools on factory and mill premises, and, ultimately in 1862, the passing by Congress of the Morrill Land Grant Act. This Act gave large tracts of federal land to states prepared to establish colleges running advanced agricultural, engineering and military science courses. Yet this activity was still not enough, for the rapid advances in technology increased pressure on both the education system and the employer-based training schools to keep pace with industrial change. Increasingly, throughout the late nineteenth and first quarter of the twentieth century, American corporations developed their own in-house training departments, some of which now, as Eurich points out:

> ... surpass many universities in their sophistication both in the range of offerings and delivery systems and methods as well. They are not factory-bound, they are global, and a single corporation may be educating in New York, Rio de Janeiro, Tokyo, and Rome. (Eurich 1985, p. 47)

The extent of American 'corporate classrooms' ranges from those offering remedial literacy and numeracy programmes to doctorates. Over two thousand corporate courses are classified according to the American academic credit weighting system under the PONSI scheme — Program on Non-collegiate Sponsored Instruction. This means that any employee who has completed a course recognised by the PONSI scheme can claim credit for it within an academic programme at a particpating college or university up to degree level. In addition, a growing number of corporations are awarding their own academic degrees and have supported the establishment of the National Technological University (NTU). From its base in Colorado, NTU beams it courses by satellite into corporate classrooms all over the country. Yet despite the billions of dollars, the impressive corporate campuses such as Xerox's Learning Center (sic) in Virginia and IBM's collection of institutes in New York, and the success of the PONSI programme, employer-based training in America is as fundamentally flawed as its British equivalent:

> This shadow education system is delivered by no single institution, is the subject of no law or policy, and functions quietly and efficiently, growing invisibly, a silent postscript to the employee's formal education. Even now, executives, managers, supervisors, and others train without the direction or assistance of training professionals. Most people involved in employer-based training do not recognize that they are part of a training system. Most trainers see themselves as managers, engineers, marketers, chemists, or sales managers, for example. They tend to be rewarded and recognized by their peers on the basis of their professional expertise, rather than their ability to train and develop employees. (Carnevale and Gainer, 1988)

Despite the growing numbers of employees with a designated training function on both sides of the Atlantic, training is still, too often, task-related and does not embrace the wider concept of human resource development. In addition, long-term training is often restricted to white-collar employees and technical élites. And, just like their colleagues in Britain, American trainers are faced with a workforce which consistently seems to lack the basic skills on which occupational training is supposed to build.

Concepts of Core and Transferability

Faced with increasing economic competition from abroad and with the knowledge that their national education and training systems are placed way down the international league table, both the UK and USA are embracing the concept of core or transferable skills. The UK has been travelling down this route for some time. Identification of these skills has been pursued and advocated since the late 1970s by the Further Education Unit, the former Manpower Services Commission in its design framework for the Youth Training Scheme and, currently, by NCVQ working with the National

Curriculum Council and the Schools Examination and Assessment Council. As has already been noted, the United States will not adopt a nationally prescribed system in the way that the UK is doing, but there appears to be a growing consensus about the concept of core or transferable skills.

That consensus has been largely fuelled by a jointly published document from the American Society for Training and Development (ASTD) and the US Department of Labor's Employment and Training Administration. *Workplace Basics: The Skills Employers Want* identifies seven skill groups which together form 'a prescription for a well-rounded worker who has acquired a number of discrete skills and who has the capability to acquire more sophisticated skills when necessary' (Carnevale *et al.*, 1988, p. 8). The seven groups are:

1 Learning to Learn
2 Reading, Writing and Computation
3 Listening and Oral Communication
4 Creative Thinking/Problem Solving
5 Self Esteem/Goal Setting-Motivation/Personal and Career Development
6 Interpersonal Skills, Negotiation and Teamwork
7 Organizational Effectiveness and Leadership.

Where once employers sought people with the traditional basic skills of reading, writing and arithmetic, they now require a far more sophisticated portfolio as *Workplace Basics* explains:

Employer complaints focus on serious deficiencies in areas that include problem solving, personal management, and interpersonal skills. The abilities to conceptualize, organize, and verbalize thoughts, resolve conflicts, and work in teams are increasingly cited as critical. Their concern is driven by the most compelling of circumstance — economic need. Competitive challenges are forcing employers to adopt an array of competitive strategies that can only be successfully implemented by an innovative and flexible workforce. Beneath the surface comments about basic skill deficiencies lie employer concerns that they will not be able to achieve their competitive goals with their existing workforce. That they will not be able to successfully integrate new technology or sophisticated production processes. That basic workplace deficiencies are beginning to affect their bottom line. (Carnevale *et al.*, 1988, p. 8)

In similar vein, the White Paper, *Employment for the 1990s* (ED, 1989), stated:

The days of a British economy with captive overseas markets are long since over. Britain is now operating in an increasingly competi-

tive international environment ... The general lesson from this is
that to meet competition at home and overseas, industry and commerce ... must be increasingly alert to the new opportunities, and
must adapt to changing technologies, changing markets and changing tastes. This requires a high degree of commercial expertise. It
also requires a more adaptable workforce, from top management to
the office or shopfloor. This in turn requires investment in training,
and an appropriate training system which will ensure the provision
of relevant skills. (p. 10)

There are similarities too in the way both nations are attempting to pursue
the goal of creating a well-trained, flexible workforce. The White Paper
went on to announce the establishment of TECs whose powers now extend
beyond running government-sponsored training programmes for the unemployed to delivering training voucher scheme for all 16–19-year-olds,
introducing action plans for final-year school pupils linked to records of
achievement, funding business growth projects, working more closely with
higher education and embedding the NCVQ framework. A 1989 national
conference of educationalists, industrialists, trade union leaders and government representatives held in Arkansas advocated the following responses to
the changing American workplace:

1 Establish state and local Councils of Worklife Education and
   Training.
2 Facilitate the transition from school to work.
3 Build demand-driven systems linked to credits.
4 Promote small businesses.
5 Promote performance-based quality standards.
6 Promote records of achievement.
7 Increase public and private investment.
   (Summarized from CBCAEL, *1989*)

The emphasis in both Britain and the United States is on employer-education
partnerships with the former being required to invest more and more at all
levels — primary school, secondary school, college, workplace, university,
post-university. In return, employers can expect education to listen to its
demands and tailor both its processes and outcomes to meet employers'
needs. In addition, both national governments are stopping short of providing any real level of public investment which is needed to support and
improve the infrastructure. Instead they are restricting their investment to the
research which is shaping the rhetorical framework within which this new
partnership is supposed to operate. The problem for both nations, and their
ultimate joint tragedy, is that while much of the rhetoric is absolutely right
and necessary, its message is being distorted and diluted at the delivery point.
  The new sophistication in terms of outlook and adaptiveness which both

governments stress is so necessary in the countries' workforces is also required by the very employers, trainers and educationalists who are expected to bring about this revolution. Instead of investing in the necessary long-term staff development to ensure trainers and educationalists are adequately prepared to deliver student-centred learning, negotiated curricula, the accreditation of prior learning and other prerequisites of a demand-driven system, both governments presume that the relevant personnel will adapt to their new roles. And, perhaps more crucially, both governments seem to believe that television advertising and glossy publications such as *BusinessWeek's* (1989) 'Children of Promise' or the Training Agency's literature will be enough to persuade employers just how high a price they are going to have to pay to get the workforce they so desperately need.

Finally, both Britain and the USA do not have a single identifiable body which can oversee and promote the necessary changes for vocational education and training. In both countries there are numerous bodies which vie for attention and influence from within the public and private sectors.

This plea from Eurich, written in 1985, applies to both nations in the 1990s:

The challenge is to create a pool of well-skilled and educated citizens from which society's requirements — including the economic — can be met for the future. Concerted action is called for from industry, labor, schools and universities, and the federal government. Such planning and projections cannot come effectively from separate states; their role comes in implementing and adjusting the programs within a great nation. No matter how appealing the new federalism may be, it abdicates leadership for America as a whole. Our country has the pattern of strategic planning bodies for the most crucial and complicated problems of national defence and security. Is it not possible to have the most basic operation of all — a Strategic Council for Educational Development in the United States? The elements are in place and all would welcome the guidance and endorse the support of national policies and leadership. Americans have a generic belief in education, as they should, in terms of the record. (Eurich, 1985, pp. 140–41)

References

BINDER, A. (1990) quoted in *Work America*, March, 7, 3, Washington DC, National Alliance of Business.

BOSTON PRIVATE INDUSTRY COUNCIL (1989) *A Summary of the Steering Committee's Proposed New Goals for the Boston Compact*, March 28th, available from Chairman, Boston PIC.

BUSINESSWEEK (1989) *Children of Promise*.

CARNEVALE, A.P. (1988) *The Learning Enterprise*, Alexandria, Virginia, The

American Society for Training and Development and the US Department of Labor Employment and Training Administration.

CARNEVALE, A.P., GAINER, L.J., MELTZER, A.S. (1988) *Workplace Basics: The Skills Employers Want*, Alexandria, Virginia, The American Society for Training and Development and the US Department of Labor Employment and Training Administration.

THE COLLEGE BOARD AND COUNCIL FOR ADULT AND EXPERIENTIAL LEARNING (1989) *A More Productive Workforce*, Highlights of a Conference Sponsored by National Governors' Association, American Council on Education, The College Board and Council for Adult and Experiential Learning, Little Rock Arkansas, May.

EDUCATIONAL TESTING SERVICE (1989) *CROSSROADS in American Education*, February, Princeton, New Jersey.

EMERSON, R.W. (1971) 'New England Reformers', in *Emerson Essays*, New York, Everyman's Library.

EMPLOYMENT DEPARTMENT (1989) *Employment for the 1990s*, Cmnd 540, London, HMSO.

EURICH, N.P. (1985) *Corporate Classrooms*, Princeton, New Jersey, The Carnegie Foundation for The Advancement of Teaching.

KIMMERLING, G.F. (1989) 'The future of HRD', *Training and Development Journal*, 43, 6, pp. 46–56.

MONTGOMERY WYNN, H. (1988) 'What makes a PIC tick?', *Transition*, November, pp. 17–19.

NATIONAL COMMISSION ON EXCELLENCE IN EDUCATION (1983) *A Nation at Risk*, Washington DC, USGPO.

NEWSWEEK (1990) *What Japan Thinks of Us — A Nation of Crybabies*, April 2nd.

US DEPARTMENT OF LABOR EMPLOYMENT AND TRAINING ADMINISTRATION, BUREAU OF APPRENTICESHIP AND TRAINING (1989) *Apprenticeship 2000*, August, Washington DC, USGPO.

Chapter 6

Cooperation, Coordination and Quality in Employer and Education Partnerships: A Role for the Regions

Ian McNay

Introduction

In this chapter, I argue that part of the explanation for Britain's economic decline lies in the failure to establish appropriate collaborative mechanisms between educators and employers. Such mechanisms are needed to provide research support to strategic economic planning, to identify training and development needs, and to train and update the workforce in relevant competences. That failure in turn relates to a failure to find the appropriate structural level for partnership, to define an acceptable set of roles for the putative partners and to analyse and promote the rewards which flow from such symbiosis. The current situation is examined: at national level there has been disengagement and little exists which is practical, flexible and relevant to diverse circumstances; at the local level there is commitment but the constraint of size. The case for a regional structure is outlined. Case examples from the UK and the rest of Europe support it. These can be seen as models for an inevitable future within the economic and constitutional framework of an integrated EC, or as pragmatic accommodations to the funding criteria for initiatives it currently sponsors.

The Current Situation: National Level

National Plans have fallen into disrepute somewhat since the days of George Brown's Department of Economic Affairs. The association of five-year plans with command economies in tightly controlled societies, and the recent collapse of that control and 'capitalizing' of several such economies have not helped. Nor has the consistent inaccuracy, at least in the UK, of projections by government of needs for qualified personnel even in occupations such as

95

teaching and medicine where it had a controlling near-monopoly of demand and supply. The free market laissez-faire approach seemed to have been vindicated, first by discrediting the alternative and second, by the growth which followed the recession of the early 1980s. Kenneth Baker, when Education Secretary, speaking to a conference at Lancaster University in January 1989, specifically eschewed planning as a government activity; 'can't plan, won't plan' was the theme, consistent with the rhetoric of rolling back the frontiers of the state.

And yet, at the start of the 1990s, the two economies among those with the poorest prospects were the flagships of 'freedom' in the 1980s: the UK and the USA, with problems of balance of payments, high unemployment compared to the EC average and considerable social inequalities. The UK in 1990 had the highest number of company bankruptcies for ten years (Beavis, 1990). It had the worst record of any EC country in developing a skilled workforce: 38 per cent of its workforce held vocational qualifications compared to over 75 per cent in Holland, Italy and France (Harper, 1990). Most UK employers had little idea of what their needs for qualified personnel would be in the middle term and only a crude concept of a graduate job (HMSO, 1990). Employers still give training low esteem and neglect it when under pressure because of cost and when buoyant because of lack of immediate need or of release time (Cassels, 1990).

This is, I believe, the result of government policy during the 1980s. Its actions, or inactions, exert considerable influence over others' plans; it is still expected to lead (Cassels, 1990) and, when it refuses to do so, a coherent sense of direction is lost. Its broad policies also have impact; employers' plans are affected by government decisions and revisions on interest rates, inflation controls, exchange rates and so on. In education, the Jarratt report (CVCP, 1985) on efficiency and effectiveness in universities pointed out that the most serious factor affecting planning in universities was lack of clarity and certainty about government policy, and its lack of continuity and consistency as and when it did emerge.

There were contradictions within policy, too, which added to uncertainty, and conflicts between the policies of different ministries. The DTI Enterprise Initiative encouraged the development of new small businesses, but Treasury policy on inflation meant high interest rates which made borrowing initial capital expensive and depressed home demand while keeping the pound high in value and exporting therefore difficult. The TVEI scheme for schools encouraged a multi-disciplinary project approach, but GCSE and the National Curriculum reinforced the traditional subject areas. Scotland managed this better with the Munn and Dunning reforms and the Action Plan.

The best explanation of government policy in the 1980s perhaps lies in contingency theory which plots the degree of certainty over ends against the degree of confidence in the means to those ends. Where there is agreement on ends but not on means, 'planning is a learning process of experimentation, innovation, responsiveness and trial and error' (Bruton, 1987). The 1980s was a decade of experimentation with policy apparently based on 'initiatives', where novelty seemed more important than quality. This was reinforced by the rapid turnover of ministers each eager to launch a scheme: YOP, UVP, WEEP, TOPS, YTS, JTS, CP, SCIP, CELP, ET, Restart, REPLAN, CEE, CPVE, PICKUP, SATUP ... the list is long, and Lord Young's 'memoirs' confirm that some schemes, e.g., TVEI and Restart were top-of-the-head impulse ideas rapidly transmuted into policy. So, there were contradictions between schemes, as in TVEI/GCSE, and short term changes in direction. For example, the Green Paper on Higher Education (DES, 1986) postulated the closure of some institutions; a year later the theme was expansion (DES, 1987a) and, for the 1990s, a doubling of student numbers.

At times, the government, whose rhetoric was to eschew planning, in reality intervened at very detailed levels of strategy, management and administration: tertiary reorganization, supplementary grants for engineering or teacher shortage areas, even the place of spelling in grading of exam scripts. It was unpredictable. It was inconsistent: LEAs and institutions had to produce plans, in detail, of several kinds and had increasing restrictions placed on them through resourcing structures and levels. There was partiality, too; employers had restrictions lifted and gained by removal of ITB levies, and by nationalized training policies which displaced apprenticeships by government funded schemes.

The result was that education institutions were driven to short term expedients and, increasingly, were dependent on short term funding (Martin, 1985). Equally, the roller coaster pattern of interest rates, to cite but one factor, made planning by employers difficult and their commitment of resource to education, training and development uncertain and uneven.

This situation was compounded by several other factors. If the various 'experiments' had been conducted within an overall agreed framework there might have been more coherence. The National Economic Development Office might have performed such a role but it was weakened by rivalry and competition between government ministries and by tensions between what in other European countries are labelled 'social partners': government, employers and trade unions who work towards consensus strategies. In the UK they were more like protagonists. The same weakness befell the former MSC when trade union representatives withdrew over industrial relations policy, and the Training Agency where major employers withdrew from Employment Training over quality and funding issues. NEDO had taken a strong interest in training and development, especially for management, but was further weakened by the non-involvement of any leaders from the education service whose support was necessary to fulfilment of any plans. One thing it has done is underline the failure of those who control capital in a capitalist country to plan its investment. There has been consistent failure for over a century to invest in renewal of capital plant and machinery or in developing the potential and performance of our human capital (NEDO/MSC, 1984, 1986) That is an English view. The record of the nation regions of the UK is much better: a result of cultural differences towards education and, specifically, towards vocational and professional education which is given much more esteem. Participation rates in post-compulsory education are much higher in Scotland, Wales and Northern Ireland: in 1990, for higher education, they are already at levels set in England as targets for the year 2000. It may also be a function of size and of integrated planning: there do not appear to have been the competitive antagonisms between arms of the Scottish Office that existed between DES, ED and DTI for England, and government is not so remote as Westminster is seen to be from the further flung provincial regions of England, though Shetlanders can also be scathing about Edinburgh based bureaucrats. In Northern Ireland the continued crisis promotes concerted action and greater government investment.

That remoteness and the exclusion of education interests from much of government thinking on training and development was another weakness and reflected a broader policy 'end' which, given the effect on the 'means' chosen to pursue initiatives, was a fatal flaw. Local authorities were virtually ignored. The work of their FE colleges was derided as out of date and unresponsive; their budgets for further education were subjected to external control by the MSC which could hold back its 25 per cent golden share until it approved the totality of plans; and the higher education provision they had built up and funded in part with ratepayers' money was nationalized without compensation by the 1988 Education Reform Act. This reflected central government's determination to reduce the power of local authorities. Yet its own top down imposed solutions needed their cooperation and participation to succeed. It is the insensitivity to local variables which is one of the failures of this centralized national policy. This might have been acceptable had the policy succeeded, but there is a patchy record at best and some singular failures if the government is judged by the criteria on which it judged others. YTS, for example, did not reduce unemployment, but displaced jobs with traineeships (DES, 1987b, 1988), displaced employers' own provision (including apprenticeships) and so had considerable deadweight and did so in a way that allowed employers to make a profit from tax borne subsidies (Deloitte, Haskins and Sells, 1987). The National Audit Office (1987) was highly critical of the Adult Training Strategy which was slow, more expensive than FE provision, unrelated to alleged skills shortages, and uncontrolled in either volume or quality.

The Current Situation: Local Level

Given these weaknesses, and their exclusion from partnership with central government, a number of local authorities have attempted to develop their own solutions a series of alternative economic strategies, a bottom up contrast to top down centralism. Many cities have development agencies, particularly where the local economy has been hit by the rapid decline of extractive and primary manufacturing industries: coal, steel, shipping. They gain support from the EC in doing so: the UK gets nearly 40 per cent of the funds available for regions in industrial decline from the European Regional Development Fund (Brunskill, 1990).

There are, however, problems here also, related to size and function:

— the different functions necessary to integrated planning do not always reside in the same authority. Some major cities looking to regeneration are not education authorities: Bristol, Southampton, Ipswich, Cambridge, are examples. That responsibility rests at county level. Planning for site development is a district level decision, as is provision of public sector housing for new workers.

— even where, in the metropolitan districts, these functions are located together, some local authorities are very small. Barnsley and Gateshead, for example, have only one FE college: a tertiary college in both cases. As noted above, LEAs now have little responsibility for higher education so that there is no guarantee of different levels of training and development. Any future role for the Training and Enterprise Councils in higher education is, as yet, unclear but they could commission work, under contract, relating to higher level NVQs, training needs analyses or the Enterprise in Higher Education scheme. However, they, too, are small, being based on travel to work areas, most about the size of an LEA, though not with identical boundaries. In Scotland, the merger of the Scottish Development Agency with the Scottish Training Agency provides a model which those south of the border might consider.

— there are problems within the organization of single-tier authorities. Involvement in economic planning is often in a separate directorate and the role of education as part of the support structure can be ignored: the bid to attract Nissan to Wearside initially made no mention of the training expertise of local colleges.

— much planning in FE is now devolved to individual colleges where the history of employer involvement in college government and advisory committees has not been good, though this may change with the provisions of the Education Reform Act. Too often, hitherto, people appointed to represent the community have little contact with that community to canvass broadly based views. In France, some colleges are sponsored, indeed were founded, by local Chambers of Commerce. In Germany the Chambers of Commerce are validating bodies and act as quality controllers. They have no such roles in the UK. The quality of branches of professional bodies varies considerably so that within any LEA the chances are poor of finding active, able, committed partners, though many professional bodies act as quality controllers at national level with varying degrees of rigour and effectiveness.

Local authorities can adopt a broker role, bringing interested parties together and promoting the cause, but many factors crucial to success remain beyond their control. A report by Segal, Quince and Wicksteed (1988) underlines the artificiality of local authority boundaries in development. The Cambridge phenomenon needed railway electrification to London, the development of Stansted airport, the growth of Felixtowe as a container port as crucial factors to add to an autonomous university and a low wage agricultural economy. All of those were beyond the city's remit, though the local authority has initiated discussions with its neighbours to try to plan housing and to spread the location of companies because the local labour pool is exhausted.

European Models

If national government is disengaging from economic planning and insensitive and over-prescriptive in educational issues especially related to employment; and if local government is too small and has insufficient levers of power, that leaves us to look for a middle-tier. Regional structures are important among the UK's partners in the EC. In part, they have historical roots: Germany and Italy have been nation states for a relatively short time; in France's system the old regional Parlements provided a basis for intermediary levels and the regional academies provide this in a centrally directed education system. Spain has regions with strong cultural identity and, post Franco, considerable autonomy.

There is also less aversion to planning, but it involves partnership between levels as in the German *Bund und Lander Kommission* which brings together regional and national interests in a common forum, as does the French *Commissariat General du Plan*.

There is, according to Bruce Millan, the EC Commissioner for regional policy a growth in economic regionalism and regional assertiveness (Hetherington, 1990). The strongest economies are those with strong provincial government which provide a focus for initiative and enterprise. French, Spanish and German regional governments have offices in Brussels lobbying the EC. North-Rhine Westphalia is among them and has gained support for regeneration of the Ruhr in a plan which links public and private sector initiatives and supports industrial rebuilding with research facilities and training through links to a science park and local colleges.

In Italy a different model can be seen: craft based small businesses in the same sector are clustered together so that regions develop specialisms and, although there is competition among them they gain from the cheaper provision of common services because of the critical mass they represent together. There is a synergetic effect, too, in the transmission of ideas by staff movement so that there is a total quality shift. In Britain this was lost with the decline of industries such as car manufacture in the West Midlands, textiles in Yorkshire (wool), Lancashire (cotton) and East Midlands (lace).

Initiatives such as these which demonstrate that wide involvement of all groups in a regional community can produce consensus and commitment have provided a model for the EC. Funding programmes in education such as LINGUA (modern languages development) ERASMUS (student exchanges) and COMETT (training for technology) all emphasize a regional base. ERASMUS gives priority to regional consortia of universities and polytechnics involved with high level technology. The Structural Funds, which by 1993 will form 25 per cent of the EC budget, are moving away from individual projects to 'programme finance, based on regional development plans drawn up by a partnership of national and local representatives' (Brunskill, 1990).

Regional Policy in the UK

The report from IPPR summarizes the effect of this drive from the EC on the UK:

> As far as Britain is concerned, the lack of a coherent national approach to regional policy has meant that the EC is effectively setting the pace.... There is no economic strategy at either a national or a regional level which sets priorities to which EC funding can clearly relate. Nor are there regional representative bodies which can contribute to EC policy formation.... The EC has effectively redrawn the regional policy map in Britain. It has obliged the DoE, DTI and the DE, to work together for the first time in drawing up regional support programmes for European funding. It has requested that programmes be drawn up in partnership with local authorities. It also wants to deal directly with regional representatives. In short, EC initiatives are setting a new framework for regional policy in Britain.... The EC has set up a Consultative Council to advise on policy, but what Britain needs is a coherent organizational approach in order to formalize dialogue between the regions and the EC. (Brunskill, 1990)

The report takes the Audit Commission (1989) comment on government urban policy: 'Programme overkill within a strategic vacuum' and tries to moderate the one and fill the other. It sees regional strategic bodies as coordinating the many different and dislocated initiatives; helping the Enterprise Agencies, where the main force has, paradoxically, been local authorities; providing a forum for the many involved agencies, from charities to the EC, multi-national companies to small advisory centres, to meet and share in

strategy discussions, to pool resources and allow economies of scale. Hitherto, structures have been 'complex, inefficient and fragmented' and 'counter
productive ... by increasing competition between similar agencies'. Such
bodies should have control of resources to make speedy decisions as necessary in rapidly changing circumstances and can apply them differently
because 'what works in one region may not work in another'. A reduction
in funding agencies by such rationalization also makes for an easier span of
control at the next tier down from government, should control need to be
reasserted, but also provides a corporate strength to 'buffer' the extremes of
ministerial enthusiasms. Currently, different schemes delivered by different
agents under different rules add up to a nightmarish bureaucratic labyrinth. A
slimmer, more efficient administration would also be more effective.

The author also sees a regional policy as having social implications:

> The Government has been ridding itself of responsibility for econo-
> mic development and thus pushing the responsibility for regional
> policy either upwards to the EC, downwards to the regional and
> local level, or sideways to the private sector.... The result of the
> Government's *laissez-faire* approach has been to compound the in-
> equalities between regions with the rapid growth of activity in the
> South sucking in the skilled workforce from the northern region.
> (Brunskill, 1990)

This contrasts with the German situation where regional responsibility is
incorporated in the Basic Law — a benefit of a written constitution — and
requires government to take measures to reduce regional differences in income and quality of life.

The main features of a regional industrial policy are given as:

a strategic body which shapes policy through partnership between

key socio-economic groups

proximity to target markets with short lines for decisions on project
approval

an integrated delivery mechanism with flexibility of response.

compatibility with UK and EC policy directions

professional support with a career structure for those involved

The combination of better coordination of local initiatives and better control
of delivery and support to national initiatives makes a convincing case. The
critical mass is sufficient for economies of scale without loss of sensitivity. It
can be argued that there is, in some parts of England, not a great regional
identity but this view is diminishing as needs are seen. The South East was
brought to collective realization of common interest by the Channel Tunnel
and its rail/road links; the South has the M4 corridor and the southcoast ports

as strengthening focuses of identity; the need for a policy for London has become ever more apparent since the abolition of the GLC and ILEA. Beyond those, identity is stronger, despite population movement, and will be reinforced by any regional constitutional structures which may emerge in the 1990s. This then gives a sense of identity, of ownership of initiatives, in contrast to the current frequent alienation or sense of conflict with national schemes.

Regional Educational Policy: Building on What is There

One of the weaknesses of the IPPR report (Brunskill, 1990) is its failure to underline the mutual service which education and employment sectors can offer. Another is to underplay the potential of structures which already exist.

If, as noted earlier, employers are vague about their personnel and training needs, colleges can provide training needs analyses and have done so (Briggs and Moseley, 1986). These are done in greater depth and in part-nership with employing organizations and so are sensitive, dynamic and developmental in a way that ED surveys often fail to be. If companies are unwilling to share commercial and technological secrets directly with rivals in the market, and if short–term secondees to promote government initiatives return with only short–term learning and short term impact, colleges can provide a continuing repository for analysing and disseminating good prac-tice while preserving commercial confidentiality. They can also save com-panies money, for example, on R&D by allowing contracting into research services which, though expensive for one company, can be developed by contracting consortia and where findings can feed into staff development for high level personnel. Sometimes this link between product, staff and company development is made; often there is no synchronization. Equally, academic and support staff and students would benefit from access to a consortium of teaching companies for work experience, professional updat-ing and case study material, to enhance their enterprise initiatives and to link credit for work based experiential learning to academic programmes.

Structures at regional level, if they are seen to be effective, are more likely to attract influential representatives from various constituents because a reduced time input will pay off better through the cascade effect of decisions on a range of lower tier operations. Major companies already have regional headquarters and the multi-nationals are very aware of EC regional policy. The same is true of organizations such as the CBI and TUC. There are regional structures in public utilities, in the health service, policing (and prisons!), broadcasting and in educational/training networks, Open College Consortia, the Regional Advisory Councils for FE, the Further Education Unit. Universities and Polytechnics increasingly meet in regional consortia to deal with policy on, for example, access, PICKUP, and may increasingly need to do so to plan and protect the availability and accessibility of opportunities by agreeing on concentration in one location of specialization in selected areas of the curriculum in the light of squeezes on resources (McNay, 1988). Staff development programmes for college staff gain from a regional organizational base (McNay, 1989).

Regions are also reaching out to Europe. The Yorkshire and Humberside Association for Further and Higher Education has, like others, appointed a European Project Officer, and is developing, with bids for EC funding, links with the French region of Franche Compte and, through that, with Tuscany in Italy. This trend will continue under EC funding and sponsorship.

Perhaps the most successful government initiatives in the 1980s were those which followed the principles outlined in this chapter. The REPLAN programme (for the adult unemployed) and the PICKUP programme (for mid-career professional development) were sponsored by the DES rather than an economic ministry. Both had a structure of regional officers coordinated by FEU who promoted the schemes in the different regions and could make speedy decisions on proposals made to them, and could provide staff development support, advice and formative monitoring. One of the early models for this was HESIN (Higher Education Services for Industry in the North) set up in 1983 and linking the three 'rival' polytechnics of Newcastle, Sunderland and Teesside, their 'competing' neighbour universities in Durham and Newcastle, and the regional centre of the Open University in a cooperative venture under the aegis of PICKUP. This collective action serves the self interest of the partners by limiting proliferation of small units where high costs would reduce success. It demonstrates a commitment to the criteria of the EC and national government schemes and enhances the income to the consortium beyond the levels possible when acting in isolation. In one case, by taking remedial action following monitoring, it has also demonstrated an objective commitment to high quality service and mutual regulation of standards. The spin-off for image and reputation management is obvious and supports marketing initiatives. Further support to the image, and the philosophy of cooperation and service is given by the high standing of its executive members who are all at the level of Pro Vice-Chancellor. This gives the 'clout' necessary to ensure delivery (Turner *et al.*, 1982).

There have been successful project bids by HESIN in the fields of training in information technology, in biotechnology, a modular engineering scheme, an integrated graduate development scheme in manufacturing systems, and marketing support to small firms. The Regional Development Agents (RDA) for PICKUP cover both HE and FE so can advise on all levels of competence development. They act as brokers for the consortium in advising on needs they see emerging and link employers into appropriate college staff. The staff development officer has helped establish a group of college staff meeting at a regional level who act as a quality circle in sharing ideas and good practice in staff development, and, collectively, sponsor the development of enterprise attitudes in colleges which have been slower to respond to new market imperatives and opportunities. There is less openness on product, where retaining market leadership conditions attitudes towards secrecy, but colleges do refer enquirers to other members. They welcome the 'neutral' forum (i.e., beyond LEAs) of the regional structure which also often provides sufficient geographical distance to allow colleges with similar expertise to cooperate because their market areas do not overlap (Bell *et al.*, 1990). The sponsorship of local initiatives leads to a diversity of activities: the imaginative approaches to working with the unemployed, a difficult field, are seen in project reports and the evaluation of REPLAN (Percy *et al.*, 1989). The Replan regional networks provide for dissemination of good practice. For example, in Yorkshire, work among the Asian community in Harehills, Leeds, has lessons for Bradford, Kirklees and Calderdale and these are passed on and developed by regular meetings of people with similar concerns — the 'cluster' argument mentioned above.

Segal, Quince and Wicksteed (1988) in reviewing HESIN conclude that:

> The higher education institutions have clearly moved into a new structured involvement with their industry. Their growing collaboration in doing so is of particular value in seeking to overcome the disadvantages of what otherwise would probably be fragmented and under resourced individual efforts.

That is universally acknowledged to be necessary. This chapter has argued that it is best achieved by regional level cooperation. HESIN provides one example. It is also a vision of the future . . . and it works!

References

AUDIT COMMISSION (1989) *Urban Regeneration and Economic Development*, London, HMSO.

BEAVIS, S. (1990) 'Company failures soar to highest level for 10 years', *The Guardian*, 9th July (reporting on figures from Dunn and Bradstreet KPMG Peat Marwick McLintock).

BELL, J., CROWCROFT, R. and McNAY, I. (1990) *Evaluation of PICKUP Inset*, unpublished, Report to FEU.

BRIGGS, M. and MOSELEY, P.A. *Increasing College Responsiveness Ananalysis of Local Training Needs due to New Technologies.* York, Longman for FEU/ PICKUP.

BRUNSKILL, I. (1990) *The Regeneration Game: A Regional Approach to Regional Policy*, London, Institute for Public Policy Research.

BRUTON, M.J. (1987) 'University planning and management in conditions of complexity and uncertainty', *Higher Education Quarterly*, 41, 4.

CASSELS, J. (1990) *Britain's Real Skill Shortage and What to Do About it*, Exeter, Policy Studies Institute.

COMMITTEE OF VICE CHANCELLORS AND PRINCIPALS (1985) *Report of the Steering*

Committee for Efficiency Studies in Universities, (The Jarratt Report) London, CVCP.

DELOITTE, HASKINS AND SELLS (1987) *The Funding of Vocational Education and Training*, Sheffield, MSC.

DEPARTMENT OF EDUCATION AND SCIENCE (1986) *The Development of Higher Education into the 1990s*, Cmnd 9524, London, HMSO.

DEPARTMENT OF EDUCATION AND SCIENCE (DES) (1987a) *Higher Education: Meeting the Challenge*, London, HMSO.

DEPARTMENT OF EDUCATION AND SCIENCE (1987b) 'Educational and economic activity of young people aged 16–18 years in England from 1975 to 1986', *Statistical Bulletin*, 2/87.

DEPARTMENT OF EDUCATION AND SCIENCE (1988) 'Educational and economic activity of young people aged 16–18 years in England from 1975 to 1988', *Statistical Bulletin*, 14/88.

HARPER, K. (1990) 'Britain worst for worker training', *The Guardian*, 6th June, (reporting on an EC Labour Market Survey).

HETHERINGTON, P. (1990) 'Bringing hope to a wasteland', *The Guardian*, 25 June.

HMSO (1990) *Highly Qualified People: Supply and Demand*, Report of an Inter-departmental Review, London, HMSO.

MARTIN, L.C. (1985) 'The funding of continuing education for adults with special reference to the Replan programme', *Studies in the Education of Adults*, 17, 2.

McNAY, I. (1988) 'Policy and administration: local and regional strategies and structures', in The Open University, *Issues in Policy, Administration and Management*, Module 4, DO5, Milton Keynes, The Open University.

McNAY, I. (1989) *Learning to Manage*, London, FEU.

NATIONAL AUDIT OFFICE (1987) *Department of Employment and Manpower Services Commission: Adult Training Strategy*, London, HMSO.

NATIONAL ECONOMIC DEVELOPMENT OFFICE/MANPOWER SERVICES COMMISSION (1984) *Competence and Competition*, London, NEDO.

NATIONAL ECONOMIC DEVELOPMENT OFFICE/MANPOWER SERVICES COMMISSION (1986) *A Challenge to Complacency*, Sheffield, MSC.

PERCY, K. with GRADDON, A., MACHELL, J. and WARD, P. (1989) *An Evaluation of the FEU REPLAN Programme*, London, FEU.

SEGAL, QUINCE, and WICKSTEED (1988) *Universities, Enterprise and Local Economic Development*, London, HMSO.

TURNER, C., FINLAYSON, J. and CHALLIS, B. (1982) *Planning Local Authority Support for YOP: MSC Exemplary Projects*, Blagdon, Coombe Lodge, FESC.

Chapter 7

Winners and Losers: The Education and Training of Adults

Richard Edwards

Since the 1970s there has been a rapid transformation of the British economy. Alongside and as part of that transformation have been changes in the provision of education and training for adults. These processes are still at work and charting their significance is increasingly important for all concerned, more so, if the prime concern is with the experience of learners and potential learners, as is the case in this chapter. This is neither easy nor straightforward, as the range and diversity of learning opportunities available to adults and the largeness of the adult population results in a web of bewildering complexity. I can examine only a few strands of that web and in the process will argue that some of the changes taking place are grounded in assumptions about the future of the economy and work which, while seemingly viewed as inevitable, are, in fact, questionable and challengeable.

This failure to debate fully some of the policy assumptions and frameworks — strands in the web — may result in the current interest in adult learners, lifelong learning and continuous training disappearing as soon as the economic imperative has lost its immediacy. At which stage, the adult population may find themselves qualitively worse off in terms of education, training and employment than they are at present. In other words, the education and training of adults will not become an embedded feature of British practice.

I shall explore this theme by an initial general discussion of the values inherent in any examination of winning and losing in education and training. This will be followed by a review of the argument that the British economy is being fundamentally reorganized on what have been termed 'post-Fordist', rather than 'Fordist', principles. Some of the ways in which education and training have been and are being used to support that reorganization (something they are themselves a part of) will then be outlined. To illustrate these themes I shall then explore a particular example, the REPLAN programme for the adult unwaged and its proposed replacement, People, Learning and

Jobs. I shall suggest that questionable policy assumptions have been introduced into the latter that were not in the former. I shall then focus on the central assumption of the need to produce multi-skilled, flexible workers which is being used to drive much of the policy and practice in the education and training of adults. I shall argue that this is an insufficient and ideologically loaded base for development. In the final section, I shall explore who are and may be some of the winners and losers among learners if current approaches are left unchallenged. A central feature of this chapter will be to suggest that current debates about education and training policy take place within a context of shared assumptions about the economy and the future of work and that a discussion about economic and social policy is necessary if the majority of adult learners are to become winners rather than losers.

Winners and Losers

The question of winning and losing in education and training cannot be divorced from the question of values. We cannot provide a final score-sheet, as in football or cricket, and celebrate the winners and give condolences to the losers. Firstly, winning and losing depends on to whom you are referring. Adults are not a homogeneous group. They are differentiated by age, geography, class, gender, race, etc., a diversity which needs to be reflected in policy and practice. Secondly, winning and losing depend on your assumptions about what adult learning is for — the role and merits of specific forms of education and training. Distinctions abound: between non-vocational and vocational, liberal adult education and training, general education and occupational competence, personal development and economic performance. Who wins and who loses are different in each possible case. We are in a contested area. The contest is over what people mean by education and training, the relative values given to and within each and what they are prepared to fund.

The issue of it being a contested area is as true for practitioners as it is for policy makers. For many practitioners in the education and training of adults, the sheer fact there appears to be recognition of the importance of their work is itself a form of winning. However, for others the spotlight is seen to have contradictory consequences. Yes, it provides recognition, but priority is given to specific areas of practice, which are viewed as being focused on narrow outcomes — learning with positive outcomes for the economy. The questions are then raised about whether the losses outweigh the gains or vica versa, and who is gaining at who's expense.

The position people take in these discussions may well reflect their institutional base — in Adult Education Centres, Extra-mural Departments, Further Education colleges, training departments, etc. — and even within organizations and departments people may vary in their opinions. For example, in a Further Education college, a general education lecturer may have a different view of the purpose of learning — to realize the potential of the individual — to a lecturer in an engineering department — to provide the skills for employment. Alternatively, both may feel they are committed to personal development, but chose different content and methods which produce different outcomes. (I am not suggesting that these generalizations inevitably hold true. They do not.)

Debates over the relative merits of the education and training of adults have had a long and unhappy history in the United Kingdom. Education was provided by schools to young people and training mediated the transition from education to employment. Education beyond school was the personal interest and responsibility of individuals, to be pursued at their leisure and to be paid for accordingly. Within the macro economic concerns of the state, these forms of learning were not a priority. The ethos of liberal adult education as an under-resourced service to meet the personal development needs of individuals developed in this situation. Funding for schooling and training came from the state and, to a limited extent, employers; funding for leisure/personal development from the state and individual. The struggle to define the principles of liberal adult education as either leisure or personal development is itself an attempt to give status to areas of practice within a pre-existing value system. The relative amounts going into training and leisure/personal development reflected their relative priorities and the lack of importance attached to notions of education beyond school:

> In the past relative government indifference and allocation of resources has confirmed education and training as lacking in prestige. Belated and determined efforts, although sometimes misdirected, are now being put into *vocational* adult education. (Stephen, 1990, p. 123, my emphasis)

The resources placed in the vocational education and training of adults — predominantly through the Training Agency — are part of the overall shift towards vacationalism in learning and has been met with varying responses in adult education circles. Some practitioners have reacted with dismay and have attempted to defend the 'faith' of non-vocational education for personal development. The involvement of others has led to and resulted from attempts to reformulate the ways in which the relationship between education and training is discussed. By demonstrating the value of educational practice to training, attempts have been made through negotiation and influence to widen the curriculum offering available to adults, much of which involves an attempt to move to a position wherein the distinction between education and training loses its relevance. Whether this is genuine negotiation or quiet annexation of one sector by another is a matter of debate and opinion, for which there are no easy answers.

Let me illustrate this point about redefining the debate, as this both reflects and reproduces some perspectives on winning and losing. There are three possibilities through which there is an attempt to move beyond the discourse of education and training with all its associated prejudices. They are (i) a shift to assessing learning outcomes; (ii) the notion of lifelong learning; (iii) theories of human resource management.

(i)   The shift towards the identification and assessment of learning outcomes is part of a wider shift towards valuing learning wherever it may take place. This is of particular importance with adults, the bulk of whose learning is likely to be in informal settings and experiential. It provides a foundation for the assessment and accreditation of prior learning, which is generally supported and welcomed by those involved in the education and training of adults. As the identification of outcomes is moved to the centre stage, the debates about education and training are marginalized.

(ii) With lifelong learning — used by UNESCO and the CBI among others — we are introduced to the idea that learning is not something which stops at the end of initial schooling, but is part of the ongoing process of life itself. This is useful insofar as it provides a basis for organizations and practitioners with very different agendas to talk with one another. However, the focus on learning discursively marginalizes questions of what forms the learning takes and for what purpose; process is valued over content.

(iii) With the practices of human resource management (HRM) employers pursue their company objectives partly through learning programmes for staff which incorporate personal development as an essential aspect of their ongoing training strategies.

The essence of HRM is that people are regarded as a competitive asset to be led, motivated, deployed and developed, together with the firm's other resources, in ways that contribute directly to the attainment of the firm's strategic objectives. (Handy *et al.*, 1989, p. 13)

Staff are developed rather than trained or educated, but within the constraints of company objectives.

The question remains whether or to what extent such formulations overcome the divisions between education and training or bury them to possibly grow again. Each of these trends discursively removes the debates about education and training and their relationship from the foreground of discussion. However, the issues themselves do not go away. They are reconstitued in different forms. For instance, what outcomes of learning are to be valued, assessed and credited? While people may be lifelong learners, to what forms of learning are they to be given access? Which must they initiate for themselves? Who benefits from human resource management and what percentage of the workforce are governed by it rather than traditional training practices — or lack of them? These are shifting sands with no easy answers.

I raise them here to demonstrate that in moving the terrain of discourse the issues may be reconstructed, but the question of values, of winning and losing, does not go away.

Shifts in the Economy

Major changes are taking place in the economy of Britain, inherent in which are trends and tensions which will no doubt continue through into the next century. However one attempts to explain those changes — demographic trends, economic restructuring, more people wanting to gain paid employment, advances in technology, increased part-time employment — the conclusion tends to be the same. It is and will become less common for people to have a single career in their working lives and the jobs they do have will change while they are doing them, all of which necessitates increased attention to adult learning. However, 'over the next 30 years ... there will be ever greater needs for a skilled, trained and educated workforce, yet we have few strategies for systematic education and training to meet these needs, and the skills gap is likely to widen' (Tucket, 1988, p. 9).

Attempts to make sense of these changes, which, in turn, are used to legitimize the trends and developments in adult learning, are ongoing. I shall briefly outline one such attempt, provocative, if controversial, put forward in an article by Robin Murray (1989) which suggests a shift in the dominant principles at work in the British economy from what are termed 'Fordism' to 'post-Fordism'. Murray argues that Fordism (epitomized in the production lines introduced by Henry Ford) was the dominant principle of manufacture and distribution in the period from the late 19th century through to the post-war boom years of the 1950s and 1960s.

With Fordism, there are standardized products manufactured by mass production plants with special-purpose machinery. Standardized products are consumed in the mass market, in which there is little scope for consumer choice unless you are wealthy enough to participate in the luxury end of the market. Fordist organizations are governed by hierarchical bureaucracies, in which the planning is done by specialists and handed down to workers and consumers alike. This results in and from authoritarian relations, pyramidal organizational structures, centralized planning and exclusive job descriptions.

Murray suggests that Fordism is no longer the dominant principle in the economy. An alternative trend has developed, made possible by advances in technology and particularly information technology. It is suggested that the emphasis in the economy has shifted from manufacturing for a mass market to the provision of services — shops, offices, leisure — for particular market segments. The principles governing this change result in and from post-Fordism.

Technological advances have increased the availability of information and the speed at which it can be collected, analysed and transmitted. This has enabled shops to introduce 'just in time' systems of ordering to meet the particular market needs at any particular time. Increases in demand for certain goods and decreases for others can be used in the ordering of supplies from manufacturers. Shops no longer keep large stocks of a narrow range of items. They have small stocks of a large range of items. Products have a shorter lifespan and there is a greater need for innovation and design. Life-style becomes a dominant motif in the marketing of specific goods to specific market segments.

Inevitably this has had an impact upon manufacturing. If manufacturers have to produce a greater range of goods and be responsive to specific demands, the mass production line and standardized product are no longer applicable. The decimation of British manufacturing capacity in the early 1980s can be seen as the attempted removal of Fordist principles from the economy or at least the strongest hint to that effect!

The new principles of post-Fordism are therefore being introduced into manufacturing. These principles involve flexible systems of manufacturing, customized design for specific segments of the market and an emphasis on quality control. The manufacturing plant in which all aspects of production are sustained under one roof is replaced by new forms of organization in which all non-essential work is sub-contracted to other organizations. There is an increase in the number of smaller organizations who act as sub-contractors for a smaller core of large organizations.

How complete or partial this analysis is is beyond the scope of this chapter. However, many of the ideas provide a context and justification for the major interventions and transformations of the education and training of adults that have and are taking place. The economic necessity for greater flexibility and innovation results in and from new organizational forms, which entail the breakdown of job demarcations and pyramidal bureaucracies. Multi-skilled, flexible workers are seen as the key to these changes, wherein, as demands change, so workers are able to drop old tasks and take up new ones. To make this happen there is thus the need for continuous training, for the support and development of lifelong learners and for the workplace to be actively constructed as a learning organization.

Shifts in Education and Training

It is unsuprising that these shifts in the economy have produced policy responses from government, as the need to provide the workforce for the restructured economy has hit home, with skill shortages reported in key areas of the economy and low investment in education and training long considered a factor in the poor performance of British capitalism in the twentieth century. 'Nationally about one in five manufacturing employers report that their output is constrained by lack of skilled labour.' (Training Agency, 1989, p. 19). To chart the full range of changes that have and are taking place is a volume in itself. However, I want to provide some illustrative examples of how learning is being harnessed to economic performance; how vocationalism is increasing its hold on education and training for adults. Adding what many would feel to be insult to injury, this trend is being supported by an ideology which appropriates the learner–centred discourses of liberal adult education for other purposes. This is not a defence of the faith, of the value of the academic above all else (Armstrong, 1990), but an attempt to sustain a critical discourse in the public sphere (Hake and Meijers, 1990). In the next section, I shall chart this influence on the development of a single programme, the DES funded REPLAN programme for extending learning opportunities for unwaged adults. Before doing so, we need to examine some of the ways in which the new flexible worker is being developed or produced.

Firstly, at an ideological and policy level, there is the emphasis placed on the need for a more highly skilled and multi-skilled, flexible workforce by state and other agencies.

> To cope with their rapidly changing skill needs, employers increasingly want multi-skilled, flexible workers with a high standard of personal competences. (Training Agency, 1989, p. 18)

> The cost of basic skills deficiencies to British industries is immense and, unless the problem is tackled, the problem will stifle our attempts to meet the challenges of new markets opening up in 1992 and in the approach to the next century. Workplace education (WPE) has a significant role to play in solving basic skills problems and in other training requirements. (Lander, 1990, p. 22)

To compete in the emerging economic order Britain will need to ensure that it has the personnel with the relevant skills and the capacity to transfer those skills as demands change. From this is drawn the requirement to fund certain types of programme rather than others, for example, the Employment Training (ET) scheme for the unemployed. The policy outcome of this ideological position is illustrated in the design framework of ET which stresses ability to transfer skills as an outcome of participation (ET/REPLAN, 1989, p. x).

Secondly, there is the development of National Vocational Qualifications. If the workplace is to be a learning organization, assessment and accreditation while at work will be motivate people to continue their learning. It also will give employers greater control over the training their employees undertake, an influence which is extended into the formal education sphere through the role played by Lead Bodies in specifying the competences against which individuals will be assessed. As part of this shift, the notion of general education is being marginalized and reconstituted as a question of core skills, which people need to support their role as part of the flexible workforce — issues which are raised in the forms of accreditation offered by

NCVQ and Open College Networks (UDACE 1989). Although, as Jallade (1989) points out,

> it is standard practice to distinguish 'occupational' skills from 'general' skills, although this distinction is somewhat arbitrary and the two categories cover very different things in each country as well as over time, since the specialized occupational skills of today may become part of general knowledge in the course of the next decade. (p. 103)

Thirdly, there is the increased power given to employers in shaping what opportunities are available to adults. I have already mentioned their role in relation to NVQs. The 1988 Education Reform Act gives employer interests a dominant role in the governance of Further Education colleges and subsumes adult education under the definition of further education. This influence is powerfully reinforced by the emerging Training and Enterprise Councils which will administer the funding of major Department of Employment schemes and promote continuous training and the acquisition of NVQs. (The local flexibility demanded by TECs itself illustrates post-Fordism in education and training — assuming they have sufficient funds to deliver (*The Guardian*, 8/8/1990).

Fourthly, there is the support for open learning, either directly through the Open Tech, Open College and Work Related Development Fund projects, or indirectly through the support for programmes, such as PICKUP, Youth and Employment Training, which encourage the development of such systems by providers. Open learning systems facilitate the training of employees without their having to attend colleges, or only for the very specific training that is required for and by them. For the flexible workforce, flexible forms of education and training are also necessary and open learning systems provide the basis for delivering opportunities when, where, and how they are needed — in theory at least!

It is argued that open learning is popular among employers because it is cost effective, allowing employees to train in their own time without having to be released from work. It also gives employers tighter control over what is learnt and means that their employees are isolated from employees in other workplaces, thereby undermining the material possibilities for discussions of shared concerns among the workforce and between different workforces (Tait, 1989).

Fifthly, the increasing emphasis on the relevance of learning to employment has placed great pressure on '21 Hour rule' provision. Largely associated with Return to Learning/Second Chance/Access opportunities, this type of provision has been developed to make use of a concession in Department of Social Security regulations, which allow the unemployed to study up to 21 hours a week as long an they continue to 'actively seek work' and are prepared to take up employment should a suitable opportunity arise. During the 1980s, there was a burgeoning of 21 Hour programmes largely targeted at adults who had missed out at the initial education stage. However, since the introduction of the Employment Training scheme in 1988, the unemployed have found themselves increasingly under pressure to abandon the learning they have entered into independently and enter ET. While what may be considered as vocational elements of 21 Hour provision may be incorporated into a person's Action Plan, other elements are not (Heywood, 1990; REPLAN, 1990).

These are some of the major forces increasingly at play in determining the winners and losers in the education and training of adults. To illustrate how such forces impact upon practice let us now examine the DES REPLAN programme for developing opportunities for learning among unwaged adults.

From REPLAN to 'People Learning and Jobs'

Begun in 1984 REPLAN has operated at various levels — local, regional and national — to increase access to learning for the unwaged. There are many reports outlining the work undertaken by the programme (for a good summary see FEU/NIACE REPLAN, 1990). What I want to suggest is that during the course of its development, the principles underlying its work, of moving beyond the education/training division, started to break down — at least at the national policy level — to be replaced by an increasing emphasis on the primacy of employment in leading the curriculum offering to the unwaged. Given the structural nature of unemployment, this is both flawed and limiting.

This shift is reflected in the proposal for a new initiative to replace the REPLAN programme — People, Learning and Jobs (NIACE, 1990) — in which adult learning is tied to servicing the supposed needs of the economy for a flexible workforce. Crucial to this process was the announcement of the Employment Training scheme. This could be viewed either as an appropriation of the discourse of learner-centredness, reworked as a mask for coercion and poor training for the increasingly marginalized unemployed sector of society, or as an introduction of adult education principles into the training of the unemployed to more fully meet their needs.

Since its inception, REPLAN has supported a specific curriculum framework model which is the foundation for the negotiation of programmes between providers/tutors and the unwaged. The elements of this model are:

1 **Employability:** to help unemployed people to develop knowled⟨ skills and attitudes which will increase their chances of finding keeping a job.
2 **Coping:** to help unemployed people to develop knowledg⟨ and attitudes which will help them to cope with being uner⟨
3 **Context:** to help unemployed people to understand the

which the responsibility for being unemployed lies with society, rather than with the individual, and to explore possible forms of social, political and community action related to unemployment.

4 **Leisure:** to help unemployed people to develop knowledge, skills and attitudes which will help them make good use of their increased 'leisure' time.

5 **Opportunity creation:** to help unemployed people to develop knowledge, skills and attitudes which will enable them to create their own livelihood. (Watts and Knasel, 1985, p. 5)

This framework is not without its critics:

> ... the idea of education for leisure is something that is not helpful (if not actually insulting and patronising) in making an educational approach relevant to unwaged adults. A more productive approach could well emphasize education for work and life, where work is seen as explicitly covering a whole spectrum from caring, house-work, further education, voluntary work, community action, 'self-sustaining life-styles', cooperative work and self-employment right up to more conventional paid employment. (Johnston *et al.*, 1988, p. 33)

This reformulation of 'work' is itself an attempt to overcome dominant views about what is recognized and valued as 'work' so that '... the work that many unwaged adults do will not be devalued and might provide a stepping-stone to paid work; and educators might no longer be slaves to the artificial distinction between vocational and non-vocational education' (Johnston *et al.*, 1988, p. 33).

However, despite the criticisms, the framework is sufficiently broad to be of use to the wide variety of agencies increasingly engaged in providing learning for unwaged adults.

> The organizations and professionals developing programmes under the REPLAN banner will often have differing views, depending on their background and philosophy, and may give emphasis to differ-ent aspects of the task in hand. There are those who see themselves primarily as educators, providing opportunities for individual de-velopment and self-improvement.... Others put more emphasis on their role as vocational trainers, shaping pegs to fit the employ-ment holes available ... others focus their attention on processes of personal and community development, emphasising their role as facilitators in a process of social change ... The overall REPLAN programme has recognized the need for a balance between educa-tional, vocational, personal and social objectives, and has sought

to accomodate a plurality of approaches and perspectives. (FEU\NIACE REPLAN, 1990, pp. 9–10)

To increase access to opportunities, REPLAN emphasizes the need for change in the structure and organization of learning for unwaged adults. These changes include:

— overcoming barriers to access
— providing ongoing guidance and counselling
— flexible starting times and year-round learning
— providing assessment of prior learning and appropriate progression routes
— collaboration and networking between organizations in contact with the unwaged
— outreach work
— negotiation of the curriculum.

This is a wide-ranging set of demands, based on the needs of unwaged learners, which had been part of the general agenda of adult educators for some time. In other words, the principles which have been promoted through REPLAN's work with unwaged people throughout the whole post-compulsory sector are those of traditional liberal adult education, therefore of relevance to adults as a whole. The spreading of adult education principles is one of the series of effects engendered by the changing situation and interest in adult learning. That is not to say that these principles are fully accepted by all adult educators. Indeed, they have come under sustained critique by feminist writers for masking the reproduction of patriarchal roles in the curriculum of liberal adult education (see Thompson, 1983).

When, in 1988, the MSC (now Training Agency) announced its new programme for the adult unemployed — Employment Training — to replace a number of schemes, the principles of liberal adult education appeared to have been accepted in the provision of training for the unemployed; the distinction between education and training had indeed been overcome. However, for people involved in the education and training of the unemployed, Employment Training was the appropriation of the discourse of adult learning to mask an inadequately funded programme to 'police' unemployment; a rhetoric which would not be matched in practice.

In theory, an unemployed adult would be invited to develop an individual action plan through a process of guidance and assessment, which would identify current areas of competence and areas in which further training was necessary. This would be provided through a combination of on- and off-the-job training and result in an outcome of occupational competence. Employment Training therefore demanded an increasing flexibility from providers of learning — a flexibility which matched the REPLAN agenda. While recognizing that ET did not encompass the REPLAN curriculum framework — concentrating on employability and opportunity creation — the programme nonetheless aligned itself at national level with the increasing pressure to provide greater flexibility and 'relevance' in learning for adults; pressure particularly exerted on Further Education colleges. In other words, because they were perceived to have similar goals, REPLAN pursued its joint interests with ET:

> Clearly some colleges and institutions are already effectively responding to the challenges of flexibility which ET presents. However, the most frequently mentioned criticisms of present FE provision include:
> * Inappropriate timing and duration of provision
> * Inability to respond to changing adult learners' needs, such as all year round provision, 'roll-on — roll off' provision
> * Lack of progression routes and modular approaches
> * Unwillingness to develop more 'open' forms of learning — flexi-distance-individualised, etc.
> * Rigidity of responsiveness due to FE conditions of service, traditional college budgeting, etc.
> * The failure to respond to the needs of the local labour market and changing industrial practice. (ET/REPLAN, 1989, pp. 5–6)

In practice, the overwhelming evidence shows Employment Training to have been a failure — in providing skilled labour for the economy and more importantly, in providing opportunities to find alternatives to their current situations for those whose lives are being wasted and destroyed through unemployment. (See for example NAEGS, 1989; Finn, 1989; Weightman and Drake, 1990; *The Guardian* 15/5/90 and 8/6/90.). However, despite its lack of 'success', we should not underestimate its impact on the unemployed and providers of learning.

In the process, the emphasis on employability, opportunity creation and increasing the flexibility of learning provision has come to dominate the REPLAN agenda at national level. At local level, it has lost a lot of its profile through the ending of DES Education Support Grant funded activity. This shift is headlined in the proposal, currently with the DES, to replace REPLAN with a new initiative, People, Learning and Jobs (PLJ) (NIACE, 1990). The latter may well be amalgamated with PICKUP to become a unified programme aimed at developing continuing education and training for the new workforce — unwaged, underemployed, or employed. The paper arguing for the resourcing of PLJ firmly accepts the dominant policy framework:

> The need for higher levels of education and skills in the workforce if Britain is to meet the economic challenges of the 1990s is acknowledged by all ... there is the need for an initiative to promote and

support the contribution education and training can make in helping adults to move from unemployment to employment and from un-skilled to more skilled work. (NIACE, 1990, pp. 1–2)

PLJ is the initiative and will pursue three inter-related objectives:

1 To promote the personal, social and vocational value of learning to adults who are unemployed, underemployed or in low-skilled jobs and not making full use of their personal potential, by working with organizations with interests in education and training.
2 To assist employers to develop educational strategies as a means of enhancing employees' motivation and readiness to learn and thus develop broader transferable competences concerned with adaptabil-ity, management of roles, creativity and flexibility.
3 To assist those planning, managing and delivering education and training opportunities to develop programmes and practices in ways that best allow these groups of adults to learn. (NIACE, 1990, p. 5)

Thus, while there is some attempt to keep alive the broad curriculum framework associated with the REPLAN programme, PLJ is much more directly involved with learning related to employment, in which education is to enable people to learn to be motivated, in order that they may be more effectively trained/developed to fulfill their role in the workforce. In a situa-tion of ongoing *structural* unemployment and underemployment is this really appropriate? The argument is usually posited as a dilemma between provid-ing people with the skills to compete more effectively for scarce jobs or to educate them for leisure. The possibility of a just distribution of paid work opportunities is rarely raised (Gorz, 1989). Will the brave new world of multi-skilled flexible working really happen? If so, for whom?

The Inevitability of the Flexible Workforce?

Over the next twenty years this country will experience profound economic and social changes, largely as a result of the increasingly rapid spread of existing and new technologies. This could lead to unprecedented shifts in economic activity, and to marked changes in the patterns of work and leisure (or non-work), with less working time needed for much more highly skilled work. Quality will have to replace quantity. Adaptability will become essential. The present scale of these changes is small compared with the future effects of the accelerating speed of change which will reach in the next few years into many more sectors of the economy to affect larger sections of the population. The idea of holding the same job for life is becoming increasingly untenable. Those with the greatest capacity to adapt will survive successfully; those least adaptable, nations as well as persons, will fail. (Advisory Council for Adult and Continuing Education, 1982, p. 181)

People need to develop a 'broader occupational competence ... concerned with adaptability, management of roles, responsibility for standards, creativity and flexibility' (CBI, quoted in NIACE, 1990, p. 2).

So far I have presented the above view of the future of the economy and working practices as though they are inevitable. There does appear to be general acceptance of the need for a more skilled, flexible workforce to meet the changing needs of the economy. As citizens, we are asked to adapt to this view, or positively support it. However, the political choices that are involved in accepting this vision of the future as the guide to our practices are not raised. They are, in fact, presented as the foundations upon which policies are built, beyond the realms of public debate.

Where, however, analyses have been undertaken into the impact of economic change on employment prospects, the result is less edifying than one might have imagined. The picture presented of the economy and labour requirements as the whole canvas is actually only part of the picture; the 'commanding heights' of the economy. When we look into the valleys, questions of winning and losing become more acute. Andre Gorz (1989) argues that unless there are substantial changes in the ideology, organization and distribution of work, current trends will result in a very different distribution of employment and learning opportunities from the impressions with which we are becoming familiar. On current trends, the future will produce a particular segmentation of the working population:

— 25 per cent will be skilled workers with permanent jobs in large firms protected by collective wage agreements;
— 25 per cent will be peripheral workers with insecure, unskilled and badly-paid jobs, whose work schedules vary according to the wishes of their employers and the fluctuations of the market;
— 50 per cent will be semi-unemployed, unemployed, or marginalized workers, doing occasional or seasonal work or 'odd jobs'. (Gorz, 1989, p. 225)

In case this may be considered unnecessarily alarmist, let me give another example from the Inner London Education Authority (now abolished) Second Further Education Development Plan of 1988:

Increasingly jobs divide into four types:
— a small number of high paid, high security posts, with in-service training, pensions, holidays, etc.

— high paid insecure posts, also few in number but expanding ...
where the worker takes responsibility for skills updating, pensions,
sick pay, etc.;
— low paid employment, with sick pay, holidays, pension but little
chance of in-service training;
— low wage insecure agency work ... with no pensions, holiday or
sick pay entitlements and no access to paid in-service training. (Tuckett, 1988, p. 9)

In other words, the flexibility and skills needed among the workforce will
vary hugely on the basis of the differential positions people occupy in the
economy. The highly educated, multi-skilled flexible workers of the future
will be the minority experience; the core workforce governed by the emerging theories of human resource management. The bulk of the workforce, by
contrast, will be consigned to marginalized positions in low skill areas,
insecure in their employment. We have already witnessed the beginnings of
this trend in Britain with the growth in employment in low paid, part-time
service sector jobs, particularly among women (*The Guardian* 6/8/1990).

In the United States, which is often taken as a model, of the thirteen
to fifteen million new jobs created in the last ten years, the majority
are in the personal-service sector and are very often insecure, badly
paid and offer no possibilities of achieving professional qualifications
or advancement — jobs as caretakers, nightwatchmen, cleaners,
waiters and waitresses, staff in 'fast food' restaurants, nursing assistants, delivery men/women, street sellers, shoeshiners, and so
on.... These 'person-to-person' services are, in reality, the jobs of
domestic or personal servants in their modernized and socialized
guise.... As in the colonies in the past and many Third World
countries today, a growing mass of people in the industrialized
countries has been reduced to fighting each other for the 'privilege'
of selling their personal services to those who still maintain a decent
income. (Gorz, 1989, p. 226)

The educators and trainers of adults are effectively being asked to support
this trend. It appears, therefore, that the core workers will be provided with
job security and training in exchange for increasing flexibility in working
practices, while the rest will need to be flexible to cope with the insecurity of
their situation, moving in and out of employment on a regular basis. (This
has disturbing, if unsurprising, echoes of the philosophy that you make the
rich work harder by giving them more, while the poor work harder if you
give them less, and the associated tax and welfare policies we have been
familiar with in Britain in the course of the 1980s). Similarly, the market for

education and training will itself be very differentiated. For the core workers, education and training will need to be available to cope with the changing demands of the market — up-skilling and development — to be able to provide relevant opportunities, as and when they are required. For the rest of the workforce, it will be there to support the movement of people in and out of employment — or at least to keep the revolving door turning!

Discourses about the multi-skilled flexible workforce of the future are therefore misleading with serious consequences for the relevance of learning available to adults insofar as this becomes the primary/sole policy goal. The minority experience is being constructed as the norm. It is for this reason that it is so important as a means of normalizing a contestable position. What these discourses do is shift the burden of responsibility for those who are not part of the core on-to them as individuals, displacing the structural issues of employment and financial reward.

> Only when a person has a positive attitude to learning and is moti-
> vated by the prospect of a different or better life can the potential
> benefits of training be fully realized. (NIACE, 1990, p. 1)

Being part of the core is the goal, as it is 'normal' to be a high-skilled worker. Persons can strive for this goal, but if they do not achieve it, it is because they lack the skills. Education and training opportunities are available as and when they need them. The responsibility for not participating in the core of the economy therefore lies with the individual. The fundamental irony is that if the adult population of Britain were to becomes highly trained flexible workers, there would not be sufficient employment opportunities for them!

We are presented with a view of the future which suggests that unemployment and under-employment can be overcome through learning and that a general increase in education and training is necessary in order to enhance the economic performance of the country as a whole. However, these approaches are actually premised on the structural conditions of un- and underemployment which they are supposedly attacking. This is not a neutral process. It is political and needs to be addressed as such. The future is not inevitable. However, to address the issue of everybody having a share in economic prosperity involves examining alternatives, alternatives which in turn involve examining the relationship between labour and payment and property relations. Policies on education and training for adults are part and parcel of policies — explicit or implicit — on employment and property relations and should be addressed as such. The current focus on education and training tends to exclude the other areas of policy from public debate, when such debates are essential if we are to benefit all members of British society in a just and fair way.

Winners and Losers — Conclusion

As mentioned in the first section of this paper, there are many who believe that the spotlight that has turned on the education and training of adults is a victory in itself. It is undoubtedly true that there are more opportunities available to adults and more adults engaging in formal education and training. Trends towards the accreditation of prior learning, modularization, increasing mature access to higher education, the rationalization of vocational qualification and their extension into new areas of employment, the development of open and flexible learning, among others, all favour the further enfranchisement of adults who wish to be formal learners. There are already many winners and potentially more in the wings.

For example, women who have been confined to the home will be able to gain credit towards qualifications for the skills of home management which may in turn be transferable to other areas of employment and learning. Older members of ethnic minorities who have qualifications and/or experience from overseas will be able to have their skills, knowledge and understanding recognized. People in unskilled work will be able to seek credit for what they can do as a starting point for further development. Opportunities to learn will not be confined to traditional settings or forms of attendance, thereby widening the scope of available learning. The workplace will become a recognized site of learning.

The possibilities are immense, shifting the emphasis from standards, élitism and exclusion to needs, access and inclusion. Within this context, learning is potentially democratized and the boundaries between education and training, which have dogged the availability and funding of learning opportunities for adults, are dissolved. There might even be some slightly hidden glee that the white middle classes who have come to dominate liberal adult education provision are being squeezed to pay more for their leisure/personal development activities.

However, perhaps we should hesitate before indulging in such glee, as much 'second chance' learning — whether or not led by equal opportunities considerations — is also being placed under increasing pressure. Let us pause to reflect on the learning that is being developed and promoted and who is likely to benefit from these trends. As I have been illustrating, because most people agree that increasing the learning available to adults is a 'good' thing, it does not mean that they all want the same thing. Debates about the relative importance of education and training and specific aspects of education and training do not go away because we start to talk of learning. They are embodied in the struggle to gain support — including state support — for the recognition of the value of specific types of learning. Further, just because education and training become more accessible, flexible and open, it does not necessarily mean that more adults will make use of them.

While the overwhelming focus on the relevance of learning to servicing the 'needs' of the economy may be relevant to members of the workforce or those seeking to enter it, there are large numbers of adults for whom this is not relevant — for example, the elderly, full-time parents and home managers. What opportunities are there for them to engage in learning, as non-work related options are marginalized and increasingly market-led, with associated fee increases? Nor is it only non-participants in paid employment who may wish to learn in other than vocational areas. We seem to be 'forgetting' that as adults we have a variety of roles — citizen, parent, football supporter, etc. — and different motivations for learning — pleasure, personal interest, social action, etc. — each of which involves forms of learning. Members of the workforce may therefore wish to pursue interests other than those related to their employment. Examples of employers (such as the Ford Motor Company and Lucas) starting to fund what traditionally are considered liberal adult education opportunities for their workers merely demonstrate the obvious. However, these are very much the exception and likely to remain so.

While opportunites to learn in the vocational sphere are being extended, in other areas they are becoming more restricted, thereby continuing to reinforce the inequalities that have always existed in the education and training system.

> Large numbers of women and men are stuck in poverty traps that do not allow them the luxury of pursuing their own research projects: namely, how to find the education opportunities they want, at a time and price they can afford — even if such things still exist in their area. Fees for adult education are being raised; classes cut; and the employment of people to carry out outreach programmes is becoming a thing of the past. (Mace, 1990, p. 89)

And, as the Employment Training scheme has demonstrated, even where opportunities to learn are made available to increase occupational competence, there is no guaranteeing their quality or meaningful outcomes for the learners involved. This is not only true of the quality of training. It is also reflected in the value given to forms of accreditation. Whether NVQs will be perceived as a debased form of qualification (as were CSEs in the secondary sector) or as a worthwhile qualification, accpeted by employers and learners alike, has yet to be tested. Much may rest on it.

The contradictory effects of the current changes in the opportunites for adults to learn make it impossible to assess precisely who are winners and losers. If the focus of development is in vocationally relevant learning, we may all be losers in fulfilling our wider roles and interests within our community with unknown consequences for the 'quality of life'. However, it may be that if more adults do participate in learning — even in a restricted field of their lives — and that participation is meaningful and relevant to them, it will place increasing demands on providers to develop more and a wider range of opportunities. In providing access to any learning, therefore, an indirect consequence may be increased demand and pressure for further learning opportunities to be made available (something which has traditionally made states very wary, as a possible threat to the status quo).

However, given what we know about current non-participants in learning, what are the chances of significant changes being encouraged solely by increased opportunities for learning?

> The 1977 OECD report, for example, identified the following non-participant typologies:
> * unemployed young adults (especially premature school leavers)
> * some rural populations
> * immigrants
> * the aged
> * urban poverty groups
> * unemployed and underemployed workers with little education
> * unskilled and semi-skilled workers
> * some groups of women (housebound mothers, women from lower socio-economic groups)
> * people with linguistic problems.
>
> Taken together, these groups add up to a large majority, whose main characteristic, according to the OECD report, is social and economic deprivation. There is a certain amount of crossover betwen groups: the least educated are often unemployed or in unskilled occupations and have low incomes; people on the lowest incomes are likely to be found among the elderly, immigrant groups and women. (McGivney, 1990, p. 15)

Many of these are precisely the groups that the government is encouraging employers to employ and train:

> Employers can no longer rely on just recruiting young people. Alternative sources of labour which may have been overlooked in the past need to be considered. These include —
> (i)   long term unemployed
> (ii) women returners
> (iii) ethnic minority groups
> (iv) people with disabilities
> (v)   older workers.
>
> ... Appropriate training will have to be provided. (Training Agency, 1989, p. 24)

However, given that the fundamental point in the OECD report is that social and economic deprivation are the main characteristics of non-participant groups, what chances of success have government exhortation, unless deprivation is also overcome?

Relative deprivation is likely to be enhanced in the economy of the future if the projections offered in the previous section are correct. While it might be argued that this deprivation may encourage adults to engage in learning to overcome their situation, experience should tell us it is only the very occassional individual who is able to do this, as deprivation has its own costs and consequences (Jeffcutt, 1990; Erlam and Hopkins, 1990). So it may well be that the winners predominantly continue to be the white middle classes, who succeed in their initial education, are in jobs where further training is provided and are able to afford to pay for their leisure/personal development interests. For the overwhelming majority of adults, dealing with the issues of social and economic deprivation (the meaning of which will vary with time, age, gender, race, class, etc.) would appear to be the key to not only opening up opportunities to learn, but also producing a culture of participation. This entails positioning educational and training policies for adults within a wider economic and social policy framework to overcome deprivation. But that's another story!

References

ADVISORY COUNCIL FOR ADULT AND CONTINUING EDUCATION (1982) *Continuing Education: From Policies to Practice*, Leicester, ACACE.

ARMSTRONG, P. (1990) 'Bridging the divide — Integrating the academic and the vocational', *Towards 1992 ... Education of Adults and the New Europe*, Proceedings of the Twentieth Annual Conference 1990, pp. 230–3, University of Sheffied, SCUTREA.

ERLAM, A. and HOPKINS, J. (Eds) (1990) *Educational Democracy: A Report on Research carried out by the Outreach Education Project, Department of Continuing and Community Education, Goldsmiths' College*, London, Outreach Education Unit Goldsmiths' College, University of London.

ET/REPLAN (1989) *Further Education and Employment Training: A Quality Response*, Sheffield, Training Agency.

FEU/NIACE REPLAN (1990) *Drawing on Experience: REPLAN Projects Review*, London, FEU/NIACE.

FINN, D. (1989) 'Employment Training — Success or failure?', *Unemployment Bulletin*, 31, pp. 9–16.

GORZ, A. (1989) *Critique of Economic Reason*, London, Verso.

HAKE, B. and MEIJERS, F. (1990) 'Adult basic education and the labour market in the Netherlands: Some contradictions in development in the 1990s', *Towards 1992 ... Education of Adults and the New Europe*, Proceedings of the Twentieth Annual Conference 1990, pp. 122–7, University of Sheffied, SCUTREA.

HANDY, L. BARHAM, K., PANTER, S. and WINHARD, A. (1989) 'Beyond the personnel function: The strategic management of human resources', *Journal of European Industrial Training*, 13, 1.

HEYWOOD, V. (1990) 'The 21 Hour Rule', *Unemployment Bulletin*, 33, pp. 17–20.

JALLADE, J-P. (1989) 'Recent trends in Vocational Education and Training: An overview', *European Journal of Education*, 24, 2.

JEFFCUTT, P. (1990) 'Transitions in a transient organization', in CORBETT, J. (Ed.) *Uneasy Transitions: Disaffection in Post-compulsory Education and Training*, pp. 147–69, London, Falmer Press.

JOHNSTON, R., MACWILLIAM, I. and JACOBS, M. (1988) *Negotiating the Curriculum with Unwaged Adults*, London, REPLAN/FEU.

LANDER, R. (1990) 'Education at work', *SCAN*, 197, pp. 22–3.

McGIVNEY, V. (1990) *Education's for Other People: Access to Education for Non-participant Adults*, A Research Report, Leicester, NIACE.

MACE, J. (1990) 'Adult literacy and mutual improvement — The challenge to higher education', *Towards 1992 . . . Education of Adults and the New Europe*, Proceedings of the Twentieth Annual Conference 1990, pp. 84–92, University of Sheffied, SCUTREA.

MURRAY, R. (1989) 'Fordism and Post-Fordism', HALL, S. and JAQUES, M. (Eds) *New Times: The Changing Face of Politics in the 1990s*, London, Lawrence and Wishart.

NATIONAL ASSOCIATION OF EDUCATIONAL GUIDANCE SERVICES FOR ADULTS (NAEGS) (1989) *Employment Training: Report of a Survey of Educational Guidance Services for Adults*.

NATIONAL INSTITUTE OF ADULT CONTINUING EDUCATION (1990) *People, Learning and Jobs: A New Initiative*, Leicester, NIACE.

REPLAN (1990) *Access Courses Within Employment Training: A REPLAN Survey*, Leicester, NIACE.

STEPHEN, M. (1990) *Adult Education*, London, Cassell.

TRAINING AGENCY (1989) *Training and Enterprise: Priorities for Action 1990/91*, Sheffield, TA.

TAIT, A. (1989) 'The Politics of Open Learning', *Adult Education*, 61, 4, pp. 308–13.

THOMPSON, J. (1983) 'Women and adult education', in TIGHT, M. (Ed.) *Opportunities for Adult Education*, pp. 145–58, London, Routledge in association with the Open University Press.

TUCKETT, A. (1988) 'The place of liberal and general adult education in special programmes for the long-term unemployed', in DE WIJS, R. (Ed.) *Report of A Conference — The Place of General and Liberal Education in Special Programmes for the Long-term Unemployed*, European Bureau of Adult Education.

UDACE (1989) *Open College Networks: Current Developments and Practice*, Leicester, UDACE.

WATTS, A. and KNASEL, E. (1985) *Adult Unemployment and the Curriculum: A Nanual for Practitioners*, London, FEU.

WEIGHTMAN, J. and DRAKE, K. (1990) *Continuing Education and Training of the Long-term Unemployed in the United Kingdom*, Berlin, CEDEFDP.

Chapter 8

Out of the Adult Hut: Institutionalization, Individuality and New Values in the Education of Adults

John Field

British adult education is at a turning point. It is not that the education of adults has gone into decline; rather that the provision systems have undergone a profound transformation, and that the conceptual and philosophical categories which underpinned the practice of adult education for several generations have become far less clear and distinct. As a result, adult education seems to have 'lost its way': it its no longer easy to identify its place in the wider order of things, or is contribution to the development of what Tawney called 'a tolerable society'. This is not just a consequence of the Thatcher government's preference for vocational education and training, clear and consistent though that policy preference has been; it also arises from the internal weakness of traditional adult education, and from its growing dependence upon the highly significant market for consumer services.

This chapter sets the consequences of government policy in the context of two broad trends in the education of adults: the institutionalization of provision on the one hand, and the increasingly individual nature of participation on the other. The strong suggestion here is that, while far from 'dead', the liberal tradition has neither a popular nor an institutional base strong enough to bear its more all-encompassing aspirations. However — and this is the third focal point of the argument — the critical and reflexive functions of the liberal tradition are now being carried out in the non-formal and self-governing practice of learning in the new social movements, and to an extent the old social movements as well.

Inevitably, such arguments also concern the involvement of the adult education organizations in the wider crisis of the welfare state. Though often conceived of as primarily fiscal in nature, or simply part of the wider Thatcherite project, the crisis of welfarism is a transnational phenomenon which is rooted deep in the wider changes in culture, affecting social values and the motivation of individuals, which has established the post-War political settlement of Europe (Offe, 1984). As a state-provided and regulated service, albeit one which is often seen as marginal, the education of adults is bound to be affected by wider crises in the welfare state; taking the wider perspective again, however, it can be seen that many of the traumas of adult education are in fact central to the present crisis of welfarism. The question is, then, whether there remains a 'public interest' in the education of adults sufficient to justify continued public fiscal support for an activity which is increasingly seen as the concern of individuals and their employers rather than of the state.

Policy Developments During the 1980s

Conservative education policies under the Thatcher government have followed a relatively consistent pattern. Whether in schools, colleges or higher education, they have pursued what a number of neo-Marxist analysts refer to as 'the new vocationalism' (e.g., Dale, 1989) within the public sector; they have sought centrally to create and reward areas of priority concern (including academic excellence); they have reduced the role of the LEA; they have attempted to create or strengthen the private sector; and they have promoted the active participation of the 'consumer'. In general, the traditional marginality of adult education has both protected it from and exposed it to this wider process of change; some parts of the adult education sub-system — for example, the long term residential colleges — were more or less ignored; yet many LEA adult education services were about the first victims of savings in the early 1980s (at one stage two LEAs proposed to extinguish their adult provision entirely), while grants to the Workers' Educational Association and university adult education programmes were steadily reduced from the mid-1980s.

By and large, in adult education the Thatcher government expects the customer to pay. It believes that, to paraphrase one junior minister, people most value that which they pay for; the best guarantee of quality in adult education is that the customer feels entitled to demand a high quality service by virtue of having paid a 'realistic' price; this in turn implies steady withdrawal of the public subsidy. Exceptions are made to the rule only where a special claim can be made on the grounds of 'disadvantage'; thus there have been small central government grants available for such areas as adult basic education or for work with the unemployed; but in practice even these limited sums are allocated largely to 'development' of initiatives which should, over time, be taken over by the LEA. However, such areas of allowable subsidy are clearly limited in size and scope; in the meantime the mainstream of provision, in whose shadows the subsidisable areas stand, is increasingly dependent upon success in the market place.

In practice, adult education is probably one of the few parts of the public education system which can successfully appeal to the market. By making a virtue of low running costs, curricular flexibility and its ability to recruit selectively, almost any adult education institution or service can develop a range of highly profitable lines of activity. This, of course, will be only a crude 'above the line' profit; adult education organizations typically external- ize most of their costs ('below the line' costs for premises and equipment are usually met by schools and other bodies; teaching costs are also partly externalized, using a largely part-time and poorly paid workforce whose training, if any, is paid for externally). More important than this essentially practical accountancy issue, though, is the dangerous assumption, implicit within all present policy, that there is no 'public interest' in the education of adults; and that the market is the best mechanism for distributing the benefits of a general adult education. Nevertheless, this assumption now pervades much of the practice of adult educators, sharpening the dissonance between their values and practice.

The Institutionalization of the Education of Adults

Adult education belongs, despite all the claims to a different status, within the framework of the welfare state. As such, it has been subjected, albeit unevenly, to the forces of bureaucratization and routinization that have affected other welfare state services. In 1942, Sir Richard Livingston de- scribed pre-War adult education in Britain as 'for the most part ... casual and episodic ... a cocktail rather than solid food' (Livingston, 1942, p. 43). Between 1945 and the 1970s, provision expanded steadily; yet it retained its characteristically 'marginal status' vis-à-vis the formal education system — a fact celebrated by many practitioners as allowing for experimentation and the testing of radical alternative approaches (Jackson, 1973). Since the 1970s there has been a marked institutionalization of adult education, with enor- mous consequences particularly for the values and purposes which shape the offering for the adult learner and its place in the wider society.

Evidence of institutionalization is apparent in the traditional adult educa- tion milieu formed by the Workers' Educational Association, the university extra-mural departments and the LEA adult centres. In each case, the 1950s and 1960s witnessed a more or less steady growth in the numbers of staff professionally employed on a full-time service to manage provision and teach, as well as in the part-time workforce. Of itself, institutional growth created new tendencies to conservatism of provision (for example, university and WEA provision tended to be concentrated in those subjects where a staff tutor had been appointed); and the existence of new career opportunities within adult education created a new instrumentalism amongst the adult educators, as individual-strategic motives displaced the love of learning or political commitments of the traditional popular educators (a process also reported in West Germany; see Kade, 1989, p. 799).

From the provider's perspective, the education of adults became more professional, less 'amateur' than in the post-War years. As a result there is now an adult education profession, if a weak and divided one, with its own lobbying bodies and even, in the UDACE, its own quango. Yet institutionalization has been much less in adult education than in other parts of the education system; it remains largely informal in its internal regulation, most of the offering does not lead to an externally-accredited qualification, and it remains hugely diverse. Some adult education services are of parallel standing to further education colleges (the larger London Institutes, for example, or the Area Colleges in Northamptonshire), but at the other end of the range is the Centre based in a comprehensive school with one full-time worker (the Centre Head), whose office system is kept in a cardboard box; the sector also includes twenty short-term residential colleges, with between one and three academic staff, and seven long-term residential colleges. No one knows for sure how many full time lecturers work in adult education, but they are vastly outnumbered by a massive penumbra of occasional part-timers, for many of whom adult education work is a secondary or tertiary activity. Decision-making is both informal and largely personalized; autonomy is enhanced by the absence of a clear and explicit framework of regulation at either the LEA or national levels. Even where there are sizeable cohorts of specialized adult education full-time staff, terms of employment vary enormously between LEAs, and where they are in trade union membership, they can be organized by one of at least three potentially competing unions. Partly because of this enormous diversity and informality, then, the education of adults has migrated into more formal institutions whose identity belongs more firmly in the educational 'mainstream'.

After a long period when adult education policy was dominated by redistributive and student-centred ethos, adult learners have moved into the markedly more instrumental and reputedly less user-friendly further education sector. The statistics are unambiguous. At some time during the mid-1990s, the number of students in centres of adult education fell below the numbers who were registered in colleges of further education. By 1987/88, when the Department of Education and Science piloted an adult education database, this process was well under way: across England and Wales, there were 2,775,000 adult students in the LEA sector; of these, 1,359,000 — just under 49 per cent — were following courses in adult education centres; a further 610,000 were following general adult education courses in colleges, and a further 806,000 over-25-year-olds were following non-advanced vocational courses. So, even if we exclude two whole groups of adults — 18–25-year-olds in the non-advanced and all adults in the advanced vocational sector — the adult centres accounted for under half of the adults in LEA provision.

On a smaller scale, similar evidence of institutionalization can be found in hihger education. Polytechnics and universities have increasingly opened up their mainstream provision to adult learners, either through greater access

to full- and part-time under- and post-graduate study, or through the development by the mainstream subject departments of new, specifically adult,
programmes. These developments have gone considerably further in the
polytechnic sector, where there has never been specialized adult education
staff; in 1989/90, though, four universities followed the polytechnic model
by ending the separate 'extra-mural' status of their adult education departments and dispersing the staff around the mainstream departments. Nonetheless, it is in the FE sector that the transformation is most advanced.

The migration process has, like all diasporas, been complex and at times
enforced. Where local authorities have chosen to relocate adult education in
the Further Education colleges, whether as a separate sub-unit or — as with
some tertiary systems — as a supposedly integrated part of the whole, adult
students have simply been transferred in a wider process of reorganization.
But at the same time, Further Education colleges have sought to recruit
adults into their institutions, whether into mainstream provision or by developing new programmes for adults, for reasons of their own. Some reflect
policy decisions, often influenced since the mid-1980s by the REPLAN
programme, to implement equal opportunities through developing new
second-chance provision such as Access courses. But there are also purely
institutional forces which derive from colleges' partial orientation towards
the market: not only are the college managers' salaries directly affected by
size — an important factor at a time of decline in traditional recruitment —
but education managers are now moving to compensate for shortfalls in the
younger age groups by recruiting older students.

The institutionalization of the education of adults has real effects upon
provision. There are very real differences in organizational forms and culture.
The typical FE college is a medium-sized organization with a tenured workforce of around 150–250, with a clear hierarchy of power, operating within a
framework of bureaucratic regulation, and commanding access to a wider
range of resources, both material and personnel (who themselves are collectively organized through NATFHE). Within the LEA area, the colleges will
have direct access to senior officers; both the DES and the Training Agency
have clear and explicit frameworks for handling relations with the further
education system, which is broadly national in its coverage and, although
its formal legal basis is thin, it is again covered through procedures of
bureaucratic regulation which are understood across the country. The college's traditional function as an agency for the routinized vocational socializa-
tion and distribution of young working class people is instantly recognizable
in the social organization of space: standardized teaching areas off long
corridors, separate facilities for staff and students, large mechanical workshops, and so on.

Most of all, institutionalization has diluted the powerful moralism of
British adult education. A good thing too, some would say (cf. Griffin,
1988). Whereas adult educators throughout the post-industrial world are
questioning the continued relevance of their values, in Britain the debate

enjoys a certain detachment from reality. The further education sector has in large measure been seen as 'value free'; this is questionable, as FE definitely has a tacit value system, but it has certainly lacked the broader value systems which have been associated with the rest of the education system; FE colleges have never, to take one obvious but still significant example, had any formal connection with the religious foundations. While individual lecturers (often of the '1968 generation') or sub-units of the further education sector expose broadly humanistic and redistributive values, the colleges' primary function remains the adaptation of young people and adults to the needs of the labour market.

Of course, there are also strong similarities, but these have tended to reinforce the instrumentality of adult learners, while fostering a comparison between the two. To put it bluntly, there is a widely held perception of FE as more efficient and business-like in delivering the (instrumental) goods. Both further and adult education are largely professionalized occupations, in that they employ a core of salaried 'experts' to run and sometimes teach the provision; in both cases, these are what might be called 'welfare state professions', starting the long period of growth to their present size in the decade after 1945. What may be described as a 'task culture' is shared by workers in both sectors, with concerns for 'getting the job done' taking precedence over abstract pedagogic and curricular conceptions. However, further educations's culture derives from the predominately youth-oriented, instrumental and vocational nature of its mainstream.

Institutionalization has a dual effect. On the one hand migration from the old educational milieu 'frees adults from the ties obligations that were justified with a pregiven idea of education' (Kade, 1989, p. 800); the learner increasingly enters into a rational contract with the provider, where s/he is able to take what s/he wishes without being made the object of what appears to be, and is, an ideologically-inspired agenda imposed by the provider. On the other hand, the new educational milieu also brings its own limits to autonomy: all large educational organizations subject learners to bureaucratic regulation, often derived from systems of government designed to contain the young; they tend to be faceless and impersonal, and thus intensify feelings of powerlessness and isolation; and they generate anxieties, inequalities and constraints through their primary involvement in the qualifications process and in labour market training.

Individuality and Personal Growth in Adult Education

What, in the meantime, is happening in what is left of the liberal adult education sector? Is the same instrumentalization not true there? In fact, in the field of liberal adult education providers increasingly operate according to market principles, and have often been surprised by the extent to which they have succeeded. Because of its concern with the expressive and affective, liberal adult education has, since its origins, but especially strongly since 1945, played a growing and significant role with respect to the growing differentiation of individual identities, the growth of personal autonomy, and the more recent strength of 'post-materialist' values. Further, liberal adult education relies on the existence of a social constituency able to back up its aspirations with solid purchasing power and free time. Essentially, then, liberal adult education providers behave in practice more and more like private, commercial agencies; yet they are staffed by people who retain a commitment to strongly held humanistic and person-centred values.

For example, it at first appears paradoxical that certain of the short-term residential colleges apparently have been able to thrive despite a huge reduction since the mid-1970s in their numbers and their levels of public funding. University provision has also, after a brief downturn in the early 1980s, recovered dramatically despite very rapid and substantial rises in fee levels. In the drive to continue the expansion of the previous period, or at least to halt decline, the providers of liberal adult education effectively mounted a practical turn to the market, seeking out areas of demand regardless of their relationship to the philosophies and values which were advanced in defence of the liberal tradition.

Market-led expansion has had two chief consequences. The first has been diversification of provision, involving the displacement of older subjects of study which have been held to epitomise the broader social purpose of liberal adult education. Economics and industrial studies, which were often though of in the inter-war years as the pulsing heart of the offering, declined steadily; the annual reports of the Universities Council for Adult and Continuing Education show that by 1974–5, courses in economics and industrial studies were 6.44 per cent of all courses offered by the universities; by 1988–9 they were a mere 1.96 per cent of the total. There has been a slight growth in literary studies over the same period, as in professional studies (management, etc.); and a very sharp and recent upswing in courses around personal growth and individual identity, such as counselling or assertiveness.

Secondly, within this wider context of change and diversification of provision it is possible to distinguish emergent trends and patterns in participation. Explanation of precisely why adult learners have migrated into the FE colleges must remain tentative; but it is possible to say something on the basis of who they are. Some adults are involuntary learners, of course, required to attend a college by their employers or the welfare agencies. What seems far more significant, though, is the extent to which adults voluntarily choose to attend a college for reasons which must be connected with the socializing and distributory functions which colleges traditionally perform for young people. These are truly 'second chance' learners. Whereas the liberal adult education tradition presupposed a willingness to learn 'for its own sake', growing numbers are treating education as an access route which is explicitly instrumental in that it offers a pathway to a recognized qualification. What little research evidence exists, though, suggests that instrumental routes appeal most strongly to younger groups in the adult population. In the case of GCSE and Access courses, for example, the student groups are characteristically female and aged between 20 and 35; in the case of GCSE, there is also above-average participation by young males from certain minority ethnic communities. (Field, 1989; Field and Hyde, 1989).

In the mainstream of WEA, university, and short-term residential college provision, on the other hand, the majority of courses now predominantly attract older adults. This development seems to have been taken furthest in the short-term residential colleges, where on average about one student in eight is aged 70 or more. Across the liberal sector, as in LEA adult provision, most participants — between two-thirds and three-quarters — are women; most are relatively well-educated, and come from middle-class backgrounds.

At the same time, provision in the liberal adult education sector has changed in its shape (long tutorial classes with required reading and even written work have been displaced by shorter and largely self-contained courses) and its content (academic disciplines and macro-social and political analysis have been replaced by a much more varied and eclectic offering, much of it concerned with personal development and growth). Overtly leisure-oriented forms of provision like the study tour are now a large, but under-theorized, form of activity, offered more or less on a commercial basis. The only exceptions to these trends of any significance are the long term residential colleges and the dwindling number of industrial day release courses. In short, what is often conventionally called 'the leisure sector' is no longer an LEA monopoly; it is increasingly commercial, and it has colonized much of the liberal adult education provision.

It is possible to see in these developments both an expression and a furthering of individualism (cf. Kade, 1989, 797–9). Qualification-bearing education has already been discussed above, but there is some evidence that the same explanation of participation is even more true in liberal adult education. Here, participation may be a reaction against the fragmentation of society, especially since the post-war years, which can create enormous personal problems of loneliness and isolation (e.g. among the highly mobile or the elderly.)

Participation can also both express and contribute to personal identity; it marks one off from others who do not attend. Adult education also constructs a series of communities through its courses, which allow access to other cultural worlds yet which embody values and aspirations which are denied in everyday life, and this also appears to be of growing significance. For example, courses on 'Celtic language and culture' made up under 15 per cent of provision in the Welsh universities in 1974–5 but over 23 per cent in 1988–9.

That adult education both expresses and fosters the process of individualization is not to imply that it has lost its previous role or that it has become contingent (cf. Kade, 1989; Keddie, 1980). The two are not mutually exclusive: liberal adult education may be a highly significant form of self-definition with regard to the public as well as the 'private' sphere. Participants in the short-term residential colleges, where older adults are a clear majority, are active in remarkably large numbers in other areas of public life — as members and officers of local voluntary bodies, even as school governors (Field, 1990). Yet they often spoke of their residential courses in terms of self-actualization, using such phrases as 'now I'm doing something for myself', 'it keeps my mind alive', and 'this is really me'. This apparent clash between public service and seeming individualism is explicable partly in terms of cultural transition: these older adults are learning, among other things, how to develop new public identities which are based on creative action but do not depend upon one's work or family role.

In fact, there is an evident congruence between adults' growing individualization and the ideology of adult educators (cf. Keddie, 1980), which is expressed in a powerfully individualistic discourse. Such notions as personal needs, self-fulfillment, and self-help pervade the public discourse of adult educators; and they are being grafted on to the rather more vocationalist discourse of at least the more influential voices in the further education community. If the relationship between the wider social process of individualization and the more specific institutionalization of welfare state agencies such as adult education has been structural and multi-faceted, as I believe, then it would seem to be of considerable significance for the future of adult education as a system and for the education of adults as a social practice.

Active Citizens as Adult Learners

A final distinguishing characteristic of adult education in Britain was its sense of a mission, of having its own special contribution to the wider society. This was long held to lie in its role in the creation of civic awareness among the adult population — not solely through its overt curriculum but also, as above all in the WEA, through its adoption of democratic organizational forms. From their privileged role in the achievement of this high mission, the liberal education institutions derived a status and leadership function within the wider adult education community which gave them a dominant position in its representative organizations and in its self-image. Has this period now ended under the pressures of institutionalization and individualization? Or, albeit in changed form, can it survive?

Ultimately, the liberal tradition of adult education was designed to produce educated citizens for a democratic world. This agenda arose from the particular constellation of forces at work in British society in the late nineteenth and earlier twentieth century, and its leading edge was for long rooted in a labour movement paradigm. At heart, both the workerists of the

Labour College movement and the quasi-Fabians of the WEA shared a view of social change that saw organized labour as the core of the forces of progress; it followed that the highest ambition for adult education was to help the working class achieve its own emancipation from ignorance and bondage (Fryer, 1990). And what underpinned the legitimacy and coherence of this paradigm was that it was shared by a sizeable minority of articulate and influential intellectuals, drawn not only from provincial institutions but from the core of the academic élite.

It is now no longer the case that any significant body of British intellectuals shares this analysis. What Andre Gorz defines as 'the working class human-ism of labour' has lost its force; it is able to inspire neither a sustained critique of capitalism and its political economy; nor, and perhaps more significantly, is it any longer able to inspire an alternative conception of social being — that is, a utopia and a means of achieving it. It is unable to inspire a living practice of adult education. It is now such a small component of the British adult education system that provision designed for working class adults is usually described and legitimated through the language of 'disadvantage'; it is also usually cleansed of any claim to have the working class itself (and its poten-tial as an agency of change) as the subject of study.

At the same time, though, newer social movements have emerged in the industrial and post-industrial nations which are clearly counter-hegemonic. Further, the values and aspirations of such movements as feminism, the gay movement, the peace movement and environmentalism have far-reaching implications for education — not least because these movements tend to be located amongst relatively well-educated sectors of the population, and often among social service professionals (including teachers) whose experience and values find expression in idealistic educational experiments (Weiler, 1988, pp. 95–6). Beyond this, though, the new social movements' critical distance from the dominant institutions and values of western capitalism (and, before Autumn 1989, of Stalinist socialism as well) mean that they can be seen as constituting free spaces which offer a profoundly radical schooling in citizenship (Evans and Boyte, 1986). Horstein (1984, pp. 156–7) has even described the new social movements as 'search movements' who invest and test new ways of living and organizing socially in and on behalf of the future interests of humanity (cf. Phillips, 1987, pp. 137–9).

Yet we cannot expect history to repeat itself; there is no intrinsic reason why the new social movements should form the basis for attempts to construct a wider adult educational coalition in the way that the labour movement did for the WEA.

More precisely because the new social movements are 'search move-ments', they are likely to prove inimical to easy partnership with the adult education profession. In so far as adult education professionals share the values of the new social movements, they are likely to have some sympathy for attempts to establish partnerships. Yet in so far as adult education has become professionalized, it increasingly seeks to manage partnership by routinizing it — a one-sided and parasitical process that is reflected linguistically in notions such as 'good practice in inter-agency cooperation' or 'voluntary-statutory collaboration'. Uncertainty and independence are the very basis of the new social movements' role as 'search movements'; such notions as 'autonomy' and 'authenticity' are key values for their participants (Offe, 1985; Phillips, 1987, p. 137). Mistrust of state agencies — even well-meaning ones like adult education — is often an act of faith; rather, feminism and ecology have produced systematic critiques of the fundamental principles of educational practice (Heinen-Tenrich and Meyer, 1988). Despite common interests at the individual level and even enormous sympathy among the professionals, it is difficult to envisage a major coalition for adult education emerging out of the new social movements.

What has happened so far might be described as an uneasy, disjointed partnership of adult education and the new social movements, based largely on the instincts of individual adult educators. It has been taken furthest by feminists, who in their experience have exposed a new set of divisions between 'reformers' and 'traditionalists' in the adult education community. The most significant fact is, though, that the new social movements are far more likely to influence adult education than benefit from it. If we look at what adults actually seem to learn about — to take two examples — complementary medicine or environmental issues, it is evident that very effective adult learning has been carried on in and around the new social movements with no resources whatever to adult education institutions; equally effective public general education has been carried out on a self-directed basis by adults using television and bookshops; it is far from evident that the involvement of adult education institution would have been, pedagogically speaking, an improvement.

To every social formation belongs its appropriate technology: it might be said that 'working class humanism' suited teachers, while the new social movements are made up of learners. Marxism and social democracy's capacity to articulate a rational-scientific utopia implied and rested upon a particular way of learning, with its appropriate pedagogy (expert-based) and curriculum (economics, history, political science) which lent themselves to codification and transmission through formal educational practices. The new social movements, on the other hand, challenge the very privileging of rational-technical thinking over and above creativity, imagination and feeling. These lend themselves to informal and reciprocal forms of learning, experienced as discovery rather than transmission, and characterized by self-management rather than external validation.

Is There a Public Interest in Adult Education?

Adult education thus finds itself in a predicament which exemplifies the wider crisis in the Welfare State. As the broad consensus which supported the

Welfare State has been eroded, adult education has found itself doubly exposed. It is reliant chiefly upon public funding, its activities are framed by public regulation, it is expected to focus itself around broad policy goals which until recently were generally egalitarian and redistributive in nature; it is now expected to turn to the market for survival. Yet for historical reasons, British adult education has been allowed to cultivate a critical, even oppositional stance; if the mainstream of provision, especially in the LEAs, was largely leisure-oriented, it long tolerated a sizeable fringe of counter-hegemonic provision, often associated (if at a distance) with the labour movement or more recently (and less distantly) with feminism; and there was a somewhat larger fringe which advocated knowledge for its own, civilizing sake. Yet now, as the state seeks to construct a new social coalition not for adult education but for adult training, involving not the students but their employers, adult education seems to have a very small role left to play. But this would be a superficial view; it would be more accurate to say that work, and ultimately training, have an ever narrower influence over our lives. Meanwhile, adult education has had perforce to serve as resources for adults, including those in their 'third age', whose identity-education and individualist aspirations only partly coincide with the goals of the providing institutions.

The 1980s, then, presented adult educators with new and worthy tasks. Yet if regulation through market forces allowed the voice of the new consumer to be heard more clearly, it has also disenfranchised those who have no power in the marketplace, and it has created a series of short-term biases in provision.

Those who are disenfranchised are, of course, also those who have had least schooling; and they received the least vocational training. It remains an open question whether the consequence has been to create a 'training underclass' of those who will and cannot participate in vocational training. Nevertheless, radical non-participation (or total exclusion) is in itself a sufficient basis to argue that some adult education is a public good, and that the state has a legitimate role to play in extending opportunities to those who are most at risk of marginalization and damage.

Over and above that, I would argue that there is a powerful public interest in the wider role of adult education in contemporary society. It is certainly in the public interest that adult participation be broadened; but is the market the best means of providing individuals with opportunities? Market decisions are inevitably short term, and lead to difficulties in the supply of trained labour, for example, that are well-known to economists (e.g. Timmermann, 1983). Moreover, if my argument is right, then adult education has a central role to play in helping overcome the multiple problems caused by the fragmentation and isolation that can arise in an increasingly individualized society. Since 1980, market forces have been remarkably successful in enabling consumers' voices to be heard; look, for instance, at the range of provision now available in identity education (personal growth, self-discovery, inter-personal relations), including the rapid growth of practical routes for self-actualization (ranging from the discovery of one's own potential to Access courses). The problem with the market place is not simply that such provision is biased towards the demands of the most powerful in the market place (and may explicitly be at the expense of provision for the less powerful); but that it may foster in providers an orientation towards fashion rather than quality, gratification rather than reflection.

Adult education has not died; in turning towards the market, it has started to identify new needs and new tasks. In so far as it has followed existing tendencies towards individualization, the adult education offering has started to empower learners to make more autonomous choices, more confidently, over more areas of their own lives. In this respect it is, in its own field, carrying out precisely that task of fostering flexibility, adaptability and creativity in adults which the vocational training system has been charged with; ironically, current policy thinking in vocational training has, in contrast, strengthened the tendencies to narrowness and fossilization that were already visible, if in less marked a fashion, earlier in the 1980s (cf. Field, 1991). Thus the institutionalization of adult education presents two apparently contradictory possibilities. The risk is that the education of adults will be sucked down the ever-narrower tube of training, in which case such fields of provision as can find a market will become more and more privatized (in both senses of the word); the opportunity is that vocational training will be influenced for the better by the humanistic and holistic goals which inspired the adult education mainstream.

References

DALE, R. (1989) *The State and Education Policy*, Milton Keynes, Open University Press.

EVANS, S. and BOYTE, H. (1986) *Free Space: The Sources of Democratic Change in America*, New York, Harper & Row.

FIELD, J. (1989) 'Finishing School: The experiences of adult students in GCSE', *Links*, 15, 1, pp. 7–8.

FIELD, J. (1990) 'Researching residential adult education', Adult Residential College Association Conference, May.

FIELD, J. (1991) 'Competency and the pedagogy of labour', *Studies in the Education of Adults*. Forthcoming.

FIELD, J. and HYDE, P. (1989) *The Financial Circumstances of Access Students*, Sheffield, Forum for Access Studies.

FRYER, B. (1990) 'The challenge to working-class education', in SIMON, B. (Ed.). *The Search for Enlightenment: The Working Class and Adult Education in the Twentieth Century*, pp. 276–319, London, Lawrence and Wishart.

GORZ, A. (1989) *Critique of Economic Reason*, London, Verso.

GRIFFIN, C. (1988) 'Recurrent education and social welfare policy', in MOLYNEUX, F. *et al.*, (Eds) *Learning for Life: Politics and Progress in Recurrent Education*, Beckenham, Croom Helm.

HEINEN-TENRICH, J. and MEYER, H. (1988) 'Okologie als Herausforderung an gesellschaft und Erwachsenebildung', *Zukunft der Weiterbildung: Eine Standortbestimmung*, Bonn, Bundeszentrale fur politische Bildung.

HORNSTEIN, W. (1984) 'Neue Soziale Bewegungen und Padagogik', *Zeitschrift fur Padagogik*, 30, 2, pp. 147–67.

JACKSON, K. (1973) 'The marginality of community development — implications for adult education', *International Review of Community Development*.

KADE, J. (1989) 'Universalisierung und Individualisierung der Erwachsenenbildung', *Zeitschrift fur Padagogik*, 35, 6, pp. 789–808.

KEDDIE, N. (1980) 'Adult education: An ideology of individualism', in THOMPSON, J. (Ed.) *Adult Education for a Change*, London, Hutchinson.

LIVINGSTONE, R. (1942) *The Future in Education*, Cambridge, Cambridge University Press.

OFFE, C. (1984) *Contradictions of the Welfare State*.

PHILLIPS, A. (1987) *Divided Loyalties: Dilemmas of Sex and Class*, London, Virago.

TIMMERMAN, D. (1983) 'Financing mechanisms and their impact on postcompulsory education', in LEVIN, H. and SCHUTZE, H.G. (Eds) *Financing Recurrent Education — Strategies for Increasing Employment, Job Opportunities and Productivity*, Beverly Hills, Sage.

WEILER, K. (1988) *Women Teaching for Change: Gender Class and Power*, South Hadley, Bergin and Garvey.

Chapter 9

Conditions for Learner Autonomy at a Distance

Lewis Elton

Editors' Note: When planning this book we came across an article by Lewis Elton which expressed many of the ideas which are central to our work in Higher Education and which we included in the Open University's Enterprise in Higher Education proposal which we were working on. The Enterprise in Higher Education (EHE) Initiative represents an important theme in current programmes which seek a closer integration between education and training, between life skills and occupational competence. We therefore invited Lewis Elton to annotate his article with specific references to EHE.

Preface

I wrote this article two years ago out of a concern that distance students in higher education might have even less opportunity to develop the skills of an autonomous learner than students in traditional educational settings. Since then, the 'Enterprise in Higher Education' programme (EHE) of the Training Agency has initiated developments in institutions of higher education designed to facilitate the learning of transferable life and work skills and to enable students to link their learning to the world of work. The conditions favourable for the acquisition of these skills and linking them to the world of work turn out to be remarkably similar to the conditions which I suggested in my article as conducive to autonomous learning. The article below, which I have annotated in a number of places, has therefore acquired an unexpected topicality.

Introduction

Learner autonomy, as a concept and how to achieve it, has received much attention over the past fifteen years, and a comprehensive and authoritative discussion of it has been given in a recent book (Boud, 1988a), from which I shall quote frequently in this chapter. Clearly it means different things to different people, but few would quarrel with the operational statement (Higgs, 1988) that:

> An accomplished autonomous learner is one who has the capabilities for learning in an independent manner, but who can recognize the advantages of choosing alternative modes of learning where these are considered more appropriate to the learning goals in question.

There is much experience of — and also some research on — autonomous learning in traditional face-to-face educational settings, and this raises for the distance educator the serious question of whether face-to-face contact with teachers is an essential condition for autonomous learning. In the Open University, the question was raised at an early stage (for instance by Farnes, 1975 as quoted by Candy, 1988):

> In the Open University, it seems paradoxical to me that the people who experience exciting and immensely demanding learning tasks are the course teams; they are acquiring and organizing knowledge, evaluating and selecting materials, designing and presenting programmes and activities. The student receives what appears to be a polished produce from this process; he has to learn from material that has been agonized over by the authors, course team members and many others ...

> If it is in the course teams that there are genuine learning experiences, should we not allow the student to participate in these learning experiences by delegating more of the job to him? ... A major effort is necessary to get students to change their passive approach to learning and to encourage them to take responsibility.

This theme was taken up by Jarvis (1981), who suggested that Open University courses should be based more on the principles of andragogy (Knowles, 1975), and by Morgan (1983) who drew attention to the value of project work in basing courses on these principles. The first OU attempt at a course which was based on these principles and used project work — course E355 on 'Education for Adults' — was started in the following year (Taylor and Kaye, 1986), and this and other attempts have been discussed recently (Elton, 1987). Valuable suggestions for overcoming the problems facing autonomy learning at a distance have been made by Enckevort (1986) and, in a different vein, Inglis (1987) has formulated a heuristic for developing student autonomous learning, which ideally:

> ... should be an instrument for student self-analysis and for sharing
> with the lecturer so that the shared understanding will promote
> lecturer and student initiatives to compensate for or enhance the
> student's milieu.

This heuristic seems to identify the qualities of students who are capable of autonomous learning; it does not attempt to help in the design of courses which aim to move students towards learning autonomy.

The words 'to compensate for or enhance' in the above quotation are significant. They are typical of the common attitude to distance education, that it is in some way deficient compared to traditional education. From this, it is a short step to looking for differences where distance education is obviously defective and trying to ameliorate these as best one can. This is false on two grounds. First, it ignores the differences where, equally obviously, traditional education is defective, and secondly, it looks for piecemeal and ad hoc improvement where comprehensive redesign would be more appropriate. The approach is similar to that which treated the motor car as a horseless carriage.

In going back to the drawing board, this chapter will start with the aims of autonomy in learning and the objectives associated with these aims. These objectives will turn out to describe processes and not products or, in the terminology of Eisner (1985), they are expressive and behavioural. They provide the basis for, first, learning strategies and, then, teaching processes and strategies which facilitate the achievement of the learning objectives. It is these processes and strategies — for both learning and teaching — which will then be interpreted in terms of teaching and learning methods from the point of view of distance education. It will be found that they differ substantially from the corresponding methods used for autonomy learning in traditional settings. This contrasts with the approach via the deficiency model of distance education, where an attempt is often made to use distance teaching methods which in some superficial way resemble corresponding face-to-face methods. A well known example of this approach — although not in connection with autonomy learning — was the intention of the Open University in its early planning to give televised lectures the status which lectures normally have in face-to-face teaching. It was soon appreciated that students, in fact, gave this status to the printed course material and that many watched television only rarely, even when they had easy access to it.

The chapter will finally illustrate the lessons learned from it by reference to two actual courses. However, as is so often the case, practice to some extent preceded theory, and experience with these courses was in many ways influential in formulating the theoretical considerations presented in this chapter.

The approach via expressive objectives and all it implies concerning processes and products is equally important for EHE.

Autonomy Learning: Aims, Processes and Strategies

Aims and processes

Dearden (1972, quoted by Boud, 1988b), in a rather more searching state-ment on autonomy learning than was given in the last section, has this to say:

> A person is autonomous to the degree, and it is very much a matter of degree, that what he thinks and does, at least in important areas of his life, are determined by himself. That is to say, it cannot be explained why these are his *beliefs* and actions without referring to his own activity of mind. This determination of what one is to think and do is made possible by the bringing to bear of relevant consid-erations in such activities of mind as those of choosing, deciding, deliberating, reflecting, planning and judging.

The phrase 'matter of degree' is very important here, for autonomy has always to be exercised within imposed constraints, and even within these it can never be said to be complete. Thus, we are dealing here with a process that has the potential for further development, rather than a finished product. It is for that reason that the associated objectives are process objectives. Boud (1988b) himself gives a list of such objectives for students whose learning is 'autonomous to a degree':

— identifying learning needs,
— setting goals,
— planning learning activities,
— finding resources needed for learning,
— working collaboratively with others,
— selecting learning projects,
— creating 'problems' to tackle,
— choosing where and when they will learn,
— using teachers as guides and counsellors rather than instructors,
— opting to undertake additional non-teacher-directed work, such as learning through independent (structured) learning materials,
— determining criteria to apply to their work,
— engaging in self-assessment,
— learning outside the confines of the educational institution, for example in a work setting,
— deciding when learning is complete,
— reflecting on their learning processes,
— making significant decisions about any of these matters, that is, decisions with which they will have to live.

The similarity of this list to most of the lists of objectives put forward by different institutions for their EHE programme is striking.

Strategies

To achieve objectives like these, the following learning strategies, as listed by Higgs (1988), may well be appropriate:

(a) to seek and utilize relevant existing learning opportunities (e.g. lectures, seminars);

(b) to seek available resource personnel and to interact with them, e.g. as 'sounding boards' and sources of ideas, feedback, stimulation and skilled/expert information;

(c) to seek and utilise available learning resources (e.g. learning modules, computer literature searches);

(d) to reflect on observations of his or her own learning experiences or the ideas and findings of others;

(e) to experiment actively with an issue or conduct an investigation of a topic of interest;

(f) to conceptualise about acquired knowledge;

(g) to seek concrete experiences which help to further his or her understanding of the topic area.

These are also good EHE strategies, except that they do not involve the world of work explicitly, although this is implied by their being considered appropriate for achieving Boud's objectives which at one point include 'a work setting'.

However, not all students at any given moment may be ready — either intellectually or emotionally — to follow such strategies; whether they are or not can be diagnosed by such instruments as the heuristic of Inglis (1987) or by a 'self-directed learning readiness' test of the kind developed for instance by Guglielmino (1977), as quoted by Higgs (1988). This tests students on the following factors:

1 Openness to learning opportunities.
2 Self-concept as an effective learner.
3 Initiative and independence in learning.
4 Love of learning.
5 Creativity.
6 Future orientation.
7 Ability to use basic study skills.
8 Ability to use problem-solving skills.

Bringing students to the point where they can learn in a self-directed manner requires a considerable reorientation from their previous dependent learning

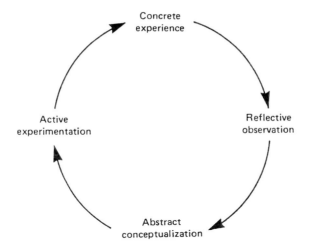

Figure 1   The Kolb learning cycle as adapted by Gibbs (1987)

methods, which is of course an aspect of the well-known educational paradox that students have to be led to autonomy. An important part of this is to learn how to learn from personal experience. In fact, strategies (d), (f), (e) and (g) above — in that order — form the experiential learning cycle of Kolb (1984) as adapted by Gibbs (1987, see Figure 1). This agreement of the quite independent work of Higgs and of Kolb and Gibbs is encouraging.

In the last paragraph I have used the words 'self-directed', 'autonomous' and 'experiential', all applied to learning. To what extent do these describe the same or different forms of learning? To me, 'self-directed' and 'autonomous' are synonymous and they include the free decision by learners to become dependent in their learning when they consider this to be appropriate. It, therefore, goes beyond independent learning, a point to which I shall return later.

Experiential learning is a learning method which can — in a slightly perverted form — be part of dependent learning, since all the experiences can be provided by the teacher who then can also guide the other stages of the learning cycle. However, such pre-digested experiences are not really experiences, and the more learners choose and use their own experiences and initiate the other stages, the more they move towards autonomy. Thus, experiential learning provides a ready and powerful means of moving learners away from dependence and towards autonomy.

Experiential learning is equally important for EHE, including the warning to eschew its 'perverted form'.

The Process of Change

How to develop students from dependence towards autonomy has been the subject of some research. The stages of development have been analysed by

Perry (1970). However, while Perry thought of these stages as developmental in general Crockett (1965) and Feldman (1980) have shown that in learning a new subject, learners again pass through the stages similar to those identified by Perry irrespective of the stage they may have reached earlier in a different subject. There is even evidence, adduced by Candy (1988), that those with higher levels of formal education feel the most frustration and loss of self-esteem when learning a new subject. This finding may well explain why university teachers tend to make very difficult students on teaching and learning courses. How learning can lead to development and change has been discussed by Ramsden (1984, 1987) who has stressed the need for a relational perspective which treats teaching and learning jointly and holistically with regard to content and context, and thereby identifies situations conducive to change. Elton (1982) has discussed the role that assessment can play as an important part of such a situation.

The process of change itself can be analysed in terms of a model such as that of Lewin (1952). The three stages of this model, with suggestions for possibly appropriate strategies are:

— *Unfreezing*: The situation is changed through a simultaneous change of the assessment methods (threatening) and of teaching methods (reassuring), both designed to encourage a development towards autonomous learning.
— *Changing*: New learning methods are introduced to match the changed assessment and teaching methods. The result should be a progressive increase in learning autonomy.
— *Refreezing*: The new teaching and assessment methods are further adjusted to match the increased learning autonomy, and are institutionalized.

The progressive changes, it may be noted, affect both students and teachers, although in different ways. Either group may reject the change at any moment and revert to earlier practices. It is most important to avoid such a situation, since the reversal of such a failure is more difficult to achieve than the original change, a point that can be understood in terms of catastrophe theory (Cryer, 1987).

The central dilemma of the teacher who wishes to encourage autonomy learning has been well put by Candy (1988):

If asked, most teachers (and especially university teachers) would state that their aim is to develop in their learners an analytical disposition along with certain skills of critical thinking: 'A questioning critical attitude is one of the hallmarks of higher education'. Lamentably, however, research has shown, more often than not, that university studies result in 'conformity' rather than critical thinking, that students seek out 'cues' as to what is required of them, and that they make 'situational adjustments' accordingly.

While it is true that some teachers are frustrated in their efforts by students who apparently prefer to remain dependent, there is another side to this coin: the students who rebel against what has been called 'the hidden curriculum' (Snyder, 1971) imposed on them by teachers who assess towards conformity, whether they teach towards it or not. A mismatch of either type is likely to lead to the kind of failure referred to above. Innovative teachers must, therefore, always endeavour to carry their students with them. The means open to them are discussed next.

The importance of basing EHE programmes on the idea of institutional and individual change cannot be overestimated. To introduce an EHE programme without an understanding of change theory is courting failure.

Autonomy Learning: The Role of the Teacher

Teaching towards Autonomy Learning

Boud (1988b) lists three teaching approaches — and there are others — which have been widely used in the pursuit of learner autonomy. In each case, they combine the process on which the approach is centred and a strategy for carrying it out:

(a) Individual-centred through a learning contract.
(b) Group-centred through group interaction and peer learning.
(c) Project-centred through problem formulation and solution.

These are not, of course, mutually exclusive. While the first and third fit in well with the list of learning strategies formulated by Higgs (1988), there is nothing in Higgs' list which corresponds to the second. It is, therefore, necessary to add an eighth item to that list (see p. 147):

(h) To cooperate with others in group and peer learning.

The reason why Higgs omitted this last item is almost certainly that she thought of autonomy in terms of independence, as is clear from the quotation with which this chapter starts. Boud, on the other hand, thinks of it in terms of interdependence, a stage beyond independence, which he considers 'a more mature relationship which places students in the world and interrelating to it rather than being apart from it'. He is clearly right, and it is important to remember this point — to which attention had already been drawn earlier — in all considerations of autonomy, particularly since group-centred work in general presents more difficulties to the distance educator than individual- or project-centred work.

The introduction of group work and the concept of interdependence also present educators with profound philosophical problem. Group work can lead to conformity which is the very opposite of independence. Some of the greatest innovators have been fiercely independent, and even lesser mortals should be aware that their genuine desire to interact constructively with others may limit their legitimate independence.

It is now generally recognized that in moving students towards autonomy, a teacher should remain an authority, but be progressively less in authority and more of a facilitator. Structures and boundaries, however, remain as features of the learning system, only these should be progressively less imposed and more negotiated. Unstructured and unlimited freedom is not freedom, but anarchy. Such structures and boundaries are obviously part of a learning contract, and they are imposed on project work through the nature of the problem to be solved and also through resource limitations. They are less apparent, but none the less real, in group work where they constitute the group. An important part of the teacher's task in guiding groups is to further the development of a group discipline that is accepted by all and not imposed.

More generally, teachers in autonomous learning must combine the roles of manager, facilitator and resource person, without ever imposing themselves or their will on their students. Students must be allowed to make their own decisions and to make mistakes; and they must be prepared to accept responsibility for their actions. All this makes the tasks of both teachers and students harder than when students accept the authority of their teachers.

Finally, as Higgs (1988) points out, following the management model of Hersey and Blanchard, teachers must exercise situational leadership. The four types of leadership identified in this model are characterized as 'telling', 'selling', 'participating' and 'delegating' and these match the teaching approaches as learner autonomy progressively increases.

At this point, EHE goes beyond autonomy learning, in that it stresses team work as well as group work. The two are not the same.

Subject Specificity

So far I have been concerned with the teacher's role in general. I now turn briefly to matters that arise from the differences between subjects and disciplines.

That learning a new subject leads to an initial regression to an earlier stage of intellectual development than had been reached in more familiar subjects has already been explained in connection with the process of change. In addition, there are significant differences between the cultures of different academic disciplines, their epistemologies and their modes of discourse (Becher, 1987). Not only does this affect, as has been said, the initial approach to an unfamiliar discipline, but it affects the detailed choice of appropriate teaching and learning methods for learning autonomy. To put it at its simplest, historians learn autonomy in the library, physicists in the laboratory, sociologists in the field. This point is of particular importance in project-oriented learning where it is often necessary to call on several disciplines in order to solve a particular problem, and it may be necessary to reconcile simultaneously a number of different academic cultures. It also has serious resource implications for attempts at achieving autonomy at a distance.

Conditions for Autonomy Learning

Autonomy learning is interdependent, i.e., autonomy learners, on their own initiative, learn both from themselves and from others; they establish a relationship of mutuality between themselves and their learning environment. In this they are quite different from 'autodidacts' who deliberately choose to teach themselves in isolation. They are also different from the students in the heady days of the 1968 student revolt, many of whom were as authoritarian towards their teachers as their teachers more usually had been and still are towards them. Mutuality implies mutual respect for each other — teacher and learner — in a common endeavour in which, in principle at least, all is negotiable. In practice, as we shall see, there are limits to what can be negotiated in any particular learning system.

How can this basic condition for autonomy learning be interpreted in terms of the four common components of course design: objectives, content, method and assessment? It is here that the practical limitations are apparent. The most obvious is that of resources. Students may have to adapt their learning objectives to the learning resources — teachers, materials, peers, etc. — available, and this will also affect content. A second limitation arises if students wish, as is almost always the case, for some certification to document their learning achievement. The extent to which assessment can then be negotiated rather than imposed is perhaps the most difficult area of autonomy learning in practice. The course design component where autonomy learning is most easily achieved is undoubtedly that of method. It is for that reason that the earlier sections of this chapter concentrated on methods — both teaching and learning. However, it is surprising how far the principles of autonomous learning can penetrate into the other components of course design, once the method component has provided a sound basis for autonomy.

I started this section by saying that the basic condition for autonomous learning lies in the word 'negotiable' and I have now said that negotiation should start with method. Such negotiation requires a radical power shift in the relationship between teachers and learners, in which teachers have to give up much of their traditional power. This in turn requires an attitudinal change on the part of teachers which is well expressed in the passage with which Boud (1988b) closes his article:

> It is not any technique or teaching methodology which is primarily needed, but an attitude of acceptance and appreciation of the views, desires and frames of reference of learners. Perhaps the single central quality which fosters autonomy is the quality of the relation-ship between teachers and learners which develops through this acceptance.

The idea of negotiation is basic to EHE, but it would be claimimg too much to say that the same is true of mutuality between teacher and learner. Most EHE programmes at present are distinctly hierarchical in this respect.

Autonomy in Distance Learning: Methods

Advantages and Disadvantages of Distance Education

In moving now to distance education, I shall use and reinterpret what has been learned from face-to-face education, as discussed previously. To this I add the important understanding that distance education has features that are usually absent from face-to-face education, or at least less easily available within it, and which may actually help in the promotion of autonomy learning. These relate to:

— flexibility of time
— flexibility of place
— the permanence of written dialogue
— life and work experience.

The deficiencies of distance education which are much better known and are constantly referred to in the literature are primarily in the areas of:

— personal contact with teachers
— contact with fellow students
— learning milieu.

Aims, Processes and Strategies

Not surprisingly, there are no differences in the aims of the autonomous learner, whether face-to-face or at a distance, and the mental activities of choosing, deciding, deliberating, reflecting, planning and judging, quoted earlier from Dearden (1972), remain the same. It is when we come to Boud's (1988b) list of learning objectives, as given earlier, that differences arise, although by no means for all of the objectives. Many can be achieved somewhat more easily when time and place are more flexible, while the following are on the whole very much more easily achieved when the learner can relate directly to life and work experience:

— creating problems to tackle (it may be noted that — in contrast to Boud — I have not put the word problems in inverted commas, for Boud's implication that in some way the problems are not real no longer applies to people who can create the problems they wish to tackle out of their life and work)
— determining criteria to apply to their work
— learning outside the confines of the educational institution, for example in a work setting
— making significant decisions with which they will have to live.

What distance learners will normally find more difficult is:

— finding resources needed for learning.

The two objectives where the balance of advantage is very much harder to assess and which will differ between students are:

— working collaboratively with others
— using teachers as guides and counsellors rather than instructors.

In the face-to-face situation, there is collaborative work with fellow students and personal contact with teachers; at a distance there is collaboration with colleagues at work as well as in other walks of life, and written dialogue with teachers.

It is worth discussing this last point more fully. The usually chosen distance substitute for personal face-to-face tutoring is telephone tutoring which, at best, is face-to-face tutoring minus visual signals. In some instances it may be the most suitable substitute, but there is no plus to balance the minus. Correspondence tutoring has many more minuses, but the permanence of the communication and the possibility to reflect on it are definitely pluses.

Appropriate learning strategies are suggested by the Kolb/Gibbs learning cycle. As was stated earlier, these are essentially unsuitable for dependent learning, whether face-to-face or at a distance, but they are equally suitable for both when learning is autonomous.

The Role of the Teacher

The general role of the teacher, as outlined in the teaching approaches listed previously and highlighted in the Boud quotation at the end of the section on 'Conditions for autonomy learning', is in no way different at a distance compared to face-to-face. However, the three teaching approaches require some adaptations at a distance. These cannot at this stage be more than tentative suggestions, although evidence for their value will be indicated here and presented in more detail later.

1　Individual-centred through a learning contract. With the greater resources available on campus, this is probably easier face-to-face (see, for instance, Percy and Ramsden, 1980), particularly if the learning is of a theoretical kind. However, if the learning is closely related to life and/or work experience, then distance learning is likely to be at an advantage. Furthermore, experience with negotiation by correspondence has shown this not to present insuperable difficulties.

2　Group-centred through group interaction and peer learning. The differences between face-to-face and distance learning situations are substantial here. The role of a local tutor at work is more often that of a facilitator or expert in practice than that of a subject or course expert. Where there is no tutor, the differences between a face-to-face peer group of students and a peer group of students and a peer group of colleagues at work, many of whom are not engaged formally in learning, are so large that no simple comparisons can be made. In addition, there are, of course, peer learning groups in distance education, such as local self-help groups, but these are more likely to work independent learning where the main question before the group is usually a variant of 'What does teacher want us to do?'

3　Project-centred through problem formulation and solution. The situation here is not very different from 1. above except that projects and problems tend to be more effective for learning if they are real, which favours distance learners with their close contact with what educationists call 'reality'. The association of projects with the work situation also helps with the provision of resources, including libraries and facilities for practical work.

Possible Areas of Difficulty

Finally, I wish to turn to the learning objectives which earlier in this section I argued as perhaps less readily achievable at a distance. Because of the difficulty that many distance learners have in obtaining learning resources, most distance teaching has been based on well-structured and highly directed learning materials which are sent to students at regular intervals. That these can achieve their learning objectives much more effectively than much of face-to-face teaching is beyond doubt, but by their very effectiveness they tend to make the student more dependent (Morgan, Taylor and Gibbs, 1982). The answer is not to abandon self instructional materials — they are far too valuable for that — but to modify them so as to allow for movement towards autonomy. Attempts at this will be described later.

The other area of difficulty concerns tutoring and counselling. If tutoring is done by correspondence, then experience indicates that it requires far more time, skill and application on the part of the tutor than may normally be found in 'essay marking' on campus. However, if this is provided, then it can be more effective than either campus essay marking or the traditional group tutorial. It all depends on how well any of these are done. Furthermore, to be done well at a distance requires considerable tutor time. The result is that for autonomous learning at a distance, the major cost is in tutoring and not in the preparation of materials. Tutor numbers must go up in proportion to student numbers, and this means that there are far fewer economies of scale. For autonomous learning, small institutions may then be more cost-effective, since they do not need so large an administrative apparatus as large ones (see, for instance, Elton, 1981). The biggest cost-saving through distance education in any case arises from students remaining in employment, as is now well recognized by employers.

What has been said for correspondence tutoring is probably not valid for counselling, where the direct interpersonal element is so important. Let me, therefore, readily concede that distance education here is a second best.

Although there are obviously features in the methods of distance learning that do not apply to face-to-face EHE, the correspondences are nevertheless striking. Independent and self-instructional learning, relating learning to life and work experience, collaborating with colleagues at work, learning contracts, project-centred learning and tutor feedback are all important features of EHE

Autonomy in Distance Learning: Objectives, Content and Assessment

I have already indicated that objectives and content in autonomous learning are circumscribed by the learning resources available, but there is no difference here, compared to face-to-face teaching. Beyond that, they cause few difficulties, since they should be either negotiated in the initial learning contract or arise naturally from the formulation of projects and problems. Again, there is no difference here between face-to-face and distance learning.

Similarly, the very real difficulties in negotiated assessment arise equally in both forms of learning. There is however, the additional difficulty at a distance of ensuring that the coursework done by students really is their own work. The solution used in dependent learning — to assess students in the main through formal examinations — is unacceptable in autonomous learning where no two students have the same learning objectives and expected outcomes. Fortunately, it is this very feature of autonomous learning which makes it difficult for students to obtain improper assistance. Their situation is very similar to that of research students who submit a thesis; during their work they have had assistance, which is right and proper, from many sources, but the final work which they present is their own. That is not to say that cheating is impossible; after all it is always possible for a student's PhD thesis to be written by someone else. Such cheating may be detectable through an oral examination on the student's work and the same remedy could be used in autonomous distance learning.

To assess students in the main through formal examinations is equally unacceptable in EHE and, as for autonomy learning, much of the assessment should be linked to negotiated learning contracts.

Autonomy Learning at a Distance in Practice

How autonomy learning at a distance has been put into practice will be illustrated through the experience with two courses: a postgraduate diploma in 'The Practice of Higher Education' at the University of Surrey (Elton, Oliver and Wray, 1986) and 'Education for Adults' at the Open University (Taylor and Kaye, 1986). Since both have been described previously, I shall concentrate here on those of their features which relate to the ideas presented in the present chapter. It is noteworthy that, in spite of the obvious similarities, the courses were developed independently of each other.

Both courses use self-instructional materials which include a wide range of readings in support of study guides that themselves provide a commentary rather than straight teaching: both allow flexibility in the order in which the material is studied and they do not have behavioural objectives. In both, most assignments require course members to relate what they have learned to personal and/or work experience. In this way the authoritarian nature of traditional course materials is much reduced. The Surrey course goes further in that all assignments relate to members' ongoing work and that members are actively encouraged to collaborate with colleagues, even if these are not taking the course. It is this feature which provides the potential for peer dialogue and group discussion. Assignments also are not necessarily accepted on first submission; but irrespective of whether they are accepted or not, they lead to extensive tutoring by correspondence. The Surrey course also allows members to re-negotiate the content of assignments if the original assignment statement is inappropriate for a particular course member.

Both courses have flexible scheduling. However, the Surrey course, which is not bound by examination regulations in the way the OU course is and where all assessment is through coursework, allows all deadlines to be negotiated. Both use project work, in which the students take the initiative, and which forms the major area of negotiation. Even here, negotiation by correspondence has been found possible, although not always easy. The Surrey course is assessed wholly on the basis of assignments and projects, the OU course substantially so.

Where the Surrey course goes beyond the OU course is that it leads on to a Master's degree, in which course members first learn research methods with the help of further course materials and then go on to a dissertation based on their own research. In this, both topic and research design are of their own choice, based on their work surroundings and agreed in negotiation with course staff. At this point, correspondence tutoring becomes supervision at a distance. From enrolment on the Diploma to the completion of the thesis there is a constant progression towards learning autonomy.

Naturally, such progression towards learning autonomy is not achieved uniformly and, particularly in the early stages of both the Surrey and OU courses, many students find the greater freedom and responsibility given to them hard to handle. Neither course has diagnostic means to assess readiness for autonomy work; experience with the Surrey course has shown that progressive tutorial guidance may well be adequate to meet this problem when it is seen to arise. This guidance may start with 'telling', but it soon goes on to 'selling' and 'participating'. At the Master's level it frequently reaches the 'delegating' stage.

Since both courses are in the education area, it has not been possible to verify the extent to which the measures taken to achieve autonomy are subject-specific. Here is a challenge for those who teach other subjects at a distance.

Conclusions

There is considerable correspondence between the ideas to achieve autonomy, put forward in the earlier part of this chapter, and the practices of the two courses described in the last section. The most important features of these practices, present in one or both of the courses are:

— negotiable structures, assignments and assessment
— modification of self-instructional materials and of assignments to allow for autonomy learning
— heavy emphasis on correspondence tutoring
— relationship of learning to ongoing life and work experience
— involvement of colleagues at work
— culmination of course in project and research work.

The conditions under which these practices can flourish are very different from those which pertain to most of distance learning. They require courses to be such that:

— there is freedom to negotiate
— there are no detailed behavioural objectives
— costing does not depend on economy of scale

— course materials encourage the use of life and work experience
— assignments benefit from students' relationships to colleagues at work
— genuinely independent activities, such as research projects, are included.

What has been demonstrated — admittedly on a limited scale — is that courses which work within these conditions exist and work successfully, and their success demonstrates that autonomy learning at a distance is possible. This is important, particularly since the only reference to distance teaching in the book (Boud, 1988a), which has been put to such good use in this chapter, is to its authoritarian form (Knapper, 1988, p. 102).

One might almost conclude that students on an EHE programme should be taught at a distance in preference to face-to-face.

Acknowledgments

My thanks are due to Dr Elizabeth Beaty and Dr Peter Jarvis for most helpful discussions — both face-to-face and at a distance — and to Dr Patricia Cryer for many suggestions which increased the clarity of this paper.

This chapter originally appeared in *Programmed Learning and Educational Technology*, 25, 3, August 1988, pp. 216–24.

References

BECHER, T. (1987) 'Disciplinary discourse', *Studies in Higher Education*, 12, 261–74.

BOUD, D. (Ed.) (1988a) *Developing Student Autonomy in Learning* (2nd edn), London, Kogan Page.

BOUD, D. (1988b) 'Moving towards autonomy', in ch. 1., BOUD, D. (Ed.) (1988a).

CANDY, P. (1988) 'On the attainment of subject-matter autonomy', in ch. 3, BOUD, D. (Ed.) (1988a).

CROCKETT, W.H. (1965) 'Cognitive complexity and impression formation', in MAHER, B.A. (Ed.) *Progress in Experimental Personality Research*, Vol. 2, pp. 47–90, New York, Academic Press.

CRYER, P. (1987) 'Insights into participants' reactions to new ideas in educational games, simulations and workshops; an application of catastrophe theory', *Simulations/Games for Learning*, 17, pp. 172–81.

DEARDEN, R.F. (1972) 'Autonomy and education', in DEARDEN, R.F., HIRST, P.F. and PETERS, R.S. (Eds) *Education and Development of Reason*, pp. 448–65, London, Routledge and Kegan Paul.

EISNER, E.W. (1985) *The Art of Educational Evaluation*, ch. 3., London, Falmer Press.

ELTON, L. (1981) 'Academic staff development through distance learning', in

PERCIVAL, F. and ELLINGTON, H. (Eds) *Aspects of Educational Technology* XV, pp. 91–5, London, Kogan Page.

ELTON, L. (1982) 'Assessment for learning', in BLIGH, D. (Ed.) *Professionalism and Flexibility in Learning*, pp. 106–35, Guildford, Society for Research into Higher Education.

ELTON, L. (1987) 'Student autonomy in distance learning', *Media in Education and Development*, March, pp. 14–15.

ELTON, L., OLIVER, E. and WRAY, M. (1986) 'Academic staff training at a distance — A case study', *PLET*, 23, 29–40.

ENCKEVORT, G. VAN (1986) 'Distance education for adult students: From old to new barriers for participation', in ENCKEVORT, G. VAN *et al.* (Eds) *Innovations in Distance Education*, section 2.4, Dutch Open University, Heerlen.

FARNES, N. (1975) 'Student centred learning', *Teaching at a Distance*, 3, pp. 2–6.

FELDMAN, D.H. (1980) *Beyond Universals in Cognitive Development*, New Jersey, Ablex, Norwood.

GIBBS, G. (1987) *Learning by Doing*, Birmingham, Educational Development Unit, Birmingham Polytechnic.

GUGLIELMINO, L.M. (1977) 'Development of the selfdirected learning readiness scale', doctoral thesis, University of Georgia.

HIGGS, J. (1988) 'Planning learning experiences to promote autonomous learning', ch. 2, in BOUD, D. (Ed.) (1988a).

INGLIS, P. (1987) 'Distance teaching is dead! Long live distance learning', *ICDE Bulletin*, 15, September, pp. 47–52.

JARVIS, P. (1981) 'The Open University Course Unit — pedagogy or andragogy?', *Teaching at a Distance*, 20, 24–9.

KNAPPER, C. (1988) 'Technology and lifelong learning', in ch. 5, BOUD, D. (Eds) (1988a).

KNOWLES, M.S. (1975) *Self-Directed Learning: A Guide for Learners and Teachers*, Chicago, Associated Press.

KOLB, D.A. (1984) *Experiential Learning — Experience as the Source of Learning and Development*, New Jersey, Prentice-Hall.

LEWIN, K. (1952) *Field Theory in the Social Sciences*, London, Tavistock Publications.

MORGAN, A. (1983) 'Theoretical aspects of project based learning in higher education', *British Journal of Educational Technology*, 14, 66–78.

MORGAN, A., TAYLOR, E. and GIBBS, G. (1982) 'Variations in students' approaches to studying', *British Journal of Educational Technology*, 14, 107–13.

PERCY, K. and RAMSDEN, P. (1980) *Independent Study*, Guildford, Society for Research into Higher Education.

PERRY, W.G. (1970) *Forms of Intellectual and Ethical Development in the College Years: A Scheme*, New York, Holt, Rinehart and Winston.

RAMSDEN, P. (1984) 'The context of learning', in MARTON, F., HOUNSELL, D. and ENTWHISTLE, N.J. (Eds) The Experience of Learning, pp. 144–64, Edinburgh, Scottish Academic Press.

RAMSDEN, P. (1987) 'Improving teaching and learning in higher education: the case for a relational perspective', *Studies in Higher Education*, 12, 275–86.

SNYDER, B.R. (1971) *The Hidden Curriculum*, Knopf, New York.

TAYLOR, E. and KAYE, T. (1986) 'Andragogy by design? Control and self-direction in the design of an Open University course', *PLET*, 23, pp. 62–9.

Chapter 10

Changes in Funding:
A College Response

Keith Cook and Geoff Crook

This chapter is a case study of the ways in which one particular public sector provider — Newham Community College — has responded to changes in funding policies.

Background

The 1950s and 1960s were a time of fairly confident and consistent growth for public sector FE. Provision was moved away from scattered, make-shift premises and classrooms borrowed from local schools into purpose-built institutions. Money was not only generally available to fund increased provision and staffing, but could be obtained via two simple routes — the Local Authority's general rate levy supplemented by central government support through the Rate Support Grant, and income derived from course fees. Elected members decided how much of their education budget they wished to spend on further education and how much could be retrieved from fees. It was certainly still possible, even in 1980, to work in a college which was an essentially publicly funded institution, running courses for students, the funding for which came in an uncomplicated way from the local council. However, major changes in funding arrangements for further education, dating from the early 1970s, produced by the mid-1980s an environment of such turbulence that some commentators were led to question the possibilities of the survival of public sector further education.

Funding Changes

One major shift has been the way in which central government has implemented political changes in funding mechanisms in order to change the shape of the educational system. The Rate Support Grant, the biggest single contributor to Local Authority finance, has been significantly affected by this process. In the early 1970s, RSG was a block grant with a built-in allowance for inflation which both allowed local authorities to increase expenditure in line with the rising costs of service provision and supplied a fair amount of local autonomy by allowing them the freedom to vire money between services. However, when it became apparent in the 1970s that the rate of inflation in Local Authority expenditure considerably exceeded that of the national economy as a whole, and possibly even that of central government, a series of controls were applied which have had the effect of decreasing the proportion of the total expenditure of local government that is supported from central government through RSG by around 15 percentage points; locally raised taxation now provides 60 per cent to the 40 per cent available through RSG, compared to the 40/60 per cent ratio in the seventies. And, in addition to squeezing the overall amount of cash available, these controls have had the further effect of making the amount of money available to a Local Authority less determined by local political decisions on how much to spend and more a consequence of national political decisions on how much grant to give.

Increasingly sophisticated and complex methods of trying to use the Rate Support Grant to influence the spending of local authorities in a downward direction were used throughout this period. 'Taper' and 'penalty' prevented Local Authorities from exceeding targets based on previous years' figures. Volume planning with cash limits (1976–1981) removed from Local Authorities the capacity to determine for themselves the money needed to supply local services (Heald, 1983). Aggregate cash planning (1982 onwards) made assumptions about inflation which tended to under-represent the reality (Henley *et al.*, 1986). The attempt to regulate 'over-spending' authorities led to the introduction of rate capping and the Community Charge, both of which further squeezed the revenue available to local authorities. It is important also to remember that, as far as FE is specifically concerned, the calculations which determine RSG take into account only the number of full-time students and part-time, day or block release students aged 16–19 and nothing else, so that the college which takes as some of its prime targets those groups of people liable to benefit from a local service — unemployed people, adult returners, evening students, people with special learning needs, etc. — receives no additional help from RSG.

Another aspect of this tightening of political control was the way in which central government attempted to ensure that resources spent at a local level tallied with nationally defined objectives. The most obvious example as far as education is concerned was the Educational Support Grant mechanism introduced in 1984 (Education Grants and Awards Act) whereby central government held back a small proportion — around 2 per cent — of overall block grant support to Local Authorities which they were then free to bid for under DES-agreed priority areas. The areas originally relating to FE were PICKUP, the development and use of information technology, guidance and educational provision for the unemployed, provision of management information systems, computer-aided learning for people with special educational needs, and the employment of staff to strength links between FE and industry. Nobody would wish to argue that the objectives were less than totally worthy. However, the money designated to achieve them was not additional to the FE budget — nor was money diverted from other activities.

Fragmentation

A second major shift taking place during these years has been the diversification of the number and location of funding sources available to the education system. There has been a great increase in the number of national bodies and 'arms' length' agencies which are able to offer money for the achievement of specific educational objectives. The effect of this, apart from continuing the process of distributing roughly the same amount of money among a proliferation of sources, has been to multiply the number of agencies which have an influence over the provision delivered by the local college and with which the college therefore needs to consult and liaise. Bower provides a comprehensive list of funding sources which have emerged since 1970 (Bower, 1985). The agency which most people will be aware of is the Training Agency (established in 1974 as the Manpower Services Commission), but Section 11 and DTI money can be considered as part of the same process.

Performance Criteria

A third major shift has been the expectation on the part of central government that colleges should both provide 'value for money' by developing mechanisms for demonstrating efficiency and effectiveness, and generate a significant proportion of their own income by engaging in entrepreneurial activities. 'Training for Jobs', 'Competence and Competition', 'Challenge to Complacency', 'The Responsive College Programme', and 'Managing Colleges Efficiently' were a series of quite major developments all of which occurred between 1984 and 1989 and all of which were pushing public sector FE to adopt the ideology of the market place.

If we consider these shifts in conjunction with other developments impacting upon the public sector at the same time, we can see that the FE context in the 1980s and 1990s is characterised by finance-led change, the fragmentation of decision-making and changes in its locations, a move towards 'privatization', the need for the college to state its objectives much more clearly and to plan and account for what it does in a much more open way, the gradual decrease in the amount of money available from traditional sources, and the increasing use of intermediaries in a situation of increasing complexity and confusion. This context has major implications for the managers of the college and has led to the concept of the 'boundary spanner', defined by David Parkes in the late 1980s:

> One increasingly finds people (who might be called 'mavericks') who need to be given a free rein, who are allowed to 'get on with it'; to act as buffers between the environment and the rest of the organization and they are people who hold some position of influence when the environment is heterogeneous and shifting. They have to manage across boundaries, bring together protagonists among different sectors and different institutions very often just for temporary solutions and only intermediate outcomes. They are the key managers of the next ten years. (Parkes, 1986)

Newham Community College

The experiences of Newham Community College in coming to terms with the new context provide an interesting case study in the management of finance-influenced change. The college itself, formed in 1986 from the merger of the two institutions which had formerly served the borough, is now one of the largest Further and Higher Education colleges in the country with a wide and varied programme of further, higher, and adult education courses; apart from secondary schools, it is the Authority's single provider of post-16 education and training. Newham itself is ranked by the DES as the second most deprived local authority in England as measured by standard socio-economic indicators. Two studies published in 1989 gave rise to great concern about the level of educational achievement (Hegarty *et al.*, 1989); in terms of exam results Newham has one of the lowest levels of performance of any LEA in England; it has the second worst record in the country for progression to higher education (Toyne *et al.*, 1989). The borough has a rich ethnic mix, with over a quarter of its population originating from the New Commonwealth and Pakistan. The southern third of Newham is undergoing massive changes as a result of the activities of the London Docklands Development Corporation; old vocational skills have become redundant and new ones are being demanded.

The overall College budget in the year preceding the introduction of the community charge and local financial management was £13.3 million, with income being split almost equally between the Local Authority and other sources. It broke down roughly as follows: —

* RSG and locally levied rates: 7.3 million combined
* Recoupment   2.4 million
* Student Fees: 1.5 million

— 40 per cent of students pay no fees (16–18 year olds on full-time courses or part-time day courses), 20 per cent pay concessionary fees, and only

40 per cent pay standard fees: the concessionary fee tranche is probably larger than the national average).

* Full cost courses   1.12 million

— these are courses charged to individuals, employers, or agencies such as the TA; the proportion of income deriving from full-cost work is probably one of the highest in the country.

* WRFE Grant   0.7 million
* Section 11 money: 0.08 million
* ESG: 0.2 Million

Protecting 'Community' Provision

An immediate issue facing the College was the extent to which it would be able to maintain its commitment to those types of provision which have a high priority in 'community' terms but which could never be self-financing — in particular, provision for people with special learning needs, adult basic education (ABE), Access, English for Speakers of Other Languages (ESOL). It is clear, at the end of the first three years of its existence, that the College has managed to protect these 'needy' areas, and has done so by means of a three-fold strategy.

The first aspect of the strategy comprises the determination by the local authority and the institution that such areas exist and that they need to be protected. If areas of community-based provision are clearly identified and prioritized, the local authority will then have to target money into the institution to enable it to deliver them. Newham Community College was, in fact, established as part of the Authority's commitment to provide a unified, community-based, post-16 education system responsive to the needs of the community and more accountable to the LEA. Some of the issues which the College was specifically created to address were as follows:

* the inaccessibility of FE to the wider community
* the changing patterns and types of employment
* the increase in long-term structural unemployment
* the retraining needs of older age-groups
* equal opportunities with special reference to the needs of women, ethnic minorities, disabled people, and those with special educational needs.

Unless both the authority and the institution have clear and unambiguous policy statements articulating their commitment to the type of provision they wish to enable locally, the danger will always exist that such provision will be marginalised or be swept away entirely by pressures inside the institution for a whole-hearted adoption of an entrepreneurial culture in the interests of survival.

The second aspect of the strategy concerns the composition of the governing body. As the crucial mechanism in ensuring the delivery of the local authority policy objectives, the governing body will also need to be committed to the protection of needy areas; it will clearly help, therefore, it its composition is sympathetic from the outset. NCC deliberately set out to establish a governing body with as high a 'community' representation as possible, within the guidelines laid down by the DES; at the moment, of the 20 governors, the balance is as follows:

* seven with experience of local industry and equipment
* one to represent the interests of people with special education needs
* one to represent the speakers of languages other than English
* one to represent adult and non-vocational education
* one to represent the interests of women seeking to enter or re-enter the labour market
* one from the Newham Commission for Racial Equality
* two staff representatives
* two student representative
* four local authority nominees

One the surface, the composition of this governing body is one that the DES could justifiably have rejected on the grounds that it would not supply a sufficiently employment-oriented leadership. The fact that it was accepted demonstrates what can be achieved given the political will, commitment, and expertise at local authority and institutional levels. DES acceptance came at the end of protracted negotiation: the fact that the college had always been assiduous in making and nurturing contacts at FESC, the FEU, and the DES itself obviously played a part; the fact that the draft Instrument of Government was carefully couched and the result of meticulous preparation was important; the name of the College — its 'community' designation — no doubt added weight; and, above all, it was the cogency of a carefully argued and tenaciously-supported case that influenced the DES into making exceptions in the case of a particular college in a particular geographical area. The balance of reasons is of less importance than the general point that the institution does not simply have to accept central government directives — creative management will always find room to manoeuvre.

The third aspect of the strategy was concerned with according the identified needy areas a high status within the institution. The College approached this in two ways. The first was to increase significantly the number and gradings of posts allocated to the development and delivery of the provision in question and to resource developments which would encourage the relevant client groups to use the institution — new approaches to marketing, more drop-in workshop delivery, access facilities for people with disabilities, etc. Within three years the College had appointed a special needs team of ten led by a Head of Department, and comprised senior lecturers in equal opportunities (for race and gender) and school links, staff at senior and principal lecturer grades for ABE, and specialist student adviser; their task has been to integrate special needs provision into departmental practices to ensure that it is a part of a college service rather than something owned and controlled by 'specialists'. Given the financial constraints mentioned earlier, this has not been easy, but it illustrates the general point that, no matter what the context, management always has choices. Clearly, in the case of NCC, choosing to resource and protect 'needy' areas has had implications for the manner in which other areas have been resourced and delivered.

The second way of according needy areas a high status within the institution has been to take advantage of a freedom allowed by ERA; if an LEA wishes to protect a needy area and the Secretary of State approves, it can be designated as a programme area, given a high weighting, and have higher FTEs allocated to it; in the case of Newham, as can be seen from the list below, this was done in respect of special needs and ABE:

* Work-related (Workshop)   1.2
* Work-related (Classroom)   1.0
* Pre-Vocational and Academic   1.0
* Essential Skills   1.3
* Community support   1.3
* Special Educational Needs   2.0

If the College chooses to deviate from its declared intention, it has to justify its actions to the authority — if deviation is judged to constitute 'a cavalier disregard of the authority's intentions', then the college stands to be substantially penalised. For example, if the authority decides to allocate 100 FTEs to ABE but the college chooses to recruit only sixty because it decides that it is more important to recruit an additional forty sheet-metal workers, the LEA would have no obligation to allocate 100 FTEs in ABE the following year — it might allocate only the sixty the college had taken on; nor would it have any obligation to pay for the forty extra sheet-metal workers that it had not decided that it wanted. This illustrates clearly that the concept of a post-ERA atmosphere in which principals are free to do much as they like is largely misguided. In the case of Newham, the authority hands over more than £7 million a year to the College, approximately half of its budget. The authority does not have to do this, any more than it has to continue using the College to deliver its post-16 provision; if it wished to resource another institution as a free-standing provider, managed directly by the LEA with no delegation and no governors, there would be nothing to stop them from so doing. The LEA will continue to be NCC's biggest customer and, just as the College has to be responsible to the needs of other paying customers, it will have to be responsive to the perceived needs of the LEA.

Very Special Grants

A second area in which the college has had a great deal of experience is in the attraction and use of specific project funding and of relatively small special grants of the ESG variety. The College has already been involved in the Responsive College Programme (TA/FESC), the Accreditation of Prior Learning Project (TA/NCVQ), the Work-Based Learning Project (TA/FESC), has attracted funding to develop Flexible Learning, Competence Led Curricula and Equity, and has made successful bids to The Institute of Education Post-16 Centre, The Training Agency (Access to HE Strategy Development), PICKUP, and many others. Such funding sources raise a number of issues related to institutional change and the management of such change. How permeable are institutions to such grants? Do programme values and processes penetrate other institutional areas? What sites of resistance are there? Are such grants actually steering individual colleges toward the achievement of what central government perceives as national priorities? The Newham experience points to the following emergent themes.

The first is that, successful though the College has been in attracting small grants and special project funding, it has never applied for any grant, large or small, just for the money. Such funding has never been viewed as a mechanism which might provide a helpful margin of manoeuvrability to a tight budget which has been committed well in advance (although it cannot be denied that the influx of such funding does sometimes have this unsought-for advantage). The funding is seen from the outset as a device which will act as a potential lever of change, but — and this is a crucial principle of strategic management which has certainly been disregarded in some institutions — the change has to be in a direction to which College senior management is committed before applying for the grant. Where management has wanted the College to go in the direction the grant promised to take it, the grant has been applied for with alacrity and the resultant funding has sometimes shown almost immediate results. For example, the College should not today have a share in a high street ABE Centre had it not been successful in bidding to ALBSU for development funding: however, it would almost certainly have had one in a year or so's time. Equally, the transformation of the College's publicity materials would have taken a lot longer to achieve had the College not been involved in the Responsive College Programme. For NCC, then, small grants and special grants do not so much shape what the College provides as allow it to provide what it wants earlier than might otherwise have been possible.

A corollary of this approach is that, where the College does have a clear and articulated set of developmental objectives, it can scrutinise funding sources available to determine whether it can present the developmental objectives in such a way that it will qualify for one of the grants being offered. For example, when the College was developing efficiency and effectiveness indicators through its involvement with the Responsive College

Programme, John Baillie, the College principal, originated the idea of 'equity', a third performance indicator dimension which would measure the extent to which a college was characterized by fairness, impartiality, and comprehensiveness in delivering its services to a local community. At this stage it was not possible to make a bid to the 'equity grant' to institute a research and development project, since such a funding source did not exist. It was possible, though, to re-shape the project objectives to make them acceptable to other funding agencies. So, what was, from the College perspective, a management information development, was divided into two, and one half sent to the TA as a market research project, and the other half sent to the FEU as a curriculum development project. This might seem a round about, and time-consuming way of attracting funding but it illustrates something which should be a source of encouragement to colleges: there can be a dialectical relationship between the agencies which have the money and the institutions which need it. The institution can help shape the national system — 'equity' has certainly become an issue of national interest and resources are now being made available to promote it. Colleges do not have to view themselves as powerless victims of inexorable external forces which are trying to change them against their will. Action at the individual college level can help shape the national scene.

A second theme is that institutions are not inherently permeable to the effects of initiatives which carry short-term funding; internal mechanisms for embedding change need to be identified by senior management as part of the agenda which leads to the original application for funding. The organizational structure of the institution can be a great barrier to change — departments, for example, are not unknown to regard the special project as a threat, something which will provoke territorial disputes and erode departmental autonomy. The size of the institution and issues of ownership — the extent to which change is perceived as being imposed from outside — will play a part. It is also quite possible for college staff to argue at least a superficial case that change is not needed: the client plays an important role in determining the FE offer, and most colleges are still finding that clients are happy to sign up for traditional courses delivered in traditional ways; every year, NCC finds that most of its courses are full within the first two days of main enrolment and that it needs to compile long waiting lists of demands that it is unable to meet. It is clear that both primary and secondary clients are to some extent acting as barriers to change — most do not seem, at the time of writing, to be ready for services like modular delivery, accreditation of prior learning, or flexible/customized delivery systems. Developments which affect the traditional curriculum offer need to be marketed to employers and potential primary clients as well as to college staff. And, in this context, marketing implies much more than arrangements for generalized consciousness raising: it is certainly the case, within Newham, that the new experiences introduced into the institution by special grants have left few staff entirely untouched, but it is equally clear that change, unless actively managed, can become institutionalized rather than institutional, something which affects surface rather than deep structures.

Two specific change-management strategies seem to have been effective within NCC. The first arises from the fact that there are now within the College a significant number of staff — around thirty — who have had experience of working on a variety of nationally-funded projects or whose posts have been temporarily funded by means of small grants. These people have been used very much in the cross-college, 'boundary-spanning' role mentioned earlier — senior management have given them free rein to disseminate project findings throughout the College via departmental staff meetings, special events, and staff training sessions, and to act as consultants to departments wishing to initiate change. It is significant that these 'boundary-spanners', although operating at main grade or senior lecturer level, have acquired status in what was at first quite a hierarchical institution and are able to interact on an equal footing with Heads of Department. The second strategy arose in 1989/90 when College management decided to apply the national 'special project' model to the internal development of the College. Three per cent of the hours which would normally have been available to departments through the curriculum offer were held back in a central pool and HoD's were invited to submit proposals indicating how they would use the hours to make their curriculum delivery more flexible. The result is that there are currently sixty-two internal development projects running in the College at the departmental level covering areas such as the development of workshops, modularized curricula, open learning packages, the accreditation of prior learning, and so on.

A third theme is that a great deal of expertise and energy is needed to attract such grants in the first place. Neither authorities nor colleges have to bid for such grants. In many cases, even at senior management level, people simply do not know that the grants exist; if the relevant LA officer is not well acquainted with current developments, or is unsympathetic to them, then news of funding opportunities might not even reach the college. Making successful bids is about much more than authorship skills or the ability to put a good submission together — important though these are. The development and maintenance of contacts is crucial — regular phone calls to relevant funding officers and regular attendance at conferences and training events where contacts can be made and renewed. The Newham experience goes against the commonly expressed view that the amount of effort required to attract the funding is wasted given the relatively small sums of money involved: success in attracting funding leads to further success, and the process becomes easier as it continues. A great deal of the funding attracted by NCC has been the result of funding obtained earlier: involvement in the Responsive College Programme led directly to funding for the Adequacy and Equity projects; involvement in the EDAP project lead to involvement in an FEU project on Advice and Guidance; the fact that senior staff were involved in consultancy work for the TA paved the way to the NVQ projects. The

College has now reached the point where it is invited to become involved in special projects by funding agencies.

Cost Recovery Activities

There is no doubt that the opportunity and the need to make money will affect the curriculum offering and balance of the individual college. The increasing costs of operating in some areas — for example, retail and construction — virtually impose an income-generating mode on public sector providers. Where the Local Authority has no commitment to community-based provision, or the sort of provision aimed at client groups who can only take it up if it is supplied at concessionary rates, then there is no doubt that such provision will be marginalized and could disappear. There is already evidence to suggest that some authorities and colleges have already decided to market themselves virtually exclusively to income-generating markets and run only those courses which are self-financing. Others are already reluctantly accepting the need to reduce the proportion of non-paying courses in the interests of survival. From the middle-1980s, some colleges were attempting to cope with the problem by adopting private company status and running part of their operation as an arms-length agency, with no apparent connection with the main college, in order to attract business from industry and commerce at commercial rates of return.

The situation in Newham is different. While the need to generate income has been embraced and has led to significant methods of delivery, a conscious decision was taken not to have two very different colleges running side by side. Senior management was determined not to segregate staff into those who were totally occupied in cost recovery activity and those who were not. Such a division would ensure that the benefits of cost recovery activity did not affect the rest of the college and the publicly funded curriculum. If cost recovery activities generate new capital equipment and better learning facilities, the view is taken that they should benefit all students and not just those fortunate enough to be able to pay full cost. Similarly, the benefits which accrue to staff from being involved in industry-related cost-recovery work — acquaintance with current developments in industry and commerce, the acquisition of new skills, and the knowledge of up-to-date techniques — should be put at the disposal of the publicly-funded curriculum and its clients.

There exists, in effect, in cost and planning terms, a Chinese wall between the cost recovery activities and the publicaly funded curriculum. Profits from short notice income generating (SNIG) work — from each individual cost recovery activity — are negotiated in advance; departments put up a proposal about how much they should retain and how much should go to the College, and the Principal then decides whether to accept that recommendation or to vary it.

A fairly extreme, but factual example, shows how the opportunity to make money can be to the unalloyed benefit of all college users. One departmental SNIG form indicates that one customer who had paid the full commercial rate for a place on a specialized vocational certification courses was attending on an infill basis, the tenth person on a course which would have run anyway with the numbers enrolled. The income was therefore surplus and had no negative effects on the balance of the institution — the course was not being run in place of something else. The institutional effects of entrepreneurialism were all positive: the host department picked up half of the total fee with which it bought some new equipment for the use of all of its students and the College will use the other half towards enhancements for the reception area of one of its centres, to the benefit of all college users.

Newham has not taken the view that it has to choose between either 'community' or 'commercial' goals; these options have always existed and the College has always combined both. ERA will undoubtedly make the difference between them clearer for most members of staff, and new systems the College has developed for recycling money should actually make the benefits of cost-recovery activities clearer. What the College will probably move towards is not so much a profit-making curriculum but one which operates at less of a loss than the traditional FE curriculum. Fees for primary clients might need to be increased slightly, or graduated scales of fees introduced.

An important aspect of cost-recovery work is the way in which profit is defined. Given that the College is still publicly funded to a very large extent, it makes sense to take marginal costs, rather than average costs, as the determining factor, since the buildings and the bulk of the staff are already paid for. In this situation, there is no reason at all why the College should not both carry on its 'ordinary' work and be much healthier financially at the same time. Clearly, though, there is a point at which lack of public funding will steer the curriculum offer of the institution more emphatically in the direction of fee-paying customers. In prosperous areas, where there is a substantial middle-class market prepared to pay high fees, community based courses could be subsidized and maintained. But where both public funding and a fee-paying audience are absent, prospects will be bleak — not just because of the absence of money but also because the energies of all staff will be consumed by developing new income generating markets.

One major effect that the opportunity to make money will certainly have, will be the need to increase the resources devoted to staff development activities. The culture and historical experience of colleges differ greatly. Some institutions have always been in the market-place and will simply find themselves extending the range of cost-recovery activities. Others, often those in the inner-city or in economically deprived areas, have perhaps been very, very slow to seize the opportunities that there are to run full-cost courses and to get business — in fact, they probably do not have the skills and expertise to do it.

The Effects of ERA

It is difficult at the time of writing to speculate on the effects that ERA will have on the situation described above. NCC will not be faced with the redistribution of money among colleges which will almost certainly be a consequence of post-ERA formula-funding in multi-college authorities. The fact that the LA will be arriving at a budget figure based on a programme-led aggregation procedure, rather than by looking at historic levels of expenditure in respect of staffing or costs as has been done in the past, will not necessarily have any significant effect on the final one-line budget figure. What will change will be how far the authority will be monitoring the extent to which the target student intake matches the reality, in order to adjust the budget in future years; there will be a clearer line of accountability than there has been up to now.

One aspect of ERA which will almost certainly cause problems arises from the fact that it makes no allowance for unforeseen, and unforeseeable, circumstances. Potential pay awards, for example, are built into the one-line budget at a level which will almost certainly fall short of the reality, a further example of central government attempting to reduce public sector spending and achieve a significant tightening of staff: student ratios. Universities and voluntary colleges have already had experience of this, and in both cases there have been redundancies and the freezing of posts in order to stay within the budget figures agreed on a basis which turned out to be quite inaccurate. There is no reason to believe that this will not happen to the FE sector.

TECs will clearly have an impact on public sector FE and it is too early to say exactly what it will be. When TECs take over the present TA area office budgets for employment training and Youth Training then a college like NCC will notice little difference: if TECs were to take over responsibility for the WRFE funding and decide to use it in the public sector, then the average college would have to make sure that the sort of provision it is prepared to offer is the sort of provision that the TEC wants to invest in or persuade its member employers to invest in. On balance, the signs are at the moment that TECs will be important as a means of steering the system rather than because of their direct contribution to the costs of maintaining and running a college.

There certainly will be changes in detail post ERA which will combine to give the college more freedom of action on a day-to-day level. But political realities are not liable to change. Successful colleges will still be those which have clear and coherent development policies and plans, and which exercise the capacity for creative choice among conflicting demands. It is significant that NCC, given its wide remit to provide for the educational and training needs of a whole community, is currently implementing a three-year development programme called 'Quality Education For ALL'.

References

BOWER, T. (1985) *Sources of Funding Education, 14–19*, Bristol, FESC.

HEALD, D. (1983) *Public Expenditure*, Martin Robertson,

HEGARTY, S. *et al.* (1989) *Boosting Educational Achievement*, Commissioned by London Borough of Newham.

HENLEY, D. *et al* (1986) *Public Sector Financing and Financial Control*, Van Nostrand Reinhold.

PARKES, D. (1986) FE — *Preoccupations and Trends in the late 1980s* Bristol, FESC.

TOYNE *et al.* (1989) *Higher Education in Newham*, Commissioned by London Borough of Newham.

Chapter 11

NVQs and the Man-Made Fibres Industry: A Case Study of Courtaulds Grafil Ltd

Lorna Unwin

This case study examines the reasons for and consequences of one company's decision to completely restructure its approach to training by introducing National Vocational Qualifications (NVQs). The case study will show how such a major shift in the company's approach to training has highlighted the need for radical changes in both the shopfloor and management organization. In financial terms the switch to a competence based system will cost the company some half a million pounds, money which comes straight out of profits. In human resource terms, the changes have led, in eighteen months, to a complete halt in labour turnover which had been averaging 25 per cent a year and in some parts of the plant as much as 50 per cent.

Background

Courtaulds Grafil Ltd, based in Coventry, is Europe's largest producer of carbon fibre and has a sister plant in Sacramento, California. Grafil is one of a number of individually managed companies which together form Courtaulds Advanced Materials and which in turn is part of Courtaulds plc, one of the UK's largest industrial enterprises.

Grafil's fibres are used in a diverse range of industries and products ranging from aeroplanes and Formula One racing cars to fishing rods and tennis racquets. In order to maintain its position as one of the world's leading carbon fibre manufacturers and meet the requirements of BS5750 quality standards, Grafil has introduced a Total Quality Management programme. Standards-based training, as encompassed in National Vocational Qualifications (NVQs) is seen by the company as the most effective vehicle for achieving the aims of that programme. In addition to the quality factor, Grafil was also looking for solutions to its large labour turnover problems which had been increasing during the 1980s due to a resurgence in the motor car industry, a major employer in the Coventry area.

Catalyst for Change

Until 1988, process operators at Grafil received a maximum of thirteen weeks on-the-job training which was designed to give them the skills they needed to do their job for the rest of their working lives. There was very little scope within the company for process operators to progress and labour turnover was high. In order to maintain and increase its profit share, Grafil traditionally had invested in plant and equipment rather than in its work-force. The increasingly high-tech nature of the man-made fibres industry meant, however, that traditional approaches to manufacturing were no longer appropriate. Geoffrey Marsh, Chief Executive of Courtaulds Grafil, stressed the need for change:

> Courtaulds Grafil is committed to establishing a reputation with customers as the leading quality supplier of carbon fibre worldwide. A vital requirement of achieving that goal is to improve the depth and professionalism of training in all parts of the organization. We must be able to use everyone at Grafil to their maximum potential and demonstrate that, as a company, we do want employees to progress beyond their initial starting grades.

In September 1988, Grafil decided to restructure its training provision and, together with the Man-Made Fibres Industry Training Board (MMFITB), developed a competence based scheme for process operators up to NVQ Level 2. A Steering Committee was established under the chairmanship of Paul Weston, Grafil's Technology Director, and a timetable for implementation was agreed, involving both the Level 1 and Level 2 NVQs which include the City and Guilds 060 Process Plant knowledge units. Geoffrey Marsh highlights four key benefits of introducing NVQs to Grafil:

* Industry-led national standards
* Credibility of externally validated qualifications
* Status of a national award
* Basis for career development for operative grades.

The company had, for some time, wanted to introduce a graded pay scheme in order to reward ability, level of contribution and initiative, three factors which are seen as vital to the company's successful future. Previously, all process operators received the same pay once they completed their training. The progressive nature of the NVQ programme was, therefore, seen as a solution to the pay problem. At the time of writing, Grafil currently make extra weekly payments of up to £10 to process operators as they achieve the Level 1 Competence and Knowledge units and £20 for achievement of Level 2.

This means a considerable shift away from the one-off, basic skills approach to operator training as Paul Weston points put:

> The plan is to systematically train all process workers in both practical and theoretical aspects of their jobs, over a period likely to be up to two years per individual dependent on ability and background in the company. This should result in an all round improvement in the quality of our production operation, with individuals becoming increasingly involved and contributing more to the performance of the production equipment. We also hope to see changes from the somewhat constrained style of traditional process worker/chargehand/ shift supervisor role to one of team working where individuals are encourgaed to act on their own initiative and develop their own natural abilities wherever this is appropriate.

Delivering the Scheme: Training the Trainers

In order to deliver the NVQ programme in-house, Grafil brought in their local College of Further Education (Hinckley) to train a team of ten managers to the point where they could deliver the City and Guilds 060 knowledge units for the NVQ Level 1. Hinckley used the City and Guilds 730 Certificate in Teacher Training as the basis of the managers' training. Grafil discovered that not only did the course achieve its primary aim, but it also encouraged a great deal of team building between the managers who are seen as the major driving force to have NVQs embedded within the company. Boris Boulstridge, a member of the management team who attended the training course, said:

> We all thoroughly enjoyed the 730 sessions. They improved our training and presentational skills but also welded us as a team. That team spirit is really helping us push forward the NVQ programme.

The managers now teach the knowledge units in-house for half a day per week over eight months of the year and still receive some support from Hinckley College. The competence units are delivered on-the-job by experienced employees of chargehand/supervisor status who have attended a MMFITB instructional techniques course and for whom training is now their sole function within the company. These nominated trainers divide their time across the four shift groups operating at Grafil who work a seven day, twenty-four hour shift system. At the time of writing, Level 1 Competence and Knowledge is being delivered in-house and Level 2 Competence and Knowledge will be phased in during the summer of 1990.

Assessment for the NVQ Level 1 takes two forms:

1   The knowledge units which form the City and Guilds 060 are assessed by a one and half hour written examination which candidates take at Grafil's training centre. The papers are marked by the managers delivering the knowledge units and are moderated by City and Guilds personnel who visit the plant. Candidates are prepared for the exam during their knowledge sessions by sitting mock examinations.
2   The competence units are assessed on-the-job by the candidates' plant managers and senior foremen, each of whom have attended an MMFITB/City and Guilds Assessor Training course. The assessors use checklists to guide their assessment and record the candidates' achievements.

Investing in Training: An Act of Faith

Making such major changes to a 20-year-old training provision within the company meant that the Grafil NVQ team had to think carefully about how they would persuade the rest of their colleagues to accept the new ideas. Geoffrey Marsh identified five groups to be targetted:

*   Grafil's Main Board
*   Management Team
*   Trainers
*   Trade Unions
*   Workforce

He stressed that the NVQ programme had to be seen as a positive opportunity which would be crucial in helping the company survive and prosper and, at the same time, would offer benefits to the workforce. A series of presentations and meetings were held with the five groups listed above and a guidebook for all employees was produced. This sets out the aims and objectives of the scheme and includes examples of the units of competence. The introduction of a graded pay structure was given full support by the Transport and General Workers Union (TGWU) which represents process operators at Grafil and the Company Board backed Geoffrey Marsh's demand for the necessary resources to run the scheme. The importance of Grafil's NVQ programme for its workforce is indicated in this quotation from a TGWU press release which heralded the programme's launch:

For the first time, process workers in the textile industry are now able to have their skills properly recognised. This is not only a first in the textile industry, it is the first national vocational qualification for process workers in any manufacturing industry. In giving formal recognition to the skills at the point of production, the industry is providing itself with a sound foundation on which to build a meaningful training programme relevant to the needs of the future. ... No doubt many thousands more textile and manufacturing workers will wish to explore the usefulness of such qualifications for themselves.

Geoffrey Marsh regards his decision to place training high on the company's agenda as a considerable 'act of faith'. He explained:

> The benefits of training are largely long-term and a company may need to wait some three to five years before those benefits are revealed. At the same time, I, as the person responsible for ensuring we make a profit, have to be prepared to commit part of that profit to something which is difficult to quantify. That's an uncomfortable feeling and one which the City and financiers generally are not sympathetic towards. The financial climate in Britain is generally not accommodating where training is concerned. It's partly to do with the short-termism of investors and the need for companies to demonstrate, annually, real returns to their shareholders. The trouble with training is that it's difficult to pin down costs and even more difficult to say exactly how successful any training scheme will be in the long run.

As a company chief executive, Mr Marsh is fully aware that he and his fellow industrialists are continually blamed, along with politicians, for Britain's poor training record. He regards the charge that British employers have consistently failed to invest adequate sums in training as too simplistic, particularly because he believes that each company has to be viewed as an individual case with individual needs and constraints. He added:

> Certainly in Britain we do not have the patient, long-term view taken by the Japanese with their very different approach to investment in the future. And, we must be much more willing to reward employees at all levels who demonstrate their commitment through hard work and ability to learn new skills. Above all, the business climate must be made more sympathetic to investment in training and to accept such investment as being equally valid to that in plant and equipment. Companies have to understand that NVQs are basically a do-it-yourself approach to delivering training. If you are going to introduce a competence based approach then you have to put in adequate resources to maintain the necessary delivery infrastructure. You also have to have commitment at the most senior

level and accept that using part of your line managers's time for training is cost-effective.

If the financiers, shareholders and company board members need to change their attitudes, so too do the employees, for effective training in changing people automatically impacts on the organizational structure in which they operate. For Grafil, the introduction of NVQs has raised significant questions about both shopfloor and management organization. Mr Marsh explained:

> By allowing people to demonstrate their competence and potential for further training, we create a much more dynamic atmosphere within the workplace. Employees from operatives through to managers are much more aware that their contribution to the company is both encouraged and valued. This means that traditional ideas about how operatives should be supervised and, in turn, ideas about how a factory's production should be managed no longer apply. We need a much more responsive structure based on teams with team leaders and reject the departmental structure which, in the past, has been devisive. Production managers need to be closer to these teams by working the same shift system. What we're aiming for is a much more co-operative spirit in which we all grow and learn together.

Grafil believes that NVQs will play a major role in achieving that co-operative spirit and the company plans to introduce them for all employees including engineers, laboratory technicians and clerical staff.

Mr Marsh emphasized the need for the company to discover much more about its employees' potential and to capitalize on the team spirit which the first NVQs have promoted. Links are being sought with the Chemical Industries Association which acts as the Lead Industry Body for process operations in the chemical industry. Other Courtaulds sites, notably at Spondon near Derby and at Grimsby, are developing similar NVQ programmes building on the foundation work which has been started by Grafil. Mr Marsh added, however, that profits still came first and that unlocking potential had to lead to better production rates.

Results and Future Goals

The first cohort of process operators began achieveing Level 1 Competence in October 1989 and the Level 1 Knowledge units are currently being delivered. Level 1 Competence is now Compulsory for all new process operators and some 60 per cent of the Level 1 Knowledge units are being used as part of the induction programme for all new employees, including graduate entrants. Mr Marsh believes that the scheme has already demonstrated significant achievements. He said:

> Grafil's NVQ programme has made a major contribution to workforce morale and motivation. We now have a structured certificated training programme which can ultimately be extended to all employees and help improve the perceived status of our operatives. In addition, there are significant management development opportunities attached to the delivery of the programme.

Grafil are so convinced of the value of NVQs that the company is currently introducing them to the United States of America. At Grafil's sister plant in Sacramento, California, process operators are taking the same Level 1 NVQ as their Coventry colleagues. Mr Marsh said that although the plant in Sacramento was much smaller, employing some forty operatives as opposed to Coventry's 140, the same competences were required.

Chapter 12

Improvements in Workforce Qualifications: Britain and France 1979–88

Hilary Steedman

Introduction

It is now widely recognized in advanced industrialized countries that the ability to exploit technological innovation competitively is dependent upon the levels of skill available in the working population. In the early 1960s, both France and Britain took steps to remedy the problem of levels of craft and technician-level skills which were inferior to those of Germany. In the intervening twenty years, these intermediate skill levels have become increasingly important, in particular for manufacturing efficiency as micro-electronic control equipment and the efficient logistical organization of production demand a new and wider range of technical services to maximize machinery utilization and to combine it with the satisfaction of more sophisticated consumer requirements.

This chapter assesses the level of formal vocational qualification of the labour force in Britain and France in 1979 and, a decade later, in 1988, on the basis of comparable national surveys of the labour force in the two countries (Labour Force Survey 1979, 1988 for Britain Recensement 1968 and 1982 and Enquête sur L'Emploi 1988 for France) and examines differing national approaches to raising qualification levels. France and Britain faced similar problems of substantial proportions of the workforce with no educational or vocational qualifications at the end of the 1960s. France chose to follow a more focused and centrally-directed policy to raise levels of vocational qualifications through the national education system. Britain persisted in keeping vocational education and training out of the education system and in relying on employers to continue to provide vocational training for manufacturing. This chapter evaluates the outcome of these two approaches. It will be concerned, in Section 1 with the workforce as a whole, and in Section 2, with three main sub-divisions: foremen, technicians and shop-floor employees in manufacturing.

Section 1
Stocks of Qualifications: Britain and France 1979–1988

In 1979, a third of the French working population held intermediate vocatio-nal qualifications compared to just under a quarter in Britain, while a smaller proportion of the French workforce held degrees. By 1988, the French position relative to Britain had changed considerably. In Britain, numbers holding general educational qualifications, particularly at lower level (GCE O-Level, CSE), had increased by 50 per cent, while stocks of intermediate vocational qualifications in the labour force showed hardly any increase; in France, over the same period, the percentage holding vocational qualifica-tions increased substantially from a higher base (by one quarter), while the proportion holding general educational qualifications (without vocational qualifications) remained below that of vocational qualifications. In both countries, proportions holding degrees increased, with the larger increase registered in Britain (Table 1). In Britain, a decade which has witnessed the largest number of government training initiatives both for young people and for adults has so far shown considerably lower growth than France of stocks of vocational qualifications in the labour force. France, on the other hand, has progressed from a level (similar to Britain in the early 1970s) of having less than half the stock of vocational qualifications of Germany to being two-thirds of the way towards the German level in 1988; France, with 40 per cent at intermediate level now (1988) lies roughly half-way between Britain (26 per cent) and Germany (64 per cent). These results require us to look carefully at differences between the two countries' policies towards the train-ing of young people — an important factor contributing to changes in stocks of qualifications in the labour force.

Flows of Vocationally-qualified Young People in Britain and France

Patterns of flows of vocationally-qualified young people in Britain relative to other advanced industrialized countries have been documented in previous work carried out by the National Institute. In brief, over the period, under half of all of 16-year-old school leavers chose to remain in full-time school or to proceed to further education. Of those who left school, few had attain-ments in basic subjects which could constitute the foundation for further on-the-job training to recognized skill levels, and for many in full-time employment such training was not available. Such skills as were acquired (mostly on the government-financed Youth Training Scheme) were at levels below internationally recognized minimum standards — City and Guilds Part II or BTEC National Level, (NVQ Level 3). As a consequence, the flows of young people obtaining recognized craft qualifications in major occupations in manufacturing in Britain hardly changed in the 12-year period

Table 1   Vocational qualifications of the labour force in Britain and France, 1979 and 1988

	Britain % 1979	Britain % 1988	France % 1979	France % 1988
No vocational or educational qualifications	46	30	52	37
No vocational qualifications but some educational qualifications	23	34	10	16
No vocational qualifications subtotal	69	64	62	53
Lower intermediate	18	20	27	33
Higher intermediate	5	6	5	7
Intermediate vocational qualifications subtotal	23	26	32	40
Degree or above	8	10	6	7
Total	100	100	100	100

Sources: Enquête-Emploi 1988 Table 01 Form, CEREQ Bulletin de Recherche sur l'Emploi et la Formation, No. 42 Table 3, page 3, own interpolations for 1979. Britain 1979 and 1988 Labour Force Survey unpublished tabulations prepared by the Department of Employment.

Notes
In Britain, those declaring no educational or vocational qualifications. In France, those declaring no educational or vocational qualifications and those holding only the CEP (Certificat d'Etudes Primaires), an almost superseded qualification formerly awarded to attest satisfactory completion of compulsory schooling at age 14.

In Britain, 0.70 of 'other qualifications', one or more CSE below Grade I, one or more O-Levels or equivalent, one or more A-Levels or equivalent. In France, BEPC (Brevet d'études du premier cycle), awarded at the end of compulsory school (16) and of O-Level standard, Baccalaureat (Series A, B, C, D, E).

In Britain, all trade apprenticeships completed (1979 all uncompleted trade apprenticeships), all City and Guilds, all BTEC ONC/OND and equivalent, 0.13 of 'other qualifications'. In France, all CAP and BEP qualifications, Baccalaureat (Series F, G).

In Britain, all BTEC HNC/HND qualifications, post A-Level Secondary and Primary teaching qualifications, Nursing qualifications. In France, all BTS and DUT, all other paramedical and other forms of professional education requiring 2 years higher education after Baccalaureat level.

In Britain, 0.17 of 'other qualifications', all degree level and postgraduate level qualifications, membership of professional institutions. In France, degree level and above.

All data taken from the Enquête-Emploi for France is based on the active population, including the unemployed. In Britain, LFS tabulations are based on the population in employment. We have calculated that adjustment of the French figures accordingly would raise the percentages with degree level and intermediate level qualifications by one percentage point and lower the percentage with no qualifications by two points. As these differences are so small the figures for France used in this study have not been adjusted.

to 1987 while in France and Germany numbers increased by 50 per cent and 30 per cent respectively.

Earlier National Institute studies have examined in detail the differences between French and British provision of initial vocational education and training. The reluctance of French employers — particularly large industrial employers — to train adequate numbers of young people in general skills led the French government to provide initial vocational education and training within the public education system. The products of this system cover the whole spectrum of skill from craft-trained worker to doctoral engineer and constitute the major source of initial skill formation.

Since 1971, the law compelling firms to devote 1.1 per cent of their payroll to the training of their employees has also played a part in helping to raise qualification levels. However, in terms of formal vocational qualifications obtained, the role of *formation continue* (continuing training) remains small. In 1984 barely 5 per cent of all CAP awards were obtained by adult employees using this route rather than through full-time initial training.

During the period in question, it was clearly easier for the French government to expand the supply of training places (subject to certain rigidities resulting from the skills of teachers in post, infrastructure, etc.) than it was for British governments to influence the British employer-based training system to expand the training provided for young people. It was also easier to monitor and maintain an agreed standard of vocational qualification when most trainees were trained in educational institutions (as in France) than where trainees were distributed widely over a large number of work places, many with no experience of training (as in Britain for the Youth Opportunities Programme, YOP, and the Youth Training Scheme, YTS).

Planning for Skills in France

Since the 1960s, French educational policy-makers have been encouraged to develop provision for education and vocational training within the overall objectives for economic growth set out in successive economic plans.

In the immediate post-war period in France a series of economic plans were drawn up to indicate the rate and type of economic growth that the government considered optimal. These plans guided the broad thrust of government legislation and investment; at no time were they more than indicative of directions to be followed. The Fifth Plan for 1966–70 was informed by awareness of the handicap imposed on French industrial and commercial development by an education system which had evolved to meet the needs of a predominantly agricultural society (in 1966 70 per cent of the population had no vocational qualifications or only a primary school leaving certificate). The 1966 Plan concentrated on the need to reduce this figure and stated as its objective that only 20 per cent of an age cohort should leave school in 1970 with no or low qualification levels, with 50 per cent at the next higher level (craft). Such proposals seemed ambitious at a time when over 50 per cent of a cohort left school with no recognized educational qualifications. Nevertheless, the resolve to raise qualification levels, particularly of the least well-qualified, was reiterated in the Sixth Plan, 1970–1975, which stated as one of its twenty-five objectives that of doubling between 1970 and 1975 the extent of post-school education and to reach the point where no child left the educational system without sufficient general education combined with the rudiments of vocational training.

A whole series of legislative measures were undertaken in the 1970s (creation of a higher qualification at craft level, the BEP, from 1968 onwards, the creation of pre-apprenticeship classes in secondary schools and the reform of apprenticeships, full recognition of the technical Baccalaureat and the creation of the University Institutes of Technology). The overriding aim was to raise numbers leaving education with some form of vocational qualification and particularly to increase the proportion with intermediate technical and commercial skills. The objective of the 1966 plan was attained in 1976 when only 19.6 per cent of school leavers left without at least completing a three-year (14–17) course of combined education and vocational training in a full-time vocational school; in 1986 the proportion was 15.1 per cent.

The Expansion of Vocational Training Places in France

A combination of clear educational objectives, centralized national administration of educational resources, nationally-recognized certification and the full-time provision of initial training within the education system enabled the French to expand the supply of vocational training places — from 212,000 pupils in the final year of full-time craft level courses in 1971, to 281,000 in 1980 and 318,000 in 1985. However, it is not obvious that any greater control could be exercised over demands from young people for vocational education and training after the completion of compulsory schooling than was the case in Britain. Nevertheless, participation rates of 16–18-year-olds in full-time education (including full-time vocational education) in France were considerably higher. 71 per cent in 1987 compared to 31 per cent in Britain in the same year.

It is beyond the scope of this chapter to analyse reasons for higher participation rates of young people in full-time education beyond the end of compulsory education at 16 in France. Labour market factors (relative youth wages and higher youth unemployment), demographic factors (higher post-war birth rates), and cultural factors have all played a part. However, it is important to note that the earliest age at which nationally recognized qualifications can normally be awarded in France is 17 — and the course in question, the CAP (craft level) may be entered upon at age 14 or 15, before the end of compulsory education at 16.

Differences in the ages at which recognized school-leaving qualifications are awarded in the two countries help to explain differential leaving rates. In Britain the CSE and GCE O-Level (growth in academic educational qualifications has particularly been concentrated on the former) are normally awarded at 16, and are widely recognized by British employers since they are the main indicators of employment potential; in France only a small proportion leave at 16 with the French qualification equivalent to GCSE (the BEPC). A majority of French 16-year-olds are already preparing for the vocationally-oriented CAP (taken at age 17) and the BEP or Baccalaureat taken at age 18 and 19 respectively and judge it worthwhile to take one or two more years to complete the course after the end of compulsory education.

Many of the French 16–18-year-olds who stay on to work for these recognized vocational and educational qualifications do so because the advantages in terms of jobs and salary can be clearly judged from employers' behaviour. This first level of vocational qualification (CAP, BEP), equivalent to NVQ Level 3, is widely recognized by employers to the extent that recognition of the CAP and of higher level vocational certificates and diplomas is written into Collective Agreements negotiated by employers and trade unions. Under these agreements, the holder of a relevant CAP qualification is entitled to be paid at a higher point on the agreed salary scale than an employee with no vocational qualifications.

Because the CAP leads to an attestation of professional competence recognized by employers, standards are rigorously maintained. Average pass-rates remain around 60 per cent. These are 'group' examinations, rather than single-subject examinations. Many leave without the CAP certificate although they have passed all the practical examinations of purely professional competence but have failed in their academic subjects. This contrasts with British willingness to count as 'qualified' a school-leaver with a single CSE or O-Level pass. If the rigorous criteria applied by the French were applied to British qualifications, that is, if we counted those who had passed their written tests and excluded those who had only 'served their time', only about 19 per cent of the British active population (instead of the 26 per cent shown in Table 1) would be considered vocationally qualified at intermediate level. This should be borne in mind when considering the higher French percentage with 'no qualifications'. Since this group contains all those who studied for but failed to obtain a CAP, many would be considered 'qualified' according to the British definition — which includes those who have completed an apprenticeship but not obtained any vocational qualifications.

The 'Rationing' of General Educational Qualifications: Consequences in France and Britain

How does the pattern of growth in qualifications in France compare with that in Britain? This question can be better understood by examining average annual percentage growth rates of the different categories of qualifications obtained by French school leavers aged 16 and over during the ten-year period 1976–1986. While numbers obtaining general educational qualifications grew by only 1 per cent per annum in this period, numbers obtaining the lower-level vocational qualification (CAP) increased by 4 per cent and higher level technical qualifications by 6 per cent. (It should be noted that these growth rates relate to increases in flows of young people with vocational qualifications and not to the growth of stocks of qualifications in the labour force. Flows contribute to the growth of stocks but are not the sole determinant).

Are these differences in growth rates the result of greater popularity of vocational and technical courses among French 16-year-olds or has the French educational structure played a part in the differential growth in numbers? There is no doubt that places in the traditionally more prestigious 16–19 secondary education courses leading to the general or technical Baccalaureat have been 'rationed' on the basis of attainments. Demand for places on these courses at the guidance point at the end of compulsory schooling invariably exceeds supply. Those pupils whose request to be allowed to continue onto Baccalaureat courses is not met, may enter the lower level vocational courses (CAP, BEP) entry to which is open to all. Within the group which accedes to Baccalaureat courses, a similar process operates, whereby access to the more prestigious general Baccalaureat courses is restricted to the more able; most growth has taken place in the newer technical Baccalaureat options.

By restricting the expansion of general educational courses in a period of steeply rising demand for post-compulsory secondary education and providing alternative vocational and teachnical routes, the French government has ensured that most of this growth has been directed into technical and vocational education. Lack of parity of esteem for the three routes open annum between 1979 and 1988 while stocks of individuals holding vocational qualifications increased by less than 1 per cent per annum over the same period. These calculations are based on analysis of 16–24-year-olds in employment taken from special tabulations of the Labour Force Survey, 1979 and 1988. In the absence of adequate national statistics on vocational qualifications gained in Britain at levels comparable to other European countries, we have had to rely on the measure of 16–24-year-olds in the labour-force holding vocational qualifications at two different dates to try to judge whether there has been any growth. Detailed analysis distinguishing City and Guilds Part II from, for example, trade apprenticeship completed is not possible because of the reordering of qualifications in the LFS analysis between 1979 and 1988.

Section 2
Stocks of Qualifications and Intermediate Qualification Levels

A larger percentage of the French labour force now holds one of the range of intermediate vocational qualifications than is the case in Britain. The division of this group into those holding higher intermediate and lower intermediate qualifications in each country allows us to identify more precisely where the British shortfall is located. Levels of stocks of higher-technician level skills in Britain are similar to those in France; the shortfall in Britain results from lower levels of 'craft-type' qualifications (Table 1).

In recruiting at intermediate skill level, French and British employers initially draw upon current stocks of skills available in the labour force — in the case of foremen, most frequently through internal recruitment and to 16-year-olds (General Baccalaureat, Technical Baccalaureat and CAP/BEP) has been a source of unease on the part of educationalists and, in particular, the vocational route, with its more limited possibilities of progression to higher-level qualifications has been criticized. Although a 'common core' of mathematics, French and a foreign language is stipulated for all qualifications offered to 16–19-year-olds and routes for transfer from CAP/BEP to Baccalaureat courses were available, the standard required was very demanding and no more than 10 per cent of CAP/BEP students normally made the transfer to the higher-level Baccalaureat courses. Dissatisfaction among employers with the narrow scope of the CAP, and the need to provide realistic progression opportunities have led to the introduction in 1986 of the Vocational Baccalaureat taken in the vocational lycée two years after the BEP, which gives access both to employment and to technical courses within higher education.

Access to higher secondary school examination courses in Britain (A levels and equivalent Scottish examinations) has been restricted in ways similar to France by the widely-applied prescription of higher grades of O-Level GCE achievement as a condition of access. As in France, the proportion of the age-group taking a range of the academically-orientated A-Level courses hardly expanded over the period. The difference between the two countries lies in the contrast between the post compulsory-school careers of 80 per cent of the age group for whom satisfactory achievement at A-Level as presently constituted is not an appropriate target.

In France, almost all this group, including those with no record of success at secondary school, enrol in a range of full-time technical or vocational courses whose structure and labour-market value is widely-recognized and understood. In Britain, offers of apprenticeships normally target the same restricted pool of leavers with 'good' O-Level passes as do A-Level courses. Further Education Colleges offering full-time vocational and educational courses might, at first sight appear to offer suitable provision and opportunity for those with few educational qualifications to move from school on to vocational courses. However, initial evidence from the Youth

Cohort Survey indicates that 16-year-olds with no, or low-level, educational attainments are unlikely to choose this route.

A clearer and more coherent system combining general education and vocational and technical qualifications and offering courses appropriate for nearly all levels of attainment at ages 15–16 has been an important factor in enabling France to enrol the 80 per cent of all pupils who are not selected for entry to an academic Baccalaureat course. The success of this 80 per cent in gaining a range of technical and vocational qualifications has made a substantial contribution to France's recent progress in increasing stocks of vocational and technical qualifications in the labour force.

In England and Wales, over the period 1979–1988, the greatest growth occurred in qualifications obtained at school and in further education, i.e., in general educational qualifications (O-Level and CSE grades 2–5). Stocks of O-Level and CSE qualifications in the labour-force increased by 4 per cent per about mid-way through working life, in the case of technicians, more frequently through external recruitment and at a younger age. We would not wish to imply that those in either country holding no vocational qualifications have no skills to offer employers. We are here merely trying to assess how far each country has gone in ensuring that the working population acquires at least some basic technical and vocational knowledge in a systematic way and has passed through national objective assessment procedures.

The study of intermediate skill level is not so far advanced that a widely accepted definition of the term has yet emerged. For the purposes of this chapter, our initial definition is qualifications-based and, more precisely, identifies a broad range of vocational qualifications which lie below first degree level and above general educational school-leaving qualifications and which together constitute the qualifications which prepare for intermediate technical and managerial positions in manufacturing industry. These positions in turn cover the spectrum of middle managerial and technical services supplied in support of those directly employed in production on the one hand (skilled and semi-skilled operators) and in research, design and development and higher management (graduates) on the other.

Lower-level intermediate qualifications usually certify a range of manual skills supported by the appropriate technical study required for the independent exercise of those skills. Technical knowledge is usually restricted to that required for a particular occupational area. By contrast, higher level technical qualifications do not train in a specific range of manual skills (although these may be acquired to a limited extent). The mathematical and scientific knowledge required encompasses sufficient theoretical understanding to allow the holder to 'problem-solve', or to devise and carry out new testing procedures and to contribute substantially to design and development.

Table 2   Qualifications of foremen and technicians (manufacturing occupations) Britain and France, 1988

| | Britain | | France | |
| | Technicians | Foremen | Technicians | Foremen |
Qualifications	%	%	%	%
No vocational qualification	55	31	44	27
Lower intermediate vocational	39	43	51	49
Higher intermediate vocational	3	14	4	21
Degree or equivalent	3	12	1	3
	100	100	100	100

Sources: Britain, Labour Force Survey 1988, unpublished tabulations. France, for foremen, Census Formation 1982 Table 08 adjusted for 1988 on basis of Table 05 Form Enquête-Emploi. For technicians, Enquête-Emploi, 1988 Table 05 Form.

For Britain, no stated qualification, 0.70 'other qualification', CSE only, O level only, A level only. For France, no stated qualification, Primary or secondary school leaving certificate only (CEP, BEPC), General Baccalaureat only.

For Britain, apprenticeship completed, 0.13 'other qualifications', City and Guilds, BECT Ordinary level. For France, CAP, BEP (craft qualifications), Technical Baccalaureat.

For Britain, HNC, HND (higher technician level) other higher education below degree level. For France, BTS/DUT (higher technician level) other higher education below degree level.

For Britain, all degree-level qualifications and above, 0.17 'other qualifications'. For France, all degree-level qualifications and above.

In Britain all first level (supervisory shop-floor employees) foremen in employment by occupation (list of occupation units available from NIESR on request) adjusted to include only manufacturing occupations and to exclude artisan occupations.

In France, all first-level foremen in active population in matched manufacturing occupational groups, CSP Numbers 4812, 4822, 4832, 4852, 4862, 4871, 4874, 4882, 4883, 4884, 4891, 4892.

Qualifications of Employees at Intermediate Skill Level

Foremen

Foremen and technicians occupy the main positions supplying intermediate skills in manufacturing. In both Britain and France, the mean age of foremen is around 42; in the case of France, their qualification levels will not reflect the full impact of the recent rise in intermediate qualification levels. Nevertheless, while in Britain around 40 per cent of first-line supervisors or foremen hold intermediate vocational qualifications, in France half do so (Table 2). In both countries, employees classified as first-level or line supervisors who hold an intermediate level qualification are more likely to hold a lower-level ('craft-type') qualification.

Technicians

A comparison of the qualifications of individuals classified as technicians in Britain and France shows that technicians are considerably more likely to hold vocational or degree level qualifications than those at supervisory level; in both countries, all but some 30 per cent hold either intermediate vocational or degree level qualifications (Table 2).

Similar proportions of technicians in both countries are qualified at lower intermediate level, but at higher intermediate level (British HNC/HND) France employs 50 per cent more than Britain. Graduates constitute 12 per cent of technicians in Britain and only 3 per cent in France. This is consonant with widely-voiced complaints that British graduates are 'under-employed' in technician-level and foremen work in Britain (a point further discussed in a forthcoming study of the deployment of technicians and foremen). It is not easy to understand why British graduates are more frequently employed in technician positions than in France when stocks of individuals with higher technician qualifications are similar in the two countries and flows of individuals with higher technician qualifications in engineering and technology in recent years are also comparable. There does not appear to be any shortage of technician skills in Britain which would justify increased deployment of graduates.

Shop-floor employees

The real explanation of why British manufacturing perceives there to be a lack of higher-technician and graduate skills may more likely be found at the level immediately below foremen and technicians. Analysis of qualifications of skilled, semi-skilled and unskilled employees in the two countries working in shop-floor positions reveals four times as many in Britain with technician-level qualifications and eight times as many with graduate qualifications in comparison with France (Table 3).

When shop-floor qualification levels are further analysed in terms of examined and non-examined vocational qualifications, considerable differences emerge. Britain has only half the total French level of shop-floor workers with examined vocational qualifications, and the higher proportions of technician and degree-level qualifications at this level may represent an attempt to compensate for low craft levels using technician-level and graduate-level skills.

In this way, technicians in British industry are 'drawn down' to lower levels by the lack of craft qualifications on the shopfloor with consequent complaints of shortages of higher technicians at technician level. Graduates are then used to compensate for this shortage at technician level. In fact, as already mentioned, flows of both graduates and technicians are similar in both countries but are differently distributed; of those employed in British manufacturing with graduate and higher technician qualifications, one third are employed in skilled and semi-skilled shop-floor work in Britain. In France, negligible numbers of higher technicians and graduates work on the

Table 3 Qualifications of shop-floor workers, manufacturing occupations, Britain and France, 1988 (000s)

Qualifications	Britain n = 6121 %	France n = 7,079 %
No vocational qualifications	66	64.5
Other vocational and apprenticeship only	14	—
Examined national vocational qualification (craft)	17.97	35
Higher technician qualifications	1.41	0.4
Degree or equivalent	0.62	0.1
TOTAL	100	100

Sources: As for Table 2.

In Britain, no qualifications, CSE below Grade 1, O-Level, A-Level, 0.70 'other qualifications'. In France, no qualifications, CEP, (Certificat d'études primaries), BEPC, General Baccalaureat.

In Britain, 0.30 'other qualifications', trade apprenticeship completed. In France, no qualifications recorded at this level.

In Britain, ONC, OND and equivalent, all City and Guilds certificates. In France, Baccalaureat de technicien, CAP, BEP.

In Britain, HNC, HND and equivalent and other higher education below degree level. HNC/HND constitutes 88 per cent of all qualifications at this level for this occupational grouping. In France, the corresponding category (BTS, DUT) constitutes some 900 per cent of all qualifications at this level. In France, DUT, BTS and other higher education below degree level.

All degree-level and above. It is not possible to disaggregate by degree subject.

On the usual assumption of random sampling, these differences are statistically significant above the 99 per cent level.

shop-floor. The craft deficit appears to have far-reaching consequences for all skill levels in manufacturing.

For all the levels of qualification considered here, deployment of qualified personnel in France appears to match position and qualifications more closely than is the case in Britain. More deliberate efforts appear to be made in France to promote holders of craft qualifications to foreman positions than in Britain where foremen are hardly more likely to hold a vocational qualification than are the shop-floor employees whom they supervise. In contrast to Britain, French managers are invariably well-informed about the different levels of skill attested by the vocational qualification system and are well-informed about their own employees' qualifications. It seems likely that the combination of a more coherent and better-understood system of vocational qualifications combined with greater managerial awareness contribute to a more efficient use of the resources available.

Pay differentials and payment structures in the two countries clearly play a part and are discussed at greater length in a forthcoming companion study. Briefly, pay differentials for technicians, foremen and skilled and unskilled workers are considerably more compressed in Britain than in France, providing both employers and employees with less reason to deploy higher level technical skills at the appropriate level. Employees in large French firms in a number of manufacturing sectors are covered by collective agreements which specify rates of pay according to qualification level and not according to job. Employers who recruit for lower level posts at high qualification levels would find themselves paying well above the average rate for that particular category and are consequently more careful to deploy skilled personnel appropriately.

Conclusions

Britain's policies to improve educational and vocational qualifications have increased numbers in employment holding lower level general educational qualifications, but has failed to increase stocks of intermediate vocational qualifications in the nine years to 1988. France has registered a 25 per cent increase in numbers with vocational qualifications over the same period. The consequences of the British shortfall for the deployment of individuals with vocational qualifications at intermediate skill level is clear. The greatest gap is at the lowest level of intermediate qualification (craft or NVQ Level 3) and there is a tendency for higher level skills to be progressively 'drawn down' in Britain to plug the gap. At foreman and technician level, disproportionate numbers of graduates are employed with consequent under-usage of their knowledge and skills and a lack of job satisfaction. The lack of a coherent and widely-understood national system of vocational qualifications also contributes to skilled manpower being more often deployed at lower levels than appears appropriate.

Policies of setting educational goals in terms of proportions qualified to different levels with strong emphasis on the upgrading of skills have served France well in the period 1960–1988 — to the extent that from a position of relative disadvantage France has now 'overtaken' Britain in all but graduate-level qualifications. The British effort has also been considerable but has failed to provide a satisfactory basis for progression for more than a small proportion of leavers. The school-leaving qualification attesting general educational attainment awarded at age 16 has been extended to include virtually the whole age group but expansion has been mainly in lower grade passes and with no increase in the tendency to continue with training to recognized levels of vocational qualification. In France, a commitment to staying-on in full-time education beyond the minimum school-leaving age to at least age 17 or 18 is necessary to obtain any vocational or general educational qualification that is recognized and accepted by employers. Employment of 16-year-olds without training or apprenticeship is now almost unheard of in France.

Damaging gaps are most apparent in Britain at the lowest level of internationally-recognized qualification (NVQ Level 3) and Britain's priority should be the promotion of broadly-based Level 3 vocational education and training to the age of 18 for most young people, giving access to the workplace or to higher education. National Curriculum provision 14–16 should, therefore, as a first priority lay the foundations for such courses — for example by preparing pupils for BTEC first certificates or modules to provide continuity and a sense of progression through to post-compulsory education or training.

The French have already set their target for the year 2000 — 75 per cent of young people to the equivalent of A Level — and intend to achieve this aim principally by expanding technical and vocational courses of an A-Level standard. In Britain, despite the lead given recently by the CBI and TUC, there is no sign of a nationally coordinated response from those responsible for education and training policy.

Changes in courses and provision for 16–19-year-olds initiated by the Department of Education and Science currently address only the issue of changing GCE Advanced Level courses in order to bring their standards and methods of assessment more into line with those of the GCSE. These initiatives seem inadequate in two respects; firstly, A Level will remain an academic course of study without the practical vocational dimension found in both the French technical and vocational Baccalaureat courses. Secondly, and more importantly, it seems doubtful whether — even in greatly revised form — it will provide an appropriate aim for more than 40 per cent of the age group. These efforts attempt to offer a strictly education-based solution to less than half the 16–19-year-old population.

In its own and artificially segregated context, the Department of Employment is preparing to promote and finance training for young people in employment through locally-based TECs. In comparison with French initiatives, two points are noteworthy here. Firstly, the stated aim for most trainees in these 2-year programmes is NVQ Level 2 while the minimum level attained in France is the equivalent of NVQ Level 3; second, the routes followed by trainees are not part of the same system of qualifications available within the education system and with opportunities for transfer between different routes as is the case in France. It seems clear to us that great benefits derive both to employers and young people from the clarity and coherence of the 16–19 framework of qualifications in France and from deliberate efforts to provide within such a framework for virtually the whole ability range — despite an education system which maintains rigorous and high academic standards. If the French can overcome the handicap of an élitist academic tradition and firmly establish that educational goals must be compatible with national economic growth, Britain should be capable of doing the same.

Acknowledgments

First published in *National Institute Economic Review*, August, 1990. We are grateful to the Training Agency, the Economic and Social Research Council and the Scottish Council Development and Industry for financial support. The views expressed are entirely the responsibility of the National Institute.

Notes

1   The German figure is taken from work in progress at the National Institute and is based upon unpublished tabulations from the 1987 Mikrozensus for Germany.

2   H. Steedman, Vocational training in France and Britain: mechanical and electrical craftsmen, *National Institute Economic Review*, No. 126, November 1988. Table 6.

3   S.J. Prais and H. Steedman, Vocational training in France and Britain; the building trades, *National Institute Economic Review*, No. 116, May 1986. H. Steedman, Vocational training in France and Britain: office work, *National Institute Economic Review*, No. 120, May 1987. H. Steedman, Vocational training in France and Britain: mechanical and electrical craftsmen, *National Institute Economic Review*, No. 126, November 1988. V. Jarvis and S.J. Prais, Two nations of shopkeepers: training for retailing in France and Britain, *National Institute Economic Review*, No. 128, May 1989.

4   This account draws heavily on W.D. Halls, *Education, Culture and Politics in Modern France*, ch. 5, Pergamon 1976 and on OECD, *Reviews of National Policies for Education: France*, pp. 133–137, Paris 1971.

5   Ministère de l'Education Nationale, Note d'Information No. 86–18, Table 1; Note d'Information No. 89–33, Table 1. In both these tables young people entering apprenticeship are counted as staying within the education system.

6   Agreements covering metal-working, the chemical industry, pharmaceuticals and the building industry are documented and analysed in F. Eyraud, A. Jobert, P. Rozenblatt and M. Tallard, *Les classifications dans l'Entreprise*, Ministère du Travail, de l'Emploi et de la Formation Professionnelle, June 1989.

7   The figure of 19 per cent comprises all higher education below degree level, all ONC certificates, all C&G passes.

8   M. Duthoit, 'Le processus d'orientation en fin de troisième' in *Education et Formation* 1987–11. Ministère de l'Education Nationale, Duthoit divides his sample into three groups. In Group I (pupils who have not repeated a school year, i.e., average and above average ability), 78 per cent opt for the Baccalaureat course and 60 per cent are successful. In Group II (pupils who have repeated the last year of compulsory schooling), 48 per cent apply and 29 per cent are successful. (Fig. i, p. 40).

9   Department of Education and Science *Statistical Bulletin* 13/88 Table 3 December 1988.

10 The relevant qualifications can be further divided into upper intermediate skills and lower intermediate skills, the former being qualifications obtained within the higher education system (French BTS, DUT, British HNC/HND); the latter being vocational qualifications normally obtained after the end of compulsory education and prior to entry to higher vocational education.

11 This conclusion is also reached in relation to a much wider range of countries but including France and Britain in S.J. Prais, *Qualified Manpower in Engineering: Britain and other industrially advanced countries*, National Institute Economic Review, No. 127, February 1989.

12 Ibid. Table I.

13 Some 165,000 pupils aged 16 or 17 left the education system in 1985 without obtaining recognized qualifications. Six months later, only 13,000 were in paid employment, the rest were in apprenticeship or other training schemes. Note d'information No. 87–34 Ministère de l'Education Nationale.

14 The complete plan for leavers from education in the year 2000 is 5 per cent without qualifications, 20 per cent with a CAP or BEP, 30 per cent with a Baccalaureat, 20 per cent with BAC plus 2 years of higher education and 25 per cent at degree level. Haut Comité Education-Economie, *Éducation-Économie: Quel système èducatif pour la société de l'an 2000?* Documentation Française, 1988, p. 30.

15 The Confederation of British Industry (CBI) set a target for the year 2000 of NVQ Level 3 or its academic equivalent by half the age group. *Towards a Skills Revolution — A Youth Charter*, Confederation of British Industry, July 1989. Trades Union Congress, *Skills 2000*, 1989.

Notes on Contributors

Dr John Burke is a Senior Research Fellow in the Institute of Continuing and Professional Education, University of Sussex. In 1988, he was awarded an NCVQ Research Fellowship. He has researched and published widely on NVQs and Core Skills. Over the past eight years he has worked on a number of externally funded research projects but has also taught on a variety of mostly postgraduate courses as well as a wide range of INSET. He began teaching in schools in 1965, and for a number of years he was a training manager in industry.

Keith Cook has worked in further education as teacher and outreach worker on research and development projects, and in publicity and marketing. He hopes one day to understand why, when learning is so simple, education is so complex.

Geoff Crook is a senior member of staff at Newham Community College. Previously he had taught in secondary school and adult education. His work within FHE has encompassed Post-16 academic and vocational education and training. His current concerns are with Progression, APL, NVQs, Educational Guidance and Quality Assurance. He also co-ordinates the college's Access to Higher Education Programme and tutors a group of adult students.

Graham Debling heads the Standards Methodology Branch within the Training, Enterprise and Education Directorate of the Employment Department. His branch supports not only the Standards Programme which underpins the development of NVQs but also other Employment Department training and education initiatives such as TVEI and Enterprise in Higher Education. Previously as a member of the HMI for Further and Higher Education in Scotland he played a major role in the evolution and implementation of the Scottish Action Plan which led to the establishment of the Scottish National Certificate. Prior to that he spent ten years at the Grimsby

College of Technology as Principal Lecturer in Food Technology. During that time he worked very closely with many third world countries.

Lewis Elton is Emeritus Professor in Higher Education at the University of Surrey and a Higher Education Adviser with the Training, Enterprise and Education Division of the Department of Employment (formerly the Training Agency) with a special concern for the Enterprise in Higher Education Initiative. His academic career has been divided equally between physics and education and he has published extensively in both fields. In 1979 he initiated an MSc in the Practice of Higher Education, which was the first British Master's degree at a distance outside the Open University. It was his experience with this degree, particularly the fact that it involved research supervision at a distance, that first alerted him to the problems of autonomy learning at a distance.

John Field is a Director of the Continuing Education Research Centre at the University of Warwick, where he has worked since 1985; previously he spent ten years as adult educator in Derbyshire and South Yorkshire. He has published widely on educational history and policy; current research interests include the development of vocational training and education for active citizenship (including especially environmental action), in the new Europe.

Richard Guy spent the early 1980s working first as a Management Trainer for industry, then in developing and setting up YTS and Adult Training in Manchester working with the MSC. He then moved to MSC's Head Office in Sheffield where has was responsible for the training design and content of YTS and ET together with the implementation and use of vocational qualifications in MSC programmes. He joined South and East Cheshire TEC as its Chief Executive in August 1989.

Ian McNay has been a teacher, trainer, learner and administrator in adult, further and higher education in England, Scotland, Belgium and Spain. He is currently seconded from the School of Education at the Open University to be Deputy Director of its Yorkshire Region.

Peter Raggatt is Director of the Centre for Youth and Adult Studies at the Open University. He combines academic interests in comparative education and vocational education and training and has published books and articles in these areas. He has recently directed a project on the implications of NVQs for staff development and is currently researching issues of quality assurance in NVQs.

Hillary Steedman, Secretary and Senior Research Fellow of the National Institute of Economic and Social Research has published comparisons of vocational qualifications of France, Britain and Germany, Productivity, machinery and skills in Britain and Germany, all in the *National Institute Economic Review*. She is currently examining 16–19 education and training provision in various European countries. She is a member of Schools Examination and Assessment Council (SEAC).

Lorna Unwin is a lecturer in Post-Compulsory Education at the Open University. She has previously taught in further education and worked as a management consultant in the public and private sectors. Her research interests include the development of work-based and experiential learning, and the staff development needs of trainers and teachers.

Index

experimentation, 96–7, 131, 138, 147, 148

Farley (1988), 29
Farnes, N. (1975), 144
Faulkner, T. (1990), 27, 38
fees, 124, 161, 164, 165, 172
Feldman, D.H. (1980), 149
feminism/feminists, 117, 138, 139, 140
FESC
    see Further Education Staff College
FEU
    see Further Education Unit
Field, J., *xiv*, 39, 129–42
    (1989), 136
    (1990), 137
    (1991), 141
    and Hyde, P. (1989), 136
finance, *x*, 14, 15, 16, **164–74**
    constraints, 167
Finegold, D. and Soskice, D. (1988), 68, 76–7, 78n2
Finn, D. (1989), 118
flexibility, 65, 119, 120, 141, 157, 169
    see also learning
Ford, H./Fordism, 111–12, 124
foreman: qualifications and skills, 182, 189, 190–2, 193, 194
Fowler, N., 87
France, *ix*, 65, 67, 68, 99, 100, 104
    -/Britain: workforce qualifications, *xv*, **182–97**
Fryer, B. (1989), 138
FTEs
    see Full Time Equivalents
Full Time Equivalents (FTEs), 167
funding, VET, *x*, 22, 48, 60, 77, 92, 95, 168, 175
    adult education, *xiv*, 53, 109, 123, 135, 139, 162
    by business/employers, 32, 49, 92, 95, 97, 171
    HE, 37, 42–3, 45
    MSC, *xv*, 48, 58, 98
    for NCVQ, 71
    public, 68–9, 139, 172
    schemes, 97, 114
    sources, 163, 170–1

YTS, 52, 78n1
    see also accountability; agencies; change; EC; EHE; employers; Employment Training Programme; government; LEA; REPLAN; values
Further Education (FE), *ix*, 9, 38, 99, 103, 104, 169, 190
    adult education in, 114, 132, 133
    funding/resources, 58, 161, 162
    -/industry links, 38, 56, 57, 99, 163
    see also employers; public sector
Further Education colleges, 50, 56, 98, 108, 118, 133, 189
    and employers, 48, 103, 114, 117
    finance, 171, 172
    see also management; Newham Community College; NVQs; YTS trainees
Further Education Staff College (FESC), 166, 168
Further Education Unit (FEU), 66, 90, 103, 166, 169
    (1984), 64
    -/NIACE REPLAN (1990), 115, 117
    and REPLAN, 104, 115, 117

GCE
    see General Certificate of Education
GCSE
    see General Certificate of Secondary Education
General Certificate of Education (GCE), 38, 183, 186, 187, 195
General Certificate of Secondary Education (GCSE), 5, 38, 66, 96, 97, 135–6, 195
general education/qualifications/skills 65, 66, 67, 108, 114, 189–90, 194
generic skills/competences, 26, 29, 32–5, 47, 57, 65, 66
    and TVEI, 55, 56
    see also core skills
Germany, *ix–x*, 64, 65, 67, 68, 131
    regional policy issues, 100, 102
    workforce skills/vocational qualifications in, 182, 183
Gibbs, G. (1987), 148, 154
Gorz, A. (1989), 119, 120, 121, 138